D0500026

PROGRAMMING IN ADA

Richard Wiener ⎯⎯⎯⎯⎯ *Richard Sincovec*

University of Colorado at Colorado Springs
Western Software Development

PROGRAMMING IN ADA

Ada is a trademark of the U.S. Department of Defense (Ada Joint Program Office).

John Wiley & Sons
New York   Chichester   Brisbane   Toronto   Singapore

QA
76.73
A35
W53
1983

To our parents,
Irving, Mary and Frank, Kathryn.
And to our families,
Sheila, Erik, Marc
and Deanna, Mary, James.

Copyright © 1983, by John Wiley & Sons, Inc.

All rights reserved. Published simultaneously in Canada.

Reproduction or translation of any part of
this work beyond that permitted by Sections
107 and 108 of the 1976 United States Copyright
Act without the permission of the copyright
owner is unlawful. Requests for permission
or further information should be addressed to
the Permissions Department, John Wiley & Sons.

Library of Congress Cataloging in Publication Data:

Wiener, Richard, 1941–
    Programming in Ada.

    Includes index.
    1. Ada (Computer program language) I. Sincovec,
Richard. II. Title.
QA76.73.A35W53 1983   001.64'24   82-20046
ISBN 0-471-87089-7

Printed in the United States of America

10 9 8 7 6 5 4 3 2 1

11-5-87

PREFACE

The primary goal of this book is to introduce and illustrate the major features of a new programming language, Ada. The book is aimed at practicing computer science and data processing professionals and students of computer science. Ada's many features for supporting software development and maintenance make the language ideally suited for those involved in large scale software projects. Although Ada builds on many concepts of Pascal and PL/1, we do not assume that the reader has programmed in either of these languages. We assume that the reader has some prior programming experience in at least one high level language such as Fortran, Basic, or Pascal.

Relatively few Ada courses are being taught at colleges or universities because of the current unavailability of Ada compilers. With the imminent completion of Ada compilers, many computer science departments will begin to offer Ada courses, since this language can be used as a vehicle for introducing advanced programming concepts (e.g., data abstraction, data hiding, concurrent processing, complex scoping, programming environments) and for teaching software engineering. When the compilers become available, we believe that Ada should be first taught at the junior or senior level. Since many computer science departments have introduced the elements of structured programming and Pascal at the freshman level and have exercised these concepts in a sophomore level data structures course, a junior or senior level Ada course that incorporates principles of advanced programming and software engineering appears to us to be most appropriate. By the time students encounter Ada, they should be concerned about the methodology associated with the development of a large software project—Ada provides an ideal mechanism for teaching such methodology—and not just about writing a "correct" program. To be able to exploit the full power of Ada, students should have some skills in numerical analysis, data structures, and algorithm design.

Ada is a more complex language than many of the languages that are currently enjoying heavy use such as Fortran, Basic, and Pascal. The military language reference manual (Reference 2) and several early Ada textbooks (e.g., References 1, 3, 6) present the details of the Ada language in a formal way. The relatively few complete Ada programs that are presented in these books are often short and sometimes trivial.

This book gives many nontrivial Ada programs to support the presentation of new Ada constructs and concepts. Application programs are presented in the areas of data structures, numerical analysis, and algorithm design. As we introduce new Ada features, some of the programs are updated to demonstrate the improvements in program design that the more sophisticated features support. We hope that the reader will acquire a faster and more meaningful appreciation of the scope and power of the Ada language by studying these Ada programs.

We employ an informal style of narrative, and we hope that the reader is not offended by our occasional attempts at humor. By concentrating on the major and significant language features and not getting bogged down on some of the fine and often complex detail(s) associated with a language feature (occasionally such details are omitted entirely), we hope to have enhanced the value of this book as a learning tool. We suggest that the reader use a current language reference manual as a supplement to this book, since we make no pretense of covering every fine detail of the language.

Chapters 1 through 8 present the basic control and data structures associated with Ada. The student who is experienced with Pascal or PL/1 should be able to go quickly through this material. The student who is unfamiliar with Pascal or PL/1 should study carefully the new concepts associated with the control and data structure features discussed in these chapters. Chapters 9 through 16 set forth powerful and advanced features of the language that set it apart from previous programming languages. Many of the concepts associated with advanced programming and software engineering are supported in the material of these later chapters, which present large Ada programs that illustrate the full power of Ada. We anticipate that the material of this book will support a one semester course in Ada programming.

We acknowledge the generous support of the Microsystems Institute, a subsidiary of the Western Digital Corporation, in helping us produce this book. In particular, we thank Alan Boal, president of the Microsystems Institute, for his confidence in us and his vision, without which this book would not be a reality. We thank William Carlson, president of the Advanced Systems Division of Western Digital, for his support. Both Western Digital and the Microsystems Institute have provided us with valuable resources and support. Many of the programs that appear in this book were tested using a Western Digital Supermicro (TM) computer and a MicroAda (TM) compiler.

Under the sponsorship of the Microsystems Institute we have been offering a series of Ada short courses for people in government and industry. Some of the useful suggestions that we have obtained from the students in these courses have been incorporated in this book. We also thank Kathleen D. Velick, of Western Digital, for her helpful suggestions and support during the production of this book. Robert Wilson, president of Hi-Country Data Systems, provided invaluable support during the production stage.

We are deeply grateful for the support of our families during the long and sometimes lonely hours that we spent writing.

Richard Wiener
University of Colorado at
Colorado Springs
Colorado Springs, Colorado

Richard Sincovec
Western Software Development
P.O. Box 953
Woodland Park, Colorado

CONTENTS

LIST OF PROGRAMS

PROGRAMMING IN ADA

Chapter 1

TOP-DOWN VIEW OF ADA

1.1 INTRODUCTION

Ada is a programming language that was designed to satisfy a variety of programming requirements including the reduction in the overall cost of software systems. It is to be used in such numerical applications as large numerical and statistical simulation packages, and it is intended to be compatible with the mathematical and statistical software libraries of the future. The development of computer operating systems and compilers is also a goal that has been set for Ada. Finally, Ada is to be used in applications with real-time and concurrent execution requirements such as those found in the avionics system of aircraft or in the coordination of complex embedded computer systems. The language is considered to be a major advance in programming technology because it brings together the best features of earlier programming languages.

The structure of Ada is simple, yet its capabilities make it one of the most powerful programming languages. Ada contains features that should significantly lower the cost of software development and maintenance. These features include the option of separate compilation of program unit specifications and program unit bodies, software packages, generics, tasks to support embedded computer systems, overloading of operators, flexible scoping and visibility rules for data objects, subprograms, and strong typing of variables.

In this book we present the features of Ada in a systematic, easy to understand manner. That is, as we introduce each new feature of the language, we usually present a complete Ada program illustrating its use. Almost every program in this book was executed and checked on a Western Digital Microengine computer using their Micro-Ada compiler. Often the examples consist of previous examples, reworked to demonstrate the use of a new language construct.

Anyone with programming experience should be able to grasp the essential details of Ada after one reading of this book. The approach we use to present Ada is carefully tailored to those readers with programming experience in almost any high level language. Our examples demonstrate the use of Ada on a variety of problems that arise in computer science, engineering, mathematics, and statistics. The programs should be easily readable, illustrating that Ada minimizes the slope of the learning curve for becoming familiar with software developed by others.

1.2 HISTORY AND THE PROBLEM ADDRESSED BY ADA

Ada was sponsored by the U.S. Department of Defense (DoD) in an attempt to reduce the rapidly increasing expense of military software systems. DoD identified language proliferation as a primary cause of the software problem. Custom languages and compilers were being developed for specific applications, but they often led to project failure because of inadequate languages and associated compiler problems. These factors prompted DoD, in 1975, to form the High Order Language Working Group (HOLWG). The HOLWG was charged with identifying and recommending solutions to DoD's language problem. Many existing languages were evaluated and found to be inadequate for the long term, and no language was found to satisfy the requirements for a common language. Additional studies indicated that a new language should be designed to meet DoD's requirements.

The language that evolved has become known as Ada. Ada is not an acronym like most computer language names. Rather it is the first name of Ada Lovelace, who worked with Charles Babbage on his difference machine. In today's terminology Ada Lovelace would probably be considered to be Babbage's programmer. That would make her the world's first female programmer. Some people say that Ada may be the last major high level language that will ever be developed, since automatic program generation techniques may be available in the not too distant future. Thus it seems fitting that the last major programming language should be named in honor of the first female programmer.

DoD is certainly not the only organization that has experienced the rapidly increasing cost of software systems. Many organizations have probably, on occasion, found their software development projects behind schedule, or the final development cost over budget, or the delivered program unreliable and/or not satisfying the original problem specifications. Another factor that has contributed significantly to increasing software cost is software maintenance. It is not unusual for the life cycle maintenance cost to exceed the original development cost. Anyone who has been involved in large software projects has probably experienced most of these dilemmas associated with computer software.

Other factors besides language proliferation have contributed to burgeoning software costs. Another principal factor has been the inability to manage complexity. Structured programming, top-down program development methodologies, and program development and analysis tools have been used to deal with this problem. Studies have shown that this approach can increase productivity by as much as a factor of five when measured with respect to the debugged number of instructions per day that are produced. However, correct methodology does not force the programmer or the programming team to organize the complexity of the problem before program development is started. The use of high order programming languages is also advocated to reduce software costs. But it is well known that the use of a high order language alone does not necessarily increase productivity unless the language is properly used in conjunction with modern programming methodologies.

The high cost of software has been accentuated by declining hardware costs. It is not unusual for an organization to discover that software costs more than 75% of its total computing budget consisting of computer hardware, software development, and software maintenance. The trend seems to indicate that eventually hardware costs will comprise only 20% of the total computing budget, with software development and maintenance accounting for 80%.

The diversity of programming languages in common use requires that programmers become expert in several different computer languages. Thus the employing organization must hire programmers with different language specialties. Often programs developed in one computer language must be translated to other languages before they can be used on a newly acquired computer system or transported to the computer of another organization. Software developed in a computer language is often not portable from one computer to another or from one compiler to another on the same computer. Some software development tools have been developed to partially solve the portability issue. In any case, such problems have contributed significantly to software development and software maintenance costs.

Another fundamental problem is that as a programmer becomes fluent or expert in one particular programming language, he or she tends to develop software in that language regardless of whether the language is suitable for the problem at hand. The resulting program is often difficult to verify and usually not very readable, hence is also difficult to maintain. These factors have a significant impact on the life cycle cost of the resulting software.

Since some languages now in common use do not support modern program development methodologies, they also contribute to high software costs. That is, the use of such languages tend to result in late, error-prone software that is costly to maintain.

1.3 WHAT IS ADA?

Ada is a software engineering language. It is a high level, structured language that incorporates modern software engineering concepts within the features of the language. The language constructs encourage top-down program development. Features were designed into the language to address such major issues of the software life cycle as the involvement of many people in large software development projects, continuous changes in the software, and maintenance by people who did not develop the original software.

To reduce the complexity of large software development projects, a problem is often partitioned into smaller, more understandable and more manageable subproblems. Facilities are available in Ada to support problem partitioning or modularization. During the evolution of large software systems, various kinds of inconsistency are often introduced. Ada does not permit this to happen, since Ada creates a compilation data base that permits program wide type checking throughout the software evolution process.

In most programming languages the procedure or subprogram is the primary means of problem abstraction. Ada introduces a new concept of problem abstraction called the package. A package consists of two components known as the specification part and the implementation part. Each part is a program unit, and so each can be compiled separately and may reside in separate files.

A package has the following structures.

```
package STRUCTURE is
        --Package specification
        --This is the part of the package that is visible to the user and indicates to
        --the user the resources that are available in the package. The package
        --specification should be written prior to the programs that use the
        --package. The specification may include data type definitions, data object
        --declarations, and subprogram specifications. Subprogram specifications
        --indicate the interface mechanism to subprograms in the package that are
        --available to the user.
private
        --The private part of the package specification is optional. It is useful when
        --the data type names must be made visible to the user but the internal
        --structure of the data type remains hidden from the user. Operations on
        --private data types may be made available to the user in the package but
        --the user does not have access to their internal representation.
end STRUCTURE;
```

In the preceding, "package", "is", "private", and "end" are key words in Ada. Comments in Ada begin with "--" and continue to the end of the line. We use lowercase boldface letters to indicate key words in Ada and capital letters to denote user-defined names. The package specification must be compiled before or concurrently with program units which use the package.

The package body is constructed as follows.

```
package body STRUCTURE is
        --Declaration of local variables and types. These are not known or usable
        --outside of the package body. Declaration of subprograms not visible
        --outside of the package.

        --Implementation of subprograms defined in the visible part of the
        --specification. The subprograms may be procedures and functions.
        --Implementation of auxiliary subprograms needed to implement the visible
        --subprograms.
end STRUCTURE;
```

The package body is the means by which the package provides the operations promised in the package specification. The package body may contain implementation details that are hidden from the user. The body can be written and compiled independent of the specification. Indeed, given the package specification, it is possible to compile programs that make use of the package before the package body is even written. This means that the implementation details can be changed without recompiling programs that use the package. For example, if a new linear systems solver is developed, it can be inserted into any package implementation independent of the programs that use the package as long as the interface remains the same.

As an example, the package specification for a package for solving a linear system of equations may have the form:

```
package LINEAR_SYSTEMS is
        MAXSIZE: constant INTEGER:=50;
        subtype INDEX is INTEGER range 1..MAXSIZE;
        type VECTOR is array (INDEX) of FLOAT;
        type MATRIX is array (INDEX, INDEX) of FLOAT;
        procedure LU_FACTOR(N: in INTEGER; A: in out MATRIX);
        procedure SOLVE(N: in INTEGER; A: in MATRIX; C: in VECTOR; X: out
        VECTOR);
        procedure MATRIX_INVERSE(N: in INTEGER; A: in out MATRIX; B: out
        MATRIX);
end LINEAR_SYSTEMS;
```

In this example, MAXSIZE is an integer constant with a value of 50, which is the largest size linear system of equations that this package can accommodate. The types MATRIX and VECTOR are introduced and used in the visible part of the specification. This package specification does not have a private part. Note that if the package specification is adequately commented, it can serve as the user's guide for the package. The procedures introduced in the specification are defined in the package body. We do not give them here but present them in Chapter 13.

A principal component of abstraction is information hiding. Ada provides two techniques for hiding the implementation details while still making the implementation available to the user. The first is the package, where the implementation of the body of the package is hidden from the user. The second technique is the private part of the package specification. The private part provides the information that a compiler must have when compiling a program that uses the resources of the package. For example, the compiler may need to allocate storage for objects declared in the private part. The information in the private part is not invisible to the user, but the user cannot use the information contained in the private part in any way that would affect the correctness of the program.

Changes to the package body do not require modifications to the source of any program that references the package or recompilation of those programs. Changes to the private part do not require any modifications in the source code of any program that references the package but may require recompilation of the source. Changes to the visible part may require changes in the source code of programs that use the package, hence recompilation of those programs.

In large programming projects and in large software libraries, a frequent and difficult problem consists of the management of names and the sharing of declarations that are to be used by many programs. Ada provides facilities for overcoming this problem by requiring each compilation unit to indicate the other compilation units that it should be compiled with and those that it depends on for resources. For example, if package C begins with the clause "with A, B;" this means that package C can refer to the names A and B if they are in the compilation library. C can also use names declared in A and B. A and B may still depend on other compilation units. Name qualification uses the dot notation, whereby a name declared in a package specification must be denoted outside the package using the name of the package and a dot as a prefix.

For example, consider the following program unit, which makes use of the LINEAR_SYSTEM package to calculate the inverse of a 10 × 10 matrix:

```
with LINEAR_SYSTEMS;
procedure SIMULTANEOUS_EQUATIONS is
        --Declaration of types and variables
begin
        --Sequence of statements that create, say, a 10 × 10 matrix, A
        LINEAR_SYSTEMS.MATRIX_INVERSE(10,A,B);
        --The inverse of A is B
        --Sequence of statements that perform desired operations
end SIMULTANEOUS_EQUATIONS;
```

The prefix may be inconvenient at times, so Ada has available a "use clause" that permits the names in a package to be used without the package name as a prefix. The preceding example may be rewritten using the "use clause" as follows.

```
with LINEAR_SYSTEMS; use LINEAR_SYSTEMS;
procedure SIMULTANEOUS_EQUATIONS is
        --Declaration of types and variables
begin
        --Sequence of statements that create, say, a 10 × 10 matrix, A
        MATRIX_INVERSE(10,A,B);
        --The inverse of A is B
        --Sequence of statements that perform desired operations
end SIMULTANEOUS_EQUATIONS;
```

If two or more packages are used together and they use the same names, the Ada compiler will detect and report the ambiguity. The program then can be changed to use qualified names where appropriate.

1.4 OVERLOADING IN ADA

In Ada, the names of subprograms and the arithmetic operators may be overloaded. This means that the subprogram name or the operator symbol may have different meanings depending on the context. The meaning that is selected by the compiler is determined by the number and types of the parameters.

We illustrate the overloading of subprogram names with the following example.

```
declare --Defines a block of code
        P: INTEGER;
        Q: FLOAT;

        procedure OVER_LOAD(X: INTEGER) is
        begin
                --Sequence of statements
        end OVER_LOAD;

        procedure OVER_LOAD(X: FLOAT) is
        begin
                --Sequence of statements
        end OVER_LOAD;
```

```
begin
      --Sequence of statements
      OVER_LOAD(P);   --Calls the version of OVER_LOAD with integer
                      --parameter; the first version
      OVER_LOAD(Q);   --Calls the version of OVER_LOAD with float parameter;
                      --the second version
end;
```

The overloading of subprogram names aids in both abstraction and name space management. Abstraction is achieved because the same subprogram name may be used for conceptually equivalent operations on different data types. Anyone who has modified a single precision Fortran program to double precision, or vice versa, has probably encountered the changes that are required in some of the built-in mathematical function routines. For example, changing SQRT to DSQRT or SIN to DSIN. In Ada, SQRT can be defined for various precisions of floating point types, thereby eliminating such conversion problems. Name management is simplified because fewer names are needed. Also the overloading of subprogram names simplifies naming conventions. Scientific subprogram libraries often contain two or more versions of the same algorithm depending on the precision or the data type. For example, there might be a routine named SOLVE, another named DSOLVE, and a third named CSOLVE depending on whether the data type is single precision, double precision, or complex. In Ada, overloading eliminates this naming problem.

To illustrate the overloading of operators, we consider the following possible package specification for performing complex arithmetic. Complex numbers are not part of standard Ada.

```
package COMPLEX_NUMBERS is
      type COMPLEX is
            record
                  REAL: FLOAT;
                  IMAGINARY: FLOAT;
            end record;

      function "+"(X,Y: COMPLEX) return COMPLEX;

      function: "*"(X,Y: COMPLEX) return COMPLEX;

            --Other functions or subprograms may also be specified.

end COMPLEX_NUMBERS;
```

In this example, the predefined operators "+" and "*" are overloaded so that they may be used with complex operands where the type COMPLEX is a user-defined type. If A, B, and C are declared to be of type COMPLEX in a program that uses package COMPLEX_NUMBERS, then statements of the form "C:=A+B;" and "C:=A*B;" are legal and cause the desired complex arithmetic operations to be performed.

The overloading of operators makes it easier to write understandable programs and permits the development of "calculus-like" features. Thus the development of packages for matrix operations, string operations, and a host of other operations is supported. In effect, the Ada language is "extended" by the new definitions of "+" and "*".

1.5 SEPARATE COMPILATION IN ADA

Program units can be separately compiled in Ada. Separate compilation refers to the ability to separately compile program units without violating the cross-checking that is fundamental to the language. For example, a subprogram defined with several parameters in one program source file cannot be called with too few parameters or with parameters in the wrong order or of the wrong type from another source file.

Ada permits individual program units to be compiled without compiling the entire program. The Ada compiler manages a data base of previously compiled units so that information is available to the compiler to verify the consistency between the various program units that comprise the entire program. For example, if program unit B uses information defined in program unit A, then unit A must be compiled before unit B. If unit A is modified and recompiled, the compiler knows via the compilation data base that unit B and all units that depend on B are no longer valid and must be recompiled.

Features in the Ada environment permit the user to query the status of the compilation data base to determine whether all program units that are required are valid. This enables the user to minimize the amount of recompilation. The compilation data base permits separate compilation with the same degree of consistency checking across separately compiled program units that is possible within a single program unit.

1.6 SOFTWARE ENGINEERING IN ADA

Ada directly supports both bottom-up and top-down software development methodologies via the package concept and program stubs and subunits.

The following scenario describes how bottom-up software development might proceed. The programming team identifies a package that is required in the software development project. The team agrees on a package specification and assigns to one member of the team responsibility for the implementation of the package. This person compiles the package specification, and the compiler inserts it into the compilation data base. Other team members may compile other program units that refer to this package specification. The team needs to meet only to discuss proposed changes in the package specification. Before the package may be used in the final executable program, the person responsible for the package must write and compile the package body.

Among the features of Ada that permit top-down development are program stubs and subprograms. A stub is a mechanism for indicating that a separately compiled program subunit must eventually be provided. To illustrate this concept, consider the following partially completed package. The package is partially completed because the procedure NOT_DONE has not yet been developed.

```
package body TOP_DOWN is
      --Declarations
procedure NOT_DONE is separate;
      --Package implementation
end TOP_DOWN;
```

The reserved word "separate" tells the Ada compiler that the procedure NOT_DONE will be compiled later. The compiler saves in the compilation data base all the contextual information needed from the package TOP_DOWN for the subsequent compilation of NOT_DONE. When the programmer develops the procedure NOT_DONE, it may be compiled as a separate program unit. The structure might be as follows.

```
separate (TOP_DOWN)
procedure NOT_DONE is
      --Declarations
begin
      --Statements
end NOT_DONE;
```

Now the reserved word "separate" and its argument TOP_DOWN inform the compiler that what follows is a subunit of TOP_DOWN and that it is to be compiled as if it were completely specified where indicated in the program unit TOP_DOWN. The compilation data base contains the information that the compiler needs to determine whether everything is contextually consistent. This means that references to objects declared in TOP_DOWN are permitted within NOT_DONE. Clearly, top-down programming may proceed in an orderly manner using these features of Ada.

1.7   PROGRAMMING IN ADA

Ada was designed to assure that efficient data access and code efficiency are possible. Both these characteristics are essential to effective scientific and systems programming. Some of the interesting features of Ada that have a significant impact in these areas were described above.

Ada supports a full complement of predefined data types. These include integer and floating point numbers, pointers, and characters. The language permits the user to define fixed point numbers. Strings are a predefined data type consisting of an array of characters. Arrays with arbitrary dimensions are permitted. Records consisting of collections of data objects of different types may be defined by the user. Arbitrarily complex data structures may be defined, such as arrays of records, arrays within records, and records within arrays.

The type system of Ada permits dynamic dimensioning of array structures. That is, descriptors that define the bounds of arrays may not be known during compilation.

Parameter passing in Ada is unique compared to most previous programming languages. Each parameter has a parameter mode of "in", "out", or "in out" indicating how the parameter will be used.

Ada contains the usual collection of operators for expressions. Since Ada is a strongly typed language, only compatible types may operate with one another. To use expressions with mixed data types, an explicit type conversion must be performed.

Both simple and compound statements are available in Ada to support sequential, conditional, and iterative control structures. The actual statements available, too numerous to mention here, include statements or variations of the usual statements that are found in many high level languages such as Pascal.

Various program units include the block, subprogram, task, and package. These logical units permit various levels of abstraction and permit the grouping of logically related items.

Exceptions are predefined and user defined. When an exception is raised, an exception handler is executed in place of the remainder of the body of the program unit in which the exception occurred.

Ada provides generic capabilities that permit the development of general purpose subprograms and packages for performing computations on abstract data types. Generics contain compile time parameters and are similar to the macro features of other programming languages.

1.8 REAL-TIME APPLICATIONS IN ADA

Ada provides facilities for logically concurrent execution via program units known as tasks. A task is similar in structure to a package in that it has two parts, a specification part and a body. The task specification contains entry declarations that define the procedure-like calls that may be made to communicate with the task. The body of the task defines the behavior of the task and may contain statements that facilitate task synchronization such as an accept statement. Concurrently executing tasks are not normally synchronized, but for one task to communicate with another, they must perform a rendezvous. One task begins a rendezvous by calling an entry to another task. When the called task is ready to perform an accept, a rendezvous occurs. To illustrate this, consider the following task specification and body.

```
task MAILBOX is
      entry SEND(MAIL: in MESSAGE);
      entry RECEIVE(MAIL: out MESSAGE);
end;

task body MAILBOX is
      BOX: MESSAGE;
begin
      loop
            accept SEND(MAIL: in MESSAGE) do
                  BOX:=MAIL;
            end;
            accept RECEIVE(MAIL: out MESSAGE) do
                  MAIL:=BOX;
            end;
      end loop;
end MAILBOX;
```

In this example, the task specification declares the entries SEND and RECEIVE for use by other tasks. The body of the task declares the local variable BOX, which is used to hold a message until it is picked up or received by another task. The code in the task body consists of an unbounded loop with two parts. The first part is an accept statement for the entry SEND. The accept statement looks similar to a procedure declaration. It has formal parameters and a body delimited by the reserved words "do" and "end". This task waits at the "**accept** SEND. . ." statement until some other task calls the entry SEND to transmit a message to the box. When this occurs a rendezvous is said to take place. After the message has been placed in the box, the rendezvous is completed, and this task and the task that called it continue their respective executions concurrently and independently. The second part of this task is an accept statement for the entry RECEIVE. The task now waits here until another task calls the entry RECEIVE to pick up a message from the box.

In this example, if the MAILBOX task is waiting at SEND, a call to RECEIVE will be queued and must wait until some task transmits a message to the box. Any number of tasks can be waiting for a given entry to be accepted. This example contains only one accept statement for each entry, but there may be any number of accept statements corresponding to each declared entry. Other features of Ada permit accept statements to be conditionally executed, or a task may wait for a call to be received for any one of a set of entries. Mechanisms for creating delays and for terminating tasks are also available. Ada also supports a conditional entry call in which the calling task is not suspended and the entry call is not made unless the called task is ready to immediately accept it. There is also a timed entry call in which the call is canceled if it is not accepted within a specified amount of time.

1.9   THE ADA ENVIRONMENT

Several of the original goals of the DoD common high level language effort that led to Ada were to reduce software life cycle costs, to improve program reliability, and to promote the development of portable software and portable software tools. It was clear that these goals could not be achieved by a new language alone, but that a total programming environment was also required.

One objective of the environment is to offer effective support to a project throughout its life cycle, from initial requirements specification through long-term maintenance. This implies that the environment must maintain complete and accurate information on the current state of the project.

Another objective of the environment is portability—that is, the capability to move software from one environment to another. A consequence of meeting this objective is that the environment software itself is largely required to be portable.

The environment architecture consists of the host operating system, a kernel Ada programming support environment (KAPSE), and a minimal Ada programming support environment (MAPSE).

The KAPSE is the minimal set of functions necessary to support the rest of the Ada environment. It provides the low level services for querying and manipulating the data base and the low level support for the input-output facilities. All services normally obtained from the host operating system are supplied by the KAPSE.

The MAPSE is the minimal set of tools and tool interfaces sufficient to support software development. It includes such functions as a command language for invoking tools, tools for editing text, tools for compiling and executing Ada programs, and tools for managing software development and maintenance.

The KAPSE/MAPSE interface separates the portable portions of the Ada environment software from the nonportable part of the Ada environment. All software in the MAPSE can be readily and inexpensively moved from one host computer to another. Software in the KAPSE is generally specific to the host computer and operating systems and is generally not portable. The KAPSE can be viewed as supplying the MAPSE software with a virtual operating system interface that is invariant across host computer boundaries.

We do not dwell on the Ada environment in this book. It suffices to say that the aim of the Ada environment is to provide an efficient implementation of the Ada language as well as a user-friendly and user-helpful environment for programming in Ada. Its intent is also to make rehosting (moving a complete environment to a new host machine) and retargeting (making the environment support a new target machine) economical. The Ada environment should significantly contribute to the solution of many critical software problems in scientific, business, and systems programming and in the development and maintenance of embedded computer systems.

1.10 ORGANIZATION OF THE BOOK

This chapter has presented a top-down view of Ada and has indicated some characteristics that distinguish it from other programming languages. We hope that this top-down view also has given the reader an overall impression of the language. In subsequent chapters, we develop Ada in a bottom-up manner. Our basic approach is to introduce a new language construct and then to present an illustrative program. Almost every program has been checked by running it on a Western Digital Microengine computer using their Micro-Ada compiler. As the book progresses the examples become more sophisticated. Quite often we rework previous examples to illustrate the new language constructs, resulting in a new program that is a significant improvement over the earlier version.

In Chapters 2 through 5 we introduce the basic language features of Ada that are needed to construct simple programs. The topics covered should be familiar to or easily understood by anyone with previous programming experience. Chapter 2 uses simple programs to present and illustrate simple input and output, identifiers, the basic intrinsic scaler types of the language, assignment statements, and the basic operators and their use in floating point, and integer expressions. We also list the reserved words in Ada. The features of Ada that permit the programmer to control the flow of a program are introduced in Chapter 3. These include IF THEN, IF THEN ELSE, IF THEN ELSIF ELSE, and the CASE statement. Chapter 4 describes Ada's powerful repetitive or loop structures: the basic LOOP, the FOR LOOP, and the WHILE LOOP. Special exiting from loops via the EXIT and EXIT WHEN mechanisms are described and illustrated. In Chapter 5 the first structured data type, the array, is presented. Several sorting algorithms are given to illustrate the array structure. The declaration of arrays, array assignment statements, constrained and unconstrained arrays, and array attributes are some of the topics discussed. Arrays permit our examples to become more complex and interesting than those in the earlier chapters.

Ada defines types in much the same manner as Pascal. In Chapter 6, we describe the predefined data types in more detail and introduce subtypes, derived types, and enumeration types. Also subranges and range, the delta and digits specification, and conversion between types are presented. We describe how the reader can define his or her own types, and we emphasize the importance of defining appropriate types for both ease of program verification and program maintenance.

Chapter 7 introduces the important features of procedures and functions. This major chapter has many serious examples that permit us to illustrate and emphasize the philosophy of structured programming. The interesting concept of operator overloading that is available in Ada is also presented and illustrated with appropriate examples. The topics covered include local and global variables, the transfer of parameters in and out of procedures, subprogram parameter types, default values for subprogram parameters, and the transfer of parameters to subprograms by name. Among the examples are sorting algorithms and string operations.

Chapters 2, 3, 4, 5, and 7 essentially cover the subset of Ada that is compatible with Fortran but, of course, Ada adds a new dimension to most of the basic features that are available in Fortran.

The more sophisticated data structure known as a record is introduced in Chapter 8. Topics include record access, initialization, positional and nonpositional assignments, passing of record variables to subprograms, deferred constants, variant size records, and variant structure records. Major programs include vector addition, linked-list maintenance using arrays of records, and the determination of duplicates in a list using a tree structure.

Predefined characteristics of named data types are known as attributes. In Chapter 9, we present scalar, discrete, fixed point, floating point, array, and special purpose attributes.

An "exception" is a situation that arises and prevents the program from continuing its normal flow. Chapter 10 covers the intrinsic exceptions defined in the language and shows users how to create their own exceptions. Topics include exception declaration and exception handling. To illustrate the use of exceptions, we present a stack operation example and a numerical example.

Tasks are program units that can be executed in parallel with other tasks. Declaration, initiation, and communication among tasks are the topics of Chapter 11. The principal example used to illustrate tasks is the classic reader–writer problem that involves reading and writing in a protected data base.

Recursion is defined and illustrated by several examples in Chapter 12. The examples include permutation of objects, greatest common divisor between integers, and adaptive numerical integration. Access types (pointers) are also introduced in this chapter. The rationale for dynamic allocation is presented. Major illustrative programs include a reworking of the linked-list maintenance program from Chapter 8, binary tree sort, and hash sorting.

Packages are the topic of Chapter 13, which treats the various constructs associated with Ada packages. The importance of packages in developing large software resources is emphasized. Topics include package specification and body, private types, limited private types, and the use clause. After describing the features of Ada for creating packages, we illustrate the power of this construct by grouping many earlier programs together and writing new programs to form packages for linear systems of equations, Pascal like input/output, and converting vectors from rectangular to polar form.

"Scope" refers to the region of text in a program where an identifier or declaration has an effect. Identifiers can be used in a portion of program text with the meaning of the identifier given elsewhere in the program, as long as the declaration is visible. The subtleties associated with scoping and visibility are the focus of Chapter 14. Scoping rules as they apply to blocks, subprograms, and packages are covered.

A generic program unit is a template for a subprogram or package whose parameter types are determined at compile time. The unique capabilities of this extremely powerful and useful feature of Ada are described in Chapter 15. Topics presented include generic types, generic parameters, generic association, and generic instantiation. We illustrate generics with a variety of programs including sorting, stacks, and adaptive numerical integration.

A compilation unit is a program unit (i.e., a subprogram, package, or task) that can be compiled as an independent entity. Compilation units are useful in creating libraries of subprograms or packages. In Chapter 16, compilation units are defined and their usefulness illustrated. The topics include compilation units, interfacing between compilation units, order of compilation, and the hierarchy of compilation units. Software design methodologies, using both bottom-up and top-down design, are presented using many previously introduced Ada concepts. We illustrate some concepts of modern software engineering using a linear systems program.

The input/output constructs used in the programs throughout the book are primitive. At the time of writing the programs, very few input/output constructs were available. This necessitated the use of intermediate variables before many "get" and "put" statements. A totally new text i/o package has been standardized in Ada 82 and is presented in Appendix B.

Now let us begin with the pleasure of learning Ada.

Chapter 2

AT THE VERY BOTTOM

In this chapter we examine some of the most basic concepts that are required to construct simple programs. The issues introduced are simple input and output, the basic scalar data types that are built into the language, assignment statements, the basic operators and their use in expressions, and the reserved words defined in Ada.

2.1 INPUT-OUTPUT; SIMPLE ADA PROGRAM

For most computations, it is necessary that the user be able to input information to the computer and receive output from the computer. In recent years, most high level languages have allowed computing to be performed in an "interactive" mode. In this mode, the user is able to input information from a terminal (keyboard) and receive output on the same terminal. Such "interactive" computing permits program execution to occasionally halt to allow the user to enter information that may affect the future course of computation. "Menu"-driven programs allow the user to determine which of several or many branches the program should pursue. Ada supports "interactive" programming, and all the programs presented in this text use this "interactive" mode of computation.

We now examine some simple mechanisms for entering information from a keyboard and printing output onto the same terminal. More elaborate procedures for input and output are given in Chapter 13. The following Ada program introduces us to three basic input-output statements, GET, PUT, and PUT_LINE. These commands are contained in a package TEXT_IO, which is predefined in Ada. TEXT_IO is a library unit that contains a variety of features for performing input and output operations. This unit is given in Appendix B.

Ada programs that reference any of the available commands in TEXT_IO must begin with the clause "**with** TEXT_IO; **use** TEXT_IO;". The command "**use** TEXT_IO" allows features of the predefined TEXT_IO package to be accessed without having to explicitly qualify the command with a prefix consisting of the package name and a dot.

PROGRAM 2.1-1

```
with TEXT_IO; use TEXT_IO;
procedure INPUT_OUTPUT is
     I,J: INTEGER;
     PI: constant INTEGER:=3.14159;
begin
     put ("Enter an integer: ");
     get(I); --In Ada 82, this becomes "get (f, I);" where f is a file type
     put_line(" "); --In Ada 82, this becomes "put_line;"
     put("Enter another integer: ");
     get(J);
     put_line(" ");
     put("The sum of the two integers is ");
     put(I+J);
     put_line(" ");
     put_line("The autumn leaves are colorful");
     put(PI);
end;
```

This simple Ada program begins with the reserved word "procedure" followed by a user-defined identifier "INPUT_OUTPUT", which names this program unit. Then two variables I and J are declared to be integers. PI is defined to be an integer constant with a value of 3.14159. Its value cannot be changed in the program.

Ada, like Pascal, is a strongly typed language. All variables used in an Ada program must be declared to be of a given type. Following the declaration part of the program (program name and definitions of various entities), the implementation part is contained between the reserved words "begin" and "end". The implementation part of the program unit consists of a sequence of executable statements, each one terminated with a semicolon. This is in contrast with Pascal, where semicolons are used to separate statements rather than to terminate them. All major Ada units (blocks, procedures, functions, packages, tasks) have a declaration section and an implementation section. We present and discuss these units in later chapters.

The first statement in Program 2.1-1 prompts the user to enter an integer. Upon encountering the "get(I);" statement, program execution halts until the user types in an integer from the keyboard followed by "return". The statement "put_line(" ");" moves the screen cursor down one line. The user is then prompted to enter another integer. When this request has been complied with, the cursor is moved down another line and the output "The sum of the two integers is", followed by the answer, is printed on the screen. After the cursor has moved down another line, the message "The autumn leaves are colorful" is printed onto the screen, followed by the value of PI.

Application software written for an "interactive" mode often has three major functional components in sequence: input, computation, then output. Although Program 2.1-1 is very simple, it contains these three basic functional components. Because of the program's simplicity, the computation and the output components are performed simultaneously.

We discuss the style of Ada programs throughout this text. Notice that in Program 2.1-1 the executable body of the program is indented with respect to the delimiters "begin" and "end". Whenever one nests a group of logically related statements within a larger group, the inner group of statements is indented with respect to the outer group. This convention is illustrated in more detail in later chapters when the complexity of our programs increase. Although the compiler does not require this indentation, the readability of the finished product, and thus ultimately its maintainability, is directly related to the style of the program.

Program 2.1-2 introduces the next section.

PROGRAM 2.1-2

```
with TEXT_IO; use TEXT_IO;
procedure MORE_OUTPUT is
begin
        put("We will next discuss identifiers and predefined ");
        put("scalar data types and assignment.");
end MORE_OUTPUT;   --One may end a program using "end" or "end" followed
                   --by the program's name.
```

2.2 IDENTIFIERS; INTRINSIC SCALAR DATA TYPES; ASSIGNMENT

Identifiers are names that are defined by the programmer for various entities such as procedures, functions, packages, tasks, types, and variables. An identifier must start with a letter, either lower case or capital, and may be followed with any number of additional letters or digits. Two adjacent characters may be separated with an underscore. Throughout this book we use capital letters for all user-defined identifiers.

Ada provides predefined data types, INTEGER, FLOAT, CHARACTER, STRING, and BOOLEAN. Other predefined types are introduced later. When the compiler encounters a variable that is declared to be any one of these types, it reserves an appropriate amount of memory to accommodate this data type. For example, a variable declared to be of type FLOAT may require more memory storage than a variable of type INTEGER.

Variables are declared to be of a given data type by writing the variable or variables of a given type, separated by commas, followed by a colon and then the data type. For example,

```
  I,J,K: INTEGER;
R1,R2: FLOAT;
 T1,T2: BOOLEAN;
    CH: CHARACTER;
NAME: STRING(1..25);
     L: INTEGER;   --Additional declarations are legal for a type
                   --previously defined.
```

Constants are defined by writing the name of the constant, followed by the reserved word "constant", followed by the type designation, followed by ":=", followed by the constant's value. For example,

```
H: constant FLOAT:=3.0;
 I: constant INTEGER:=3;
```

In the body or implementation section of a program we may assign values to variables by using the sequence of characters ":=", which is read "is assigned the value." These assignment symbols are to be contrasted with the simple equal sign, "=", which is used to compare two entities. In many early high level languages such as Fortran, the curious statement "I=I+1" caused considerable consternation among many mathematicians using the language. In Ada, such a statement would be written "I:=I+1" and would be read "I is assigned a value equal to its old value plus one."

Program 2.2-1 illustrates both the assignment statement and the predefined data types INTEGER, FLOAT, BOOLEAN, CHARACTER, and STRING. Initial values may be assigned to any variable during the variable declaration, as shown.

Comments may be inserted on any line of an Ada program by using a sequence of two dashes. The comment continues to the end of the line.

PROGRAM 2.2-1

```
with TEXT_IO; use TEXT_IO;
procedure DATA_TYPES is
         I: INTEGER:=1;   --We may initialize a variable when it is declared
         R: FLOAT;
       CH: CHARACTER;
        B: BOOLEAN;
    S1,S2: STRING(1..80);
begin
     R:=0.1;
         --A number of type FLOAT cannot start with a decimal point
     CH:='A';
         --Note the single quotes surrounding the character variable
     B:=FALSE;
         --A Boolean variable may only be assigned "TRUE" or "FALSE"
     S1:="This is an example of a string.                                        ";
     S2:="This is another string.                                               ";
         --S1 and S2 must have 80 characters. Blanks must be added to pad
         --out S1 and S2.
     put_line(S1);
     put("CH="); put(CH); put_line(" ");
     put("R=");   put(R);   put_line(" ");
     put("I=");   put(I);   put_line(" ");
     put_line(S1&S2);
         --The operator "&" is used to concatenate two strings
end DATA_TYPES;
```

2.3 EXPRESSIONS; OPERATORS

An expression is a formula that computes a value. Expressions are usually built up by connecting variables by operators. The operators that are defined in Ada are listed below.

ADA OPERATORS

+, −, **not**	--unary
abs	--unary
*, /, **mod**, **rem**	--multiplication and division
+, −	--addition and subtraction
**	--exponentiation to integer power
&	--concatenation of two strings
=, /=, <=, >=, <, >	--relational

in, not in	––membership
and, or, xor	––logical
or else	––short-circuit
and then	––short-circuit

2.3.1 Integer Expressions

Integers may have a positive exponent designated by the letter "E" or "e" followed by a signed or unsigned decimal integer. For example, 2100 could be written as 21E2, 210e+1, or 2100E0.

We assume that I and J have been declared to be variables of type INTEGER. The operators $+$, $-$, $*$, $/$ have the usual meanings. When two integer variables are divided, the result is truncated to the integer part of the answer. Thus 8/3 will equal 2. The operators **mod**, **rem**, and ** have the following sign conventions.

I **mod** J	––Answer has the sign of J
I **rem** J	––Answer has the sign of I
I**J	––J must be nonnegative

The **mod** operator is defined as follows: A **mod** B equals the remainder when the integer A is divided by the integer B. So, for example, 20 **mod** 3 = 2, since 20 $-$ (6 $\times$ 3) = 2. The **rem** operator is the same as **mod** for positive operands, but, as the definition above suggests, differs from **mod** for negative operands. An example of **rem** is given in Program 2.3-1, which illustrates the basic integer operators.

PROGRAM 2.3-1

```
with TEXT_IO; use TEXT_IO;
procedure INTEGER_EXPRESSIONS is
      I,J,K,L: INTEGER;
begin
      I:=3;
      I:=I**4;                          ––I now equals 81
      put("I="); put(I); put_line(" ");
      J:=-50;
      K:=I mod J;                       ––K will be -19
      L:=I rem J;                       ––L will be 31
      put("K="); put(K); put_line(" ");
      put("L="); put(L); put_line(" ");
      K:=I/9+J*2;                       ––K will be -91
```

```
    L:=abs(J);                         --L will be 50
    put("K="); put(K); put_line(" ");
    put("L="); put(L); put_line(" ");
end INTEGER_EXPRESSIONS;
```

The key word ''end'' at the termination of a program may be followed by the name of the program. The inclusion of the program name is optional.

2.3.2 Floating Point Expressions

Floating point numbers must have at least one digit on either side of the decimal point.

The operators +, −, *, / have the usual meanings. The exponentiation operator raises a floating point number to an integer power. Integer and floating point variables cannot be mixed in the same expression. The following Ada program illustrates the basic floating point operators.

PROGRAM 2.3-2

```
with TEXT_IO; use TEXT_IO;
procedure FLOATING_POINT_EXPRESSIONS is
    A,B,C,D: FLOAT;
begin
    A:=3.3;
    B:=−7.0E2;                         --We can use scientific representation
    C:=4.0;
    D:=A/1.1;
    put("D=");
    put(D);
    put_line(" ");
    D:=abs(B−A);
    put("D=");
    put(D);                            --Answer 703.3
    put_line(" ");
    D:=C**3;
    put("D=");
    put(D);
    put_line(" ");
    D:=A*B+C*2.0;
    put("D=");
    put(D);
    put_line(" ");                     --Answer −2302.0
end FLOATING_POINT_EXPRESSIONS;
```

2.3.3 Boolean Expressions

Very often in Ada programming one has to evaluate a Boolean (logical) expression. A Boolean expression is composed of Boolean clauses connected by the operators **and**, **or**, **xor**, and the unary operator **not**. A Boolean clause is a subexpression that is either true or false. For example, the clause (A=B) is either true or false. The clause (A>=0) is either true or false. The clause (A>B−C/D) is either true or false. The following program illustrates some examples of Boolean expressions.

PROGRAM 2.3-3

```
with TEXT_IO; use TEXT_IO;
procedure LOGICAL_EXPRESSIONS is
      A,B,C: BOOLEAN;
        I1,I2: INTEGER;
      S1,S2: CHARACTER;
begin
      I1:=3;
      I2:=2;
      A:=I1>I2;                    --A will have the value true
      S1:='A';
      S2:='H';
      B:=S1<S2;                    --B will have the value true
      C:=(A xor B) or (not A);     --C will have the value false
      A:=I1/=I2;                   --A will have the value true
end LOGICAL_EXPRESSIONS;
```

The clause (A **xor** B) will be false when both A and B are true. The clause (**not** A) will be false when A is true, thus the Boolean expression (A **xor** B) or (**not** A) will be false.

Suppose that in a Boolean expression containing two clauses, we do not wish to test the second clause if the first clause is true. We can use short-circuiting to accomplish this. For example, in the expression

(I = 0) **or else** (J/I > 10)

if I=0 then we will never test to see whether J/I>10. We can also use short-circuiting with an AND operator.

(I /= 0) **and then** (J/I > 10)

Our next program uses the if-then and if-then-else constructs to illustrate short-circuiting. We will formally introduce these control constructs in Chapter 3. See whether you can predict the output of Program 2.3-4.

PROGRAM 2.3-4

```
with TEXT_IO; use TEXT_IO;
procedure SHORT_CIRCUITING is
        I: INTEGER;
        J: INTEGER:=10;                 --We initialize this variable
        A: BOOLEAN:=TRUE;               --We initialize this variable
begin
        I:=3;
        I:=I**4;
        if (I=81) and (A) then
                put_line("We have gotten off to a good start");
        end if;
        I:=0;
        If (I = 0) or else (J/I>4) then
                put_line("J/I>4 or I=0");
        else
                put_line("It appears that J/I<4");
        end if;
        if (I>2) and then (J/I>2) then
                put_line("J/I>2 and I>2");
        end if;
        I:=3;
        if (I=0) or else (J/I>4) then
                put_line("J/I>4 or I=0");
        else
                put_line("It appears that J/I<4");
        end if;
        if (I>2) and then (J/I>2) then
                put_line("J/I>2 and I>2");
        end if;
end SHORT_CIRCUITING;
```

2.4 LEXICAL UNITS AND RESERVED WORDS

The Ada character set that is assumed to be available consists of 56 characters: 26 letters, 10 decimal digits, the space character, and " # & ' ( ) * + , - . / : ; < = > _ |. There may also be an extended character set that contains the lower-case letters and the following symbols: ! $ @ ~ [ ] ^ \ { } % ? ' .

A lexical unit is the finest grain component Ada construct that has linguistic meaning. Identifiers, numbers, strings, and reserved words such as "begin" and "procedure" are all examples of lexical units. Spaces may not appear within lexical units. Reserved words may not be used as identifiers in Ada programs.

RESERVED WORDS IN ADA

abort	exit	raise
abs	for	range
accept	function	record
access	generic	rem
all	goto	renames
and	if	return
array	in	reverse
at	is	select
begin	limited	separate
body	loop	subtype
case	mod	task
constant	new	terminate
declare	not	then
delay	null	type
delta	of	use
digits	or	when
do	others	while
else	out	with
elsif	package	xor
end	pragma	
entry	private	
exception	procedure	

Pragmas are statements contained in a program that act as messages to the compiler. In Appendix A we list all Ada pragmas.

2.5 SUMMARY

- Statements are terminated by a semicolon.
- Mixed mode arithmetic is not allowed. Conversion (explained and illustrated in Chapter 6) must be used.
- Spaces are allowed only in comments, strings, and character literals.
- Some scalar types are INTEGER, FLOAT, BOOLEAN, and CHARACTER.
- Real literals must have a decimal point preceded by an integer and followed by an integer.

- Identifiers may be of any length, must start with a letter, and may use the spacer symbol _ to connect two characters.
- To add to program clarity, the names chosen for identifiers should be as descriptive as possible. A few extra keystrokes invested in typing a descriptive name for an identifier may save a great deal of time in later program debugging and maintenance.
- The predefined package TEXT_IO (which is connected to the program using "**with** TEXT_IO; **use** TEXT_IO;") contains, among others, the basic input-output commands: **put, put_line,** and **get.**
- Arithmetic expressions may be evaluated in an output statement.
- The short-circuit logical operators "**or else**" and "**and then**" may be used to eliminate evaluation of parts of a Boolean expression. These operators are generally used to protect a program from a divide-by-zero error or other illegal operations.

Exercises for Chapter 2

1. Write an Ada program that performs each of the following steps.
   - **(a)** The user inputs a floating point number.
   - **(b)** The number is multiplied by 7.5 and printed out.
   - **(c)** The user inputs a second floating point number.
   - **(d)** The previous result is multiplied by this new number and the result printed out.

2. Find as many errors as you can in the following program.

   procedure BAD
           X,Y=INTEGER;
           Z=FLOAT;
   begin;
           B:=X+Y;
           Z:=2*X;
   end BAD;

3. What is the output of Program 2.3-4?

4. When might short-circuiting be desirable?

5. Which of the following are not legal identifiers? Explain why.
   - **(a)** 1E7
   - **(b)** E17
   - **(c)** A_
   - **(d)** A_B
   - **(e)** BUSTER_KEATON
   - **(f)** FLOAT
   - **(g)** NEW_INTEGER
   - **(h)** HELLO_MAN

6. Evaluate the following expressions.

    A: INTEGER:=3;
    B: INTEGER:=−4;
    C: INTEGER:=6;

    (a) A + B/C   **(d)** A + 21 **rem** B
    (b) A/B + C   **(e)** B **rem** 3
    (c) A + 21 **mod** B   **(f)** A**C + B

Chapter 3

IF THEN WHAT ELSE?
MAYBE ELSIF.
WE'LL BUILD A CASE

In applications software it is often important to be able to conditionally transfer (either locally or globally) from one segment of a program to another. Often the result of some test(s) during the execution of the program determines which program path will be followed. Ada offers the programmer a rich variety of conditional control constructs, which we examine in this chapter. We also examine the "goto" construct, which allows the programmer unconditional control of path flow in a program.

3.1 IF THEN

Whenever one wishes to execute a statement or statements subject to a contingency, the IF THEN construct may be appropriate. The IF THEN command is constructed as follows.

```
if Boolean_expression then
      executable statement(s);
end if;
```

The Boolean expression may be a complex interconnection of Boolean clauses, but if the entire Boolean expression is true, the executable statement(s) will be performed. Otherwise the executable statement(s) will be skipped and program control will pass to the statement directly below the "end if" terminator. Often the major portion of a program segment is embedded

29

within an **IF THEN** construct if some basic condition on a variable must be satisfied before computation can continue. We present such an example in Program 3.1-1.

PROGRAM 3.1-1

```
with TEXT_IO,MATH_LIB; use TEXT_IO,MATH_LIB;
procedure IF_THEN is
        NUMBER: FLOAT;
begin
            --We read in a real number and print its square root if the number is
            -->= 0
        put("Enter a real number");
        put_line(" ");
        get(NUMBER);
            --If the number is >= 0, then we calculate its square root
        if NUMBER >= 0.0 then
            put("The square root of ");
            put(NUMBER);
            put(" =");
            put(sqrt(NUMBER));
                --We assume sqrt is available in package MATH_LIB
            put_line(" ");
        end if;
            --If the number is < 0, then we print an error message
        if NUMBER < 0.0 then
            put("Cannot calculate the square root of a negative number");
        end if;
end IF_THEN;
```

3.2   IF THEN ELSE

Whenever a branching decision involving a choice between two different program paths depends on the value of a Boolean expression, the IF THEN ELSE construct may be appropriate. The command is constructed as follows.

```
if Boolean_expression then
        executable statement(s);
else
        executable statement(s);
end if;
```

To illustrate the IF THEN ELSE construct, we present a program that builds a simple truth table using the basic Boolean operators.

PROGRAM 3.2-1

```
with TEXT_IO; use TEXT_IO;
procedure IF_THEN_ELSE is
        A,B,C: BOOLEAN;       --We define three Boolean variables
        ANSWER: CHARACTER;   --Variable for user response to questions
begin
        put_line("Truth Table for Boolean Operators");
        put_line("---------------------------------");
        put_line(" ");
        put("Is variable A true(y/n)? ");
        get(ANSWER);
        put_line(" ");
                --We allow for either lower- or uppercase answer
        if (ANSWER='y') or (ANSWER='Y') then
                A:=TRUE;
        else
                A:=FALSE;
        end if;
        put("Is variable B true(y/n)? ");
        get(ANSWER);
        put_line(" ");
        if (ANSWER='y') or (ANSWER='Y') then
                B:=TRUE;
        else
                B:=FALSE;
        end if;
        put_line(" ");
        C:=A or B;
        put("A or B is ");
        if C then
                put("true");
        else
                put("false");
        end if;
        put_line(" ");
        C:=A xor B;
        put("A xor B is ");
        if C then
                put("true");
        else
                put("false");
        end if;
        put_line(" ");
        C:=A and B;
```

```
    put("A and B is ");
    if C then
            put("true");
    else
            put("false");
    end if;
    put_line(" ");
    C:=(not A) xor B;
    put("not A xor B is ");
    if C then
            put("true");
    else
            put("false");
    end if;
end IF_THEN_ELSE;
```

In Program 3.2-2 we ask the user to input three real coefficients A, B, and C. Then we compute the roots of a quadratic equation A*X*X + B*X + C = 0. Program 3.2-2 presents another example of the IF THEN ELSE construct.

PROGRAM 3.2-2

```
with TEXT_IO,MATH_LIB; use TEXT_IO,MATH_LIB;
procedure QUADRATIC_EQUATIONS is
        A,B,C,D,REAL_1,REAL_2,IMAG_1,IMAG_2: FLOAT;
                            REALROOTS,DONE: BOOLEAN;
begin
    put_line("Solution of A*X*X + B*X + C = 0");
    put_line(" ");
            --We input the coefficients
    put("Enter the coefficient A: ");
    get(A); put_line(" ");
    put("Enter the coefficient B: ");
    get(B);put_line(" ");
    put("Enter the coefficient C: ");
    get(C); put_line(" ");
    put_line(" ");
    DONE:=FALSE;
    if (A=0.0) and (B /= 0.0) then
            put("X=");                      --Only one root
            put(-C/B);
            put_line("Since A=0 there is only one root.");
            DONE:=TRUE;
    end if;
```

```
if not DONE then
        D:=B*B−4.0*A*C;                 −−The discriminant
        if D>=0.0 then
                REALROOTS:=TRUE;
                REAL_1:=(−B+sqrt(D))/(2.0*A);
                REAL_2:=(−B−sqrt(D))/(2.0*A);
        else
                REALROOTS:=FALSE;
                D:=−D;
                REAL_1:=−B/(2.0*A);
                REAL_2:=REAL_1;
                IMAG_1:=sqrt(D)/(2.0*A);
                IMAG_2:=−IMAG_1;
        end if;
        if REALROOTS then          −−Two real roots
                put("The roots are both real.");
                put_line(" ");
                put("ROOT_1 =");
                put(REAL_1);
                put(" ROOT_2 =");
                put(REAL_2);
                put_line(" ");
        else                          −−Two complex roots
                put("The roots are complex.");
                put_line(" ");        −−We use "J" to represent sqrt(−1)
                put(REAL_1); put("+J"); put(IMAG_1); put_line(" ");
                put(REAL_2); put("+J"); put(IMAG_2); put_line(" ");
                put_line(" ");
        end if;
    end if;
end QUADRATIC_EQUATIONS;
```

3.3 GOTO

The unconditional transfer statement "goto" forms the central fabric of an unstructured language like Basic. The extensive use of "goto" commands has created what many computer scientists call the spaghetti syndrome, in which control is shuttled back and forth among labeled segments of a program. In debugging or maintaining such software, it is often quite difficult to follow the flow of logic. With the advent of Pascal, PL/1, and other structured languages, the use of unconditional transfer "goto" has been discouraged. Likewise, we discourage the use of "goto" statements in Ada. There are occasions when the well-chosen use of a "goto" command actually simplifies programming and makes a program easier to read and maintain. The goto command cannot transfer control into an "if", "loop", or "case" statement.

Any statement may be labeled to give it a name by enclosing the name in double angle brackets.

```
⟨⟨MARK⟩⟩ statement;
        sequence of statements;
goto MARK;
```

The statements connected by a "goto" command and a label must be in the same logical unit body (same subprogram, package body, or task body—these logical units are introduced in later chapters).

3.4   IF THEN ELSIF ELSE

Often a programmer wishes to create a branch point in a program that allows several alternative program paths to be followed. The more general IF THEN ELSIF ELSE construct may then be appropriate. The construct is built as follows.

```
if Boolean_expression then
        executable statement(s);
{elsif Boolean_expression then
        executable statement(s);}              ––Zero or more elsif blocks
{else
        executable statement(s);}              ––Optional
end if;
```

In Program 3.4-1 we illustrate the IF THEN ELSIF ELSE construct. Ordinarily, this program would have been written using a loop. Since we do not introduce loop constructs until Chapter 4, we must simulate a loop by using a "goto" command. Besides, this gives us the unusual opportunity to include at least one token "goto" command in this book!

Suppose we wish to perform an income survey. From the keyboard we type in annual income data. We have five categories of income and we wish to determine the income distribution of our given population. The income categories are the following.

Category 1: $0.000–$1999.99
Category 2: $20000–$29999.99
Category 3: $30000–$49999.99
Category 4: $50000–$79999.99
Category 5:   >= $80000.00

PROGRAM 3.4-1

```
with TEXT_IO; use TEXT_IO;
procedure INCOME_SURVEY is
            INCOME: FLOAT;
               C1: INTEGER:=0;   --C1, C2, C3, C4, C5 are used to count the
               C2: INTEGER:=0;   --number of entries in income categories
               C3: INTEGER:=0;   --1, 2, 3, 4, and 5, respectively
               C4: INTEGER:=0;
               C5: INTEGER:=0;
            COUNT: INTEGER:=0;   --Used to count the amount of data
            ANSWER: CHARACTER;   --Used to answer a yes/no question

begin
      《START》 COUNT:=COUNT+1;
      put_lIne(" ");
      put("Enter income for person ");
      put(COUNT);
      put(": ");
      get(INCOME);
      if INCOME <= 19999.99 then
            C1:=C1+1;
      elsif (INCOME>=20000.0) and (INCOME<=29999.99) then
            C2:=C2+1;
      elsif (INCOME>=30000.0) and (INCOME<=49999.99) then
            C3:=C3+1;
      elsif (INCOME>=50000.0) and (INCOME<=79999.99) then
            C4:=C4+1;
      else
            C5:=C5+1;
      end if;
      put_line(" ");
      put("Enter more data(y/n)? ");
      get(ANSWER); put_line(" ");
      if (ANSWER='y') or (ANSWER='Y') then
            goto START;
      end if;
      put_line("The survey results are");
      put_line("---------------");
      put("category 1: "); put(C1); put_line(" ");
      put("category 2: "); put(C2); put_line(" ");
      put("category 3: "); put(C3); put_line(" ");
      put("category 4: "); put(C4); put_line(" ");
      put("category 5: "); put(C5); put_line(" ");

end INCOME_SURVEY;
```

3.5 NOW WE BUILD A CASE: THE CASE STATEMENT

The IF THEN ELSIF ELSE construct presented in Section 3.4 allows one to create a branch point with several alternative program paths. The value of Boolean expressions formed the basis for determining which program path would be followed. Whenever these exists a branch point with alternative program paths, and the program path to be taken will be decided by the value that is assumed by a discrete type (integer, character, or enumeration type— see Chapter 6), the CASE construct may be appropriate. This construct is built as follows.

```
case DISCRETE_VARIABLE is
when VALUE_1 | POSSIBLE_VALUE_2 | · · · | POSSIBLE_VALUE_N =>
      executable statement(s);
when VALUE_N+1 | POSSIBLE_VALUE_N+2 | · · · | POSSIBLE_VALUE_M =>
      executable statement(s);
when others =>                      --Covers all other possible values
      executable statement(s);
end case;
```

In the preceding, DISCRETE VARIABLE is the name of an identifier of discrete type that can take on the values VALUE 1, POSSIBLE VALUE 2, . . . , POSSIBLE VALUE M, as well as other values not listed. The executable statements must contain at least one statement. If no action is required, the reserved word "null" must be used.

As an example,

```
case I is
      when 1 | 2 | 3 | 4          => put("alternative 1");
      when 5 | 6                  => put("alternative 2");
      when 7 | 8 | 9 | 10 | 11    => put("alternative 3");
      when others                 => put("alternative 4");
end case;
```

It is possible to have a range specification for alternatives. As an example, the preceding may be rewritten thus:

```
case I is
      when 1..4                   => put("alternative 1");
      when 5..6                   => put("alternative 2");
```

```
    when 7..11                    => put("alternative 3");
    when others                   => put("alternative 4");
end case;
```

Case statements are often used in building program menus. The user is presented with a choice of major options and asked to enter either an integer or character. Then, depending on the entered choice, control is passed to one procedure or another through a "case" command. Program 3.5-1 is a rework of Program 3.4-1 using a "case" command.

PROGRAM 3.5-1

```
with TEXT_IO; use TEXT_IO;
procedure INCOME_SURVEY_USING_CASE is
        INCOME,RCHOICE: FLOAT;
                    C1: INTEGER:=0;      --C1, C2, C3, C4 and C5 are used
                    C2: INTEGER:=0;      --to count the number of entries
                    C3: INTEGER:=0;      --in income categories 1, 2, 3, 4,
                    C4: INTEGER:=0;      --and 5, respectively
                    C5: INTEGER:=0;
                CHOICE: INTEGER;
                 COUNT: INTEGER:=0;      --Used to count the amount of data
                ANSWER: CHARACTER;       --Used to answer a yes/no question
begin
        《START》 COUNT:=COUNT+1;
        put_line(" ");
        put("Enter income for person ");
        put(COUNT);
        put(": ");
        get(INCOME);
        --We now convert the floating point variable RCHOICE to an integer variable
        --CHOICE
        RCHOICE:=INCOME/10000.0;
        if RCHOICE<1.0 then
                CHOICE:=1;
        elsif (RCHOICE>=1.0) and (RCHOICE<2.0) then
                CHOICE:=2;
        elsif (RCHOICE>=2.0) and (RCHOICE<3.0) then
                CHOICE:=3;
        elsif (RCHOICE>=3.0) and (RCHOICE<4.0) then
                CHOICE:=4;
        elsif (RCHOICE>=4.0) and (RCHOICE<5.0) then
                CHOICE:=5;
        elsif (RCHOICE>=5.0) and (RCHOICE<6.0) then
                CHOICE:=6;
```

```
      elsif (RCHOICE>=6.0) and (RCHOICE<7.0) then
            CHOICE:=7;
      elsif (RCHOICE>=7.0) and (RCHOICE<8.0) then
            CHOICE:=8;
      else
            CHOICE:=9;
      end if;
      case CHOICE is
            when 1|2    => C1:=C1+1;
            when 3      => C2:=C2+1;
            when 4|5    => C3:=C3+1;
            when 6|7|8  => C4:=C4+1;
            when others => C5:=C5+1;
      end case;
      put_line(" ");
      put("Enter more data(y/n)? ");
      get(ANSWER); put_line(" ");
      if (ANSWER='y') or (ANSWER='Y') then
            goto START;
      end if;
      put_line("The survey results are");
      put_line("---------------");
      put("category 1: "); put(C1); put_line(" ");
      put("category 2: "); put(C2); put_line(" ");
      put("category 3: "); put(C3); put_line(" ");
      put("category 4: "); put(C4); put_line(" ");
      put("category 5: "); put(C5); put_line(" ");
end INCOME_SURVEY_USING_CASE;
```

3.6 SUMMARY

- The IF THEN control construct allows one to execute a block of code after a Boolean expression has been found to be true. Thus a test must be passed before the block of code will be executed.
- The IF THEN ELSE control construct allows one of two blocks of code to be executed depending on the evaluation of a Boolean expression.
- The IF THEN ELSIF ELSE control construct allows one of several blocks of code to be executed depending on the evaluation of several Boolean expressions.
- The CASE control construct allows one of many alternative blocks of code to be executed, depending on the value of a discrete variable. All possibilities in the CASE statement must be accounted for.
- If "others" is used in a CASE statement, it must be last.

Exercises for Chapter 3

1. What is the output of the following program?

```
procedure QUESTION1 is
        A,B,C,D: INTEGER;
begin
        A:=3;
        B:=4;
        C:=5;
        D:=6;
        if A*B-C*C<13) then
                put_line("A");
        elsif (A*A*B*B-D**3)>0 then
                put_line("B");
        else
                put_line("C");
        end if;
end;
```

2. Write a program that performs each of the following.
   (a) The user inputs two integers.
   (b) If the two numbers are of opposite sign, the ratio of the two numbers is printed out.
   (c) If the two numbers are both even, the product of the two numbers is printed out.
   (d) If the two numbers are both odd, the positive difference between the two numbers is printed out.
   (e) If one number is odd and the other number is even, the sum of the numbers is printed out.
   (f) If the two numbers are of the same sign and both are even, the message "We are done." is printed out.

3. "Walk" your way through Program 3.5-1 and explain how it works.

4. Refer to Program 3.2-1. If A is true and B is false, what is the output of the program?

5. Write a "truth table" type of program modeled after Program 3.2-1 that uses five BOOLEAN variables A, B, C, D, and E.

6. Write a program to determine whether an entered integer is even or odd.

7. Modify Program 3.1-1 so that both real and complex roots may be printed out.

Chapter 4

ROUND AND ROUND WE GO: LOOPS

One of the major powers of a digital computer is its ability to perform repetitive tasks quickly. At the core of many important computer algorithms is iteration. Generally, in an iterative approach to solving a problem, successive approximations are obtained that converge to a solution. The heart of iteration is looping. Often the same sequence of steps is repeated many times, each time updating or refining the values of certain variables.

The earliest high level languages provided constructs for looping. In Fortran the famous DO loop allows programmers to perform iteration. In Basic the DO loop is recast as the FOR NEXT loop, which essentially performs the same function as the Fortran DO loop. Let us briefly examine the structure of the Basic FOR NEXT loop. In particular, let us see how one is able to abort execution of the loop prematurely. We create a fictitious situation to illustrate the basic (pun intended) idea.

```
100    FOR I=1 TO 5000
110..250  executable statements that change variable A
260    IF A>=789 THEN 340
270..320  more executable statements
330    NEXT I
340    first statement outside the loop
```

The possible premature jump out of the loop in the foregoing segment of a Basic program was accomplished with a conditional transfer statement embed-

41

ded in the middle of the loop. It was necessary to have a label for line 340 to accomplish the transfer out of the loop. But we know that labels and "goto" statements make for poor program structure and a consequent lack of readability. It would be desirable to be able to transfer out of a loop without using a label. It would also be desirable to perform a test before entering a loop to see whether we wish to execute the loop, even once. In the Basic FOR NEXT loop or the Fortran DO loop, the loop must be at least partially executed before exiting. This requirement has caused confusion and misunderstanding in reading programs.

Pascal, an important structured programming language, has some additional loop constructs, the WHILE LOOP and the REPEAT LOOP, in addition to the DO LOOP. Ada has extended the variety of loop constructs even further by creating conditional exit commands that may be used within a loop without the need for a label.

In this chapter we examine the rich variety of looping constructs that are available in Ada. It has been our experience that the mastery of loop control is an important cornerstone in becoming a competent programmer.

4.1 THE SIMPLE LOOP

Perhaps the simplest loop construct in Ada is the "loop" construct. It is implemented as follows.

```
loop
      executable statement(s);
end loop;
```

Generally a simple loop structure, like the one above, requires a conditional exit statement within the loop. Otherwise program execution would continue forever or until the plug is pulled from the computer (whichever occurs first). We discuss conditional exit statements in Section 4.4.

4.2 FOR LOOP

For Fortran or Basic programmers, a familiar loop construct is the definite loop. In such a loop the number of cycles is known by the programmer in advance. In Ada, definite loops (FOR loops) are controlled by a discrete variable of type INTEGER, CHARACTER, or some user-defined enumeration type (presented in Chapter 6). The FOR loop is built as follows.

```
for DISCRETE_VARIABLE in RANGE_DEFINED_BY_USER loop
      executable statement(s);
end loop;
```

Some typical loop segments are:

```
for I in 1..100 loop
        executable statement(s);
end loop;
for G in 'A'..'H' loop
        executable statement(s);
end loop;
```

In these examples the variables I and G are implicitly defined. That is, they are not declared in the procedure heading as are other variables. If a loop variable has the same name as a declared variable, the compiler treats these as two distinct entities. That is, when the loop variable is incremented, the declared variable retains its original value.

Within each of the loops above the variables I and G are constants whose values are modified in each new cycle in the loop. Both the lower and upper limits in a FOR loop may be expressions or variables that are assigned before starting the loop. This allows the same program structure to be used for many different size problems.

To illustrate the FOR loop in the context of a full program, we present a program that allows the user to input a list of N real numbers. Then the program calculates the average value and the variance of the data set.

PROGRAM 4.1-1

```
with TEXT_IO; use TEXT_IO;
procedure AVERAGE_VALUE is
        SUM: FLOAT:=0.0;   --Sum of the numbers
        SUMSQ: FLOAT:=0.0;   --Sum of squares of the numbers
    NUMBER: FLOAT;
    N_REAL: FLOAT;
        N: INTEGER;       --Size of list
begin
        put_line("      Average and Variance of Data Set");
        put_line("      ----------------------");
        put_line(" ");
        put("What is the size of your data set: ");
        get(N);
        put_line(" ");
        --The following loop performs a running sum of the data and a running sum
        --of the squares of the data
        for I in 1..N loop
            put("Enter number "); put(I); put(": ");
```

```
                get(NUMBER);
                SUM := SUM + NUMBER;
                SUMSQ := SUMSQ + NUMBER*NUMBER;
         end loop;
         put_line(" ");
         N_REAL := FLOAT(N);   ––Converts the integer N to a float N_REAL
         put("The average value of the data=");
         put(SUM/N_REAL);
         put_line(" ");
         put("The variance of the data=");
         put((SUMSQ-SUM*SUM/N_REAL)/(N_REAL-1.0));
end AVERAGE_VALUE;
```

In Program 4.1-1 the loop control variable "I" was not declared in the declaration section of the program. It was defined implicitly in the loop construct. Within the loop, "I" acts like a constant (with new values each cycle), and upon exit from the loop it no longer exists.

It is possible to reverse the direction of loop traversal as follows.

```
for DISCRETE_VARIABLE in reverse RANGE_DEFINED_BY_USER loop
      executable statement(s);
end loop;
```

For example,

```
for K in reverse 1..25 loop
      put(K);
      put_line(" ");
end loop;
```

The integers 25, 24, 23, . . . , 2, 1 will be printed one beneath the other.

Ada only permits loop increments of size one in its FOR loop. Loops that require different increments may be programmed using constructs presented in the next sections.

4.3   WHILE LOOP

At times it may be important to perform a test on a Boolean expression before entering a loop. If the Boolean expression proves to be true, the loop will be entered; otherwise the entire loop will be passed over. Only the WHILE loop allows such a precondition test to be performed. The WHILE loop may be built as follows.

```
while Boolean_expression loop
      executable statement(s);
end loop;
```

It is important when constructing a WHILE loop to carefully determine what initial conditions must be set before entering the loop, since a test will be performed before the first execution of the loop.

To illustrate the WHILE loop, we present a program that allows the user to input a written text. All the vowels {A,E,I,O,U} used in the text will be counted.

PROGRAM 4.3-1

```
with TEXT_IO; use TEXT_IO;
procedure VOWEL_COUNT is
            CHAR: CHARACTER;
        VOWELCOUNT: INTEGER:=0;
begin
      put_line("Please enter your text below in uppercase.");
      put_line(" End with ""/"".");
      put_line(" ");
      get(CHAR);
      while (CHAR /= '/') loop
            if (CHAR='A') or (CHAR='E') or (CHAR='I') or
               (CHAR='O') or (CHAR='U') then
                  VOWELCOUNT := VOWELCOUNT + 1;
            end if;
            get(CHAR);
            --To avoid an infinite loop, we change the value of CHAR
      end loop;
      put_line(" ");
      put("The number of vowels in the text=");
      put(VOWELCOUNT);
end VOWEL_COUNT;
```

Take note of the double quotes on each side of the "/" in the user prompt in Program 4.3-1. Whenever you wish to use a set of quotes in a put statement, they must be doubled up. Also note that it was necessary to input the first character before constructing the WHILE loop. This is because the WHILE loop tests the value of the variable CHAR and compares it to "/".

4.4 DIFFERENT KINDS OF EXIT FROM LOOPS

Ada provides the programmer with several different mechanisms for exiting from within a loop. In this section we examine four of these mechanisms.

4.4.1 Simple EXIT

A simple EXIT statement may occur in the following context.

```
loop--For loop or while loop may also be used
      executable statement(s);
      if Boolean_expression then
            executable statement(s);
            exit;
      end if;
      executable statement(s);
end loop;
```

Upon encountering the "exit" statement, control is transferred to the statement directly following the "end loop". Thus, no label is required after the loop. We demonstrate a practical use of the exit command by reworking Program 3.5-1 and eliminating the "goto" statement from that program.

PROGRAM 4.4-1

```
with TEXT_IO; use TEXT_IO;
procedure INCOME_SURVEY_WITHOUT_GOTO is
      INCOME,RCHOICE: FLOAT;
                  C1: INTEGER:=0;   --C1, C2, C3, C4, and C5 are used to
                  C2: INTEGER:=0;   --count the number of entries in income
                  C3: INTEGER:=0;   --categories 1, 2, 3, 4, and 5,
                  C4: INTEGER:=0;   --respectively
                  C5: INTEGER:=0;
              CHOICE: INTEGER;
               COUNT: INTEGER:=0;   --Used to count the amount of data
              ANSWER: CHARACTER;    --Used to answer a yes/no question
begin
      loop
            COUNT:=COUNT+1;
            put_line(" ");
            put("Enter income for person ");
            put (COUNT);
```

```
      put (":");
      get(INCOME);
      RCHOICE:=INCOME/10000.0;
      if RCHOICE<1.0 then
            CHOICE:=1;
      elsif (RCHOICE>=1.0) and (RCHOICE<2.0) then
            CHOICE:=2;
      elsif (RCHOICE>=2.0) and (RCHOICE<3.0) then
            CHOICE:=3;
      elsif (RCHOICE>=3.0) and (RCHOICE<4.0) then
            CHOICE:=4;
      elsif (RCHOICE>=4.0) and (RCHOICE<5.0) then
            CHOICE:=5;
      elsif (RCHOICE>=5.0) and (RCHOICE<6.0) then
            CHOICE:=6;
      elsif (RCHOICE>=6.0) and (RCHOICE<7.0) then
            CHOICE:=7;
      elsif (RCHOICE>=7.0) and (RCHOICE<8.0) then
            CHOICE:=8;
      else
            CHOICE:=9;
      end if;
      case CHOICE is
            when 1|2     => C1:=C1+1;
            when 3       => C2:=C2+1;
            when 4|5     => C3:=C3+1;
            when 6|7|8   => C4:=C4+1;
            when others  => C5:=C5+1;
      end case;
      put_line(" ");
      put("Enter more data(y/n)? ");
      get(ANSWER); put_line(" ");
      if (ANSWER='n') or (ANSWER='N') then
            exit;
      end if;
   end loop;
   put_line("The survey results are");
   put_line("----------------");
   put("category 1: ");   put(C1);   put_line(" ");
   put("category 2: ");   put(C2);   put_line(" ");
   put("category 3: ");   put(C3);   put_line(" ");
   put("category 4: ");   put(C4);   put_line(" ");
   put("category 5: ");   put(C5);   put_line(" ");
end INCOME_SURVEY_WITHOUT_GOTO;
```

4.4.2 EXIT WHEN

Another technique for conditionally exiting from within a loop, the EXIT WHEN construct, is built as follows.

```
loop--For loop may also be used
      executable statement(s);
      exit when Boolean_expression;
      executable statements;
end loop;
```

To illustrate the EXIT WHEN statement, Program 4.4-2 presents two loops; each loop performs the same function.

PROGRAM 4.4-2

```
with TEXT_IO; use TEXT_IO;
procedure EXIT_WHEN_ILLUSTRATION is
      SUM: INTEGER:=0;
begin
      for I in 1..150 loop
            SUM:=SUM+I;
            if I=27 then
                  exit;
            end if;
      end loop;
      put("SUM=");
      put(SUM);              --378 is printed
      SUM:=0;                --We will begin again
      put_line(" ");
      for I in 1..150 loop
            SUM:=SUM+I;
            exit when I=27;
      end loop;
      put("SUM=");
      put(SUM);              --378 is printed
end EXIT_WHEN_ILLUSTRATION;
```

It is evident, in Program 4.4-2, that the second loop is more natural to use and requires less code than the first loop.

4.4.3 EXIT (NAME OF LOOP) WHEN

Ada allows us to provide user-defined names for a loop. Thus it becomes possible to use another mechanism for exiting from within a loop, as follows.

```
USER_DEFINED_NAME: loop
      executable statement(s);
         exit USER_DEFINED_NAME when Boolean_expression;
      executable statement(s);
end loop USER_DEFINED_NAME;
```

This exit mechanism may also be used with a "for loop" or a "while loop."
We rework Program 4.4-2 to illustrate this new exit mechanism.

PROGRAM 4.4-3

```
with TEXT_IO; use TEXT_IO;
procedure LABELED_LOOP is
      SUM,I: INTEGER:=0;
begin
      SAMPLE: loop
                    I:=I+1;
                    SUM:=SUM+I;
                    exit SAMPLE when I=27;
             end loop SAMPLE;
      put("SUM=");
      put(SUM);
end LABELED_LOOP;
```

Using the EXIT WHEN construct, one can exit an outer loop from within an inner loop by naming the outer loop in the exit statement that appears in the inner loop. We illustrate this control with Program 4.4-4.

PROGRAM 4.4-4

```
with TEXT_IO; use TEXT_IO;
procedure OUTER_LOOP_INNER_LOOP_CONTROL is
      SUM,I: INTEGER:=0;
begin
      OUTERLOOP: loop
                    I:=I+1;
                    for J in 1..I loop
                          SUM:=SUM+J;
```

```
                          put("PARTIAL SUM=");
                          put(SUM);
                          put_line(" ");
                          exit OUTERLOOP when SUM>2500;
                    end loop;
                end loop OUTERLOOP;
        put("SUM=");
        put(SUM);
end OUTER_LOOP_INNER_LOOP_CONTROL;
```

It is instructive to walk your way through Program 4.4-4. To begin, both I and SUM are initialized to zero. Then I is incremented to 1. The first excursion of the inner loop has J going from 1 to 1. The sum will be 1. Now I will be incremented to 2. The inner loop will go from 1 to 2 and sum will go from its old value of 1 to 2 and then 4. Now I will be incremented to 3. The inner loop will go from 1 to 3 and sum will go from its old value of 4 to 5, then 7 and then 10. This will continue until the sum exceeds 2500. Can you calculate the final value of SUM?

Whenever you wish to exit conditionally from a loop that is contained by some outer loop (the inner loop may be nested several levels within the outer loop), it may be appropriate to use the EXIT WHEN construct.

4.4.4 Unconditional EXIT

It is possible to unconditionally exit from a labeled loop by using the statement

exit USER_DEFINED_LOOP_NAME;

in some inner loop. Generally, this construct would be used within an IF THEN or IF THEN ELSIF ELSE control structure. See whether you can modify Program 4.4-4 so that the EXIT construct can be used as a substitute for the EXIT WHEN statement.

4.5   ADA PROGRAMS TO ILLUSTRATE VARIOUS LOOPS

Since mastery of loop control is fundamental to becoming a good software developer, we now present a series of programs that use many of the loop control constructs given in Sections 4.1 through 4.4. We have chosen problems that are interesting in their own right. Perhaps you have already written programs in other languages to solve some of these problems.

4.5.1   Series Approximation to the Exponential

The mathematical function exp(x), read "e raised to the xth power," has a well-known approximation as a sum of a series. The series approximation to exp(x) is:

$$\exp(x) \sim 1 + x + \frac{x*x}{2!} + \frac{x**3}{3!} + \cdots + \frac{x**n}{n!}$$

The symbol "!" means factorial with $N!$, defined as follows.

$$N! = N*(N-1)*(N-2)* \cdots *2*1$$

The symbol $\sim$ means approximated by. If one examines the terms in this series approximation for exp(x), it is evident that the terms eventually get smaller and smaller, and, in fact, approach zero. Program 4.5-1 allows the user to determine (within the limits of the computer) any accuracy desired. In this example, accuracy refers to absolute error rather than relative error.

PROGRAM 4.5-1

```
with TEXT_IO; use TEXT_IO;
procedure EXPONENTIAL_APPROXIMATION is
        EPS,X,TERM,SUM,N: FLOAT;
            ANSWER: CHARACTER;
begin
        put("Enter the smallest term you wish to add to the series");
        put_line(" ");
        put("approximation to exp(x)-->");
        get(EPS);
        ANSWER:='Y';          --Just to get the process started
        while (ANSWER='Y') or (ANSWER='y') loop
            SUM:=1.0;
            TERM:=1.0;
            N:=1.0;
            put_line(" ");
            put("Enter the argument x for exp(x): ");
            get(X);
            loop
                    TERM:=X*TERM/N;
                    exit when abs(TERM)<EPS;
                    SUM:=SUM+TERM;
                    N:=N+1.0;
            end loop;
```

```
            put_line(" ");
            put("The approximation to exp(x)=");
            put(SUM);
            put_line(" ");
            put("Enter another argument(y/n)? ");
            get(ANSWER);
            put_line(" ");
        end loop;
end EXPONENTIAL_APPROXIMATION;
```

Have you carefully walked through the loops of Program 4.5-1? One could, of course, exit the inner loop after a certain number of terms had been summed. Do you see how to make such a modification to the program?

4.5.2 Prime Number Series

Our next problem is to generate a series of prime numbers. A prime number is a positive integer that can be divided evenly only by itself and 1. The first several prime numbers are:

1 2 3 5 7 11 13 17 19 23 29 31 37 41 43

Only odd integers (except 2) may be prime. In Program 4.5-2, we test successive odd integers and print out those that satisfy the basic condition of not being divisible by a smaller integer. We note that the trial divisors must be odd integers only up to the square root of the candidate integer. This follows because if a trial divisor larger than the square root of the candidate were to exist, a trial divisor smaller than the square root of the candidate would also exist, since the product of the two numbers must equal the candidate integer.

PROGRAM 4.5-2

```
with TEXT_IO; use TEXT_IO;
procedure PRIME_NUMBERS is
        CANDIDATE: INTEGER:=3;
          DIVISOR: INTEGER;
            PRIME: BOOLEAN;
begin
        put_line("This program generates all the prime integers up to 1999");
        put_line("----------------------------------------------------------");
        put_line(" ");
        put("2");
        put_line(" ");
        put("3");          --We take care of 2 and 3 separately
        put_line(" ");
```

```
loop
        DIVISOR:=1;
        CANDIDATE:=CANDIDATE+2;
        PRIME:=TRUE;
        --Assume the candidate is innocent until proved guilty
        while DIVISOR*DIVISOR <= CANDIDATE loop
                DIVISOR:=DIVISOR+2;
                if CANDIDATE mod DIVISOR = 0 then
                        PRIME:=FALSE;
                        exit;                    --No need to keep testing with more
                                                 --divisors
                end if;
        end loop;
        if PRIME then                    --We may exit from loop for two reasons:
                put(CANDIDATE);          --1) We have disqualified the candidate
                put_line(" ");           --2) We have exhausted all divisors and
                                         --have a prime.
        end if;
        exit when CANDIDATE=1999;
    end loop;
end PRIME_NUMBERS;
```

The first "exit" statement, contained within the WHILE loop, will transfer control to the line just below the WHILE loop; that is, "**if** PRIME . . .". If we had wanted to exit the outer loop from within the WHILE loop, we would have had to label the outer loop and then use the EXIT WHEN construct.

4.5.3 Square Root of a Real Number

The next program allows us to compute the square root of a real number, N. Program 4.5-3 utilizes a famous algorithm called the Newton algorithm. During each iteration, in the Newton algorithm, the new value of X (renamed X0 in the program) is set to $(X0*X0+N)/(2.0*X0)$, where X0 is the old value of X. Two tests are performed during each iteration. First, if the function X0*X0-N is very small, we exit from the iteration. Second, if the value of ABS(X0-XOLD) is less than or equal to EPS*X0 (where XOLD is the old value of X), then we exit from the iteration.

PROGRAM 4.5-3

```
with TEXT_IO; use TEXT_IO;
procedure SQUARE_ROOT is
        EPS: FLOAT;
        NMAX: INTEGER:=8;   --We will have, at most, eight iterations
        X0,XOLD,N: FLOAT;
```

```
begin
      EPS:=0.000001;
      put("Enter real number: ");
      get(N);
      put_line(" ");
      if N >= 0.0 then
            X0:=N/2.0;    --This is just an initial guess
            XOLD:=X0;
            for I in 1..NMAX loop
                  exit when abs(X0*X0-N) <= EPS*N;
                  X0:=(X0*X0+N)/(2.0*X0);
                  exit when abs(X0-XOLD) <= (EPS*X0);
                  XOLD:=X0;
            end loop;
            put("The square root=");
            put(X0);
      end if;
end SQUARE_ROOT;
```

4.5.4 Sum of a Series

For our last program we determine how many terms are required in the series
$1*1 + 2*2 + 3*3 + 4*4 + \cdots + N*N$ so that the sum just exceeds 10000.

PROGRAM 4.5-4

```
with TEXT_IO; use TEXT_IO;
procedure SUM_EXCEEDS_10000 is
      SUM: INTEGER:=0;    --Keeps track of the running sum
      TERM: INTEGER:=1;   --Keeps track of the term number
begin
      loop
            SUM:=SUM+TERM**2;
            exit when SUM>=10000;
            TERM:=TERM+1;
      end loop;
      put("The number of terms required=");
      put(TERM);
end SUM_EXCEEDS_10000;
```

4.6 SUMMARY

• The loop parameter in a FOR loop acts as a constant during each iteration of
  the loop.

- The WHILE loop requires that a test be performed before entering the loop. This allows for the possibility that the entire loop will be bypassed. Generally, careful attention must be paid to setting up initial conditions before a WHILE loop.
- One may exit from a loop by using a simple EXIT, or an EXIT WHEN, EXIT (NAME OF LOOP) WHEN, or an EXIT (NAME OF LOOP). The two latter constructs are used when several loops are nested and the programmer wishes to exit an outer loop from within an inner loop.
- A loop with a name must have the name at both ends of the loop.

Exercises for Chapter 4

1. What is the value of SUM after the following loop?
   ```
   N:=0;
   SUM:=10;
   while N<6 loop
         N:=N I 1;
         SUM:=SUM+N;
   end loop;
   ```

2. Write an Ada program that prints on a video terminal the sequence of numbers 0, 5, 10, 15, 20, 25, 30, . . . , 500.

3. Write an Ada program that prints on a video terminal the reverse sequence of that required in Exercise 2.

4. The mathematical function sin(x) has a series approximation

   $$\sin(x) = 1 - \frac{x}{1!} + \frac{x^{**}3}{3!} - \frac{x^{**}5}{5!} + \cdots$$

   Write an Ada program that approximates the sin(x) function. Your program should allow the user some control over the accuracy of the approximation.

5. What is the value of SUM after the following loops?
   ```
   SUM:=0;
   OUTER1: for I in 1..1000 loop
         SUM:=SUM+I;
         for J in 1..200 loop
               SUM:=SUM+I;
               for K in 1..2 loop
                     SUM:=SUM+K;
                     exit OUTER1 when J=5;
               end loop;
         end loop;
   end loop OUTER1;
   ```

6. How many terms are required before the series 3*3*3 + 6*6*6 + 9*9*9 + 12*12*12 + · · · first exceeds 30000? Write an Ada program to obtain the answer.

7. Write an Ada program that inputs a text (sequence of characters) and determines the number of words in the text. Assume that exactly one space separates each word in the text and that the first character in the text is not a space.

8. Rewrite Program 4.5-4 using the WHILE loop and no exit statements.

9. Compute the value of SUM in Program 4.4-4.

10. Compute the sum of the series $1/i$ from $i = 1$ to n for values of n equal to:
    (a) 10
    (b) 20
    (c) 30

Chapter 5

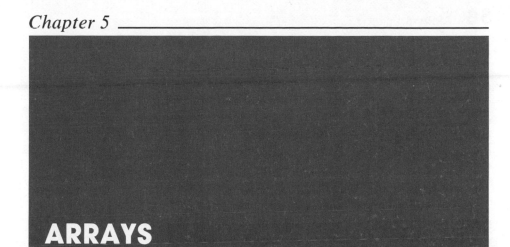

ARRAYS

Previous chapters have introduced some of Ada's predefined data types (integer, string, Boolean, float, and character). With these data types we have been able to solve some fairly simple problems. As the complexity of problems increases, we must have available more complex data structures in our arsenal of tools. The array is the first structured data type that we present. Virtually every high level language provides the programmer with the array data structure. As this chapter shows, Ada extends the scope of array manipulations beyond the boundaries established in Pascal.

Whenever one needs to store/or manipulate a set of data objects where each data object is of the same type, the array structure may be appropriate. For example, the appropriate mechanism for storing 1500 examination scores for later statistical processing may be the array. Arrays may be unidimensional or multidimensional. Multidimensional arrays are often called matrices. An important feature of the array data structure is the ease with which one may fetch a data object from an array. This is accomplished through array addressing. For example, A(4) represents the data object stored in the fourth "slot" of the array A; B(3,7) represents the data object stored in the third row and seventh column of the two dimensional array B.

Ada allows both static and dynamic dimensioning of arrays. The dynamic dimensioning feature, which is illustrated in this chapter, allows software library modules to be more easily written.

The subject of arrays allows us to enter a realm of more complex and interesting problems. In this chapter we present programs that deal with problems that are important in their own right.

57

5.1 CONSTRAINED ARRAYS

Constrained arrays are dimensioned using any discrete index type (discrete variables are formally introduced in Chapter 6). An array may contain any type of data object, but all entries in the array must be of the same type. Later chapters introduce a rich variety of data object types, all of which may be contained within an array. Chapter 8 presents a more sophisticated data structure known as a record, which can contain data objects of different types.

The array data structure may be declared as follows.

type USER_DEFINED_NAME **is array**(USER_DEFINED_RANGE) **of** [data type];

Some examples:

type RARRAY **is array**(1..2000) **of** FLOAT;
type STRING_OF_CHAR **is array**(1..30) **of** CHARACTER;
type MATRIX **is array**(−25..25,−2..2) **of** INTEGER;
type TRUTH_TABLE **is array**(1..20,1..5,1..3) **of** BOOLEAN;

Each type declaration creates a template. To activate such a template, a variable declaration naming the array type must exist. This process, called elaboration, sets space aside for the declared variables. Some examples:

A,B,C: RARRAY;
  D,E: STRING_OF_CHAR;
    F: MATRIX;
    G: TRUTH_TABLE;

Whenever variables representing constrained arrays (statically dimensioned) are elaborated, memory space is set aside for each variable elaborated. For example, when the declaration "A,B,C:RARRAY;" is elaborated, memory space for 6000 floating point numbers is set aside, since each of the variables A, B, and C requires 2000 floating point numbers. On a machine that requires 4 bytes per floating point number, each of the variables A, B, and C will require 8000 bytes of memory space before the program execution begins. If 2 bytes of memory is required to store an integer variable, the elaboration "F: MATRIX;" requires $51 \times 5 \times 2 = 510$ bytes of memory space. If each Boolean variable requires 1 byte of memory, the variable G requires $20 \times 5 \times 3 = 300$ bytes of memory when it is elaborated.

It is evident that the programmer must be cautious in declaring variables to be an array type, since all machines are limited in memory. Although Ada imposes no constraint on the number of dimensions in an array, it is obvious that the amount of memory space utilized by a high order array may exceed the capacity of a particular computer. A statically dimensioned array requires memory space determined by the array declaration. This space is independent of how much of the array the program actually uses.

Arrays can also be declared without defining a type. For example,

```
A,B: array (1..2000) of FLOAT;
  C: array (1..2000) of FLOAT;
```

These arrays are said to be of anonymous type. Anonymous types cannot be mixed in expressions because each is considered to have a separate identity and therefore is a separate type. For example, the expression

```
A:=C;
```

would be illegal.

Let us illustrate the use of arrays by considering Program 5.1-1, which allows a user to input a list of names, each name represented as an array of characters. Later we extend this program to allow the list of names to be alphabetized.

PROGRAM 5.1-1

```
with TEXT_IO; use TEXT_IO;
procedure INPUT_LIST_OF_NAMES is
        type NAME is array(1..100,1..20) of CHARACTER;
            N: NAME;
        SIZE,J: INTEGER;
        CHAR: CHARACTER;
begin
        ——We initialize the two dimensional array to blanks
        for ROW in 1..100 loop
            for COLUMN in 1..20 loop
                N(ROW,COLUMN):=' ';
            end loop;
        end loop;
```

```
        put("How many names will be alphabetized: ");
        get(SIZE);
        put_line(" ");
        --We input the list of names
        for I in 1..SIZE loop
                put("Enter name ");
                put(I);
                put(". Terminate name with '/-->");
                get(CHAR);
                J:=0;
                while CHAR /= '/' loop
                        J:=J+1;
                        N(I,J):=CHAR;
                        get(CHAR);
                        exit when J=20 ;   --A name cannot have more than 20
                                           --characters
                end loop;
                put_line(" ");
        end loop;
        put("List of names successfully input.");
end INPUT_LIST_OF_NAMES;
```

The two dimensional array of characters is initialized to blanks because later when we print out each name (in alphabetical order) we can print out all 20 columns in each row of the matrix without having to worry about how many nonblank characters are in each row.

To complete Program 5.1-1 and make it an alphabetizing program, we must discuss sorting. For now, we present two simple methods for sorting a group of discrete objects (a set of objects for which a natural ordering exists). Then we will add alphabetizing to Program 5.1-1.

5.1.1 Sorted Tales

Program 5.1-2 presents a sorting method called "exchange sort." The algorithm is described by the following (we use an informal algorithm language that should be self-explanatory):

Input array A of size N
index:= N+1
loop
        index:= index−1
        find position of maximum value in array A from 1 to index
        exchange elements A(index) with A(position)
        exit when index=2
end loop

By continuing to exchange the maximum value in the array from 1 to index (where index is decremented by one each time around the loop), with the contents of the last position, we are assured that the elements in the array A will be in ascending order when we are done. Program 5.1-2 translates this algorithm into an Ada program.

PROGRAM 5.1-2

```
with TEXT_IO; use TEXT_IO;
procedure EXCHANGE_SORT is
        type IARRAY is array(1..50) of INTEGER;
                                A: IARRAY;
        SIZE,TEMP,INDEX,MAXIMUM,POSITION: INTEGER;
begin
        put("How many integers will be sorted: ");
        get(SIZE);
        put_line(" ");
        for I in 1..SIZE loop
                put("Enter A(");
                put(I);
                put("): ");
                get(TEMP);
                A(I):=TEMP;
        end loop;
        INDEX:=SIZE+1;
        loop
                INDEX:=INDEX-1;
                --We find the maximum value in array A from 1 to INDEX
                MAXIMUM:=A(1);
                POSITION:=1;
                for I in 1..INDEX loop
                        if A(I) >= MAXIMUM then
                                MAXIMUM:=A(I);
                                POSITION:=I;
                        end if;
                end loop;
                --We exchange A(POSITION) with A(INDEX)
                TEMP:=A(POSITION);
                A(POSITION):=A(INDEX);
                A(INDEX):=TEMP;
                exit when INDEX=2;
        end loop;
        --We output the sorted array
        put_line(" ");
        put_line("The sorted integers");
        put_line("--------------");
```

```
     for I in 1..SIZE loop
          TEMP:=A(I);
          put(TEMP);
          put_line(" ");
     end loop;
end EXCHANGE_SORT;
```

We have chosen integers to be the objects of our sort procedure in Program 5.1-2. This was done to permit the reader to concentrate on the sorting algorithm. Have you walked your way through Program 5.1-2?

Our next sorting algorithm is called the "bubble-sort" algorithm. It goes as follows.

Input the array of objects stored in A, from 1 to SIZE
outer_loop_counter:=1
outer loop
    i=0
    b:=false
    inner loop
        i:=i+1
        if A(i) > A(i+1) then
            exchange A(i) with A(i+1)
            b:=true
        end if
        exit when i=SIZE-outer_loop_counter
    end inner loop
    outer_loop_counter:=outer_loop_counter+1
    exit when (outer_loop_counter = SIZE) or (b=false)
end outer loop

At the end of the first outer loop cycle we are guaranteed that the maximum value in the array A is in the A(SIZE) position. At the end of the second outer loop cycle we are guaranteed that the second largest value is in the A(SIZE-1) position. And so forth. The number of possible exchanges in the inner loop decreases by one for each iteration of the outer loop.

The number of exchanges that may be required is the sum of the series $n + (n - 1) + (n - 2) + \cdots + 2 + 1$ whose sum is a second order polynomial in n [i.e., $n(n + 1)/2$]. This suggests that if you double the size of the array to be sorted, you will quadruple the amount of time needed to perform the sorting when n is large. This algorithm, like the exchange algorithm that preceded it, is said to be of complexity n^2.

The purpose of the Boolean variable b in the bubble-sort algorithm above is to determine whether an interchange was required in the inner loop. If an outer cycle is possible without an interchange occurring (*b* remains false), then the list of objects is already sorted and there is no point in continuing with the outer loop.

We translate the algorithm above into an Ada program.

PROGRAM 5.1-3

```
with TEXT_IO; use TEXT_IO;
procedure BUBBLE_SORT is
        type IARRAY is array(1..500) of INTEGER;
                        A: IARRAY;
        SIZE,TEMP,OUTER_COUNT,I: INTEGER;
                        B: BOOLEAN;
begin
        put("Enter the size of the array of integers: ");
        get(SIZE);
        put_line(" ");
        --We input the array of integers
        for I in 1..SIZE loop
            put("Enter integer "); put(I); put(": ");
            get(TEMP);
            A(I):=TEMP;
        end loop;
        --We begin the bubble-sort algorithm
        OUTER_COUNT:=1;
        loop
            I:=0;
            B:=FALSE;
            --B will be changed to true if an interchange occurs
            loop
                I:=I+1;
                if A(I)>A(I+1) then
                --We exchange A(I) with A(I+1)
                    TEMP:=A(I);
                    A(I):=A(I+1);
                    A(I+1):=TEMP;
                    B:=TRUE;        --The numbers are not yet sorted
                end if;
                exit when I=SIZE-OUTER_COUNT;
            end loop;
            OUTER_COUNT:=OUTER_COUNT+1;
            exit when (OUTER_COUNT=SIZE) or (not B);
        end loop;
        --We output the sorted array
        put_line(" ");
```

```
        put_line("The sorted integers");
        put_line("---------------");
        for I in 1..SIZE loop
             TEMP:=A(I);
             put(TEMP);
             put_line(" ");
        end loop;
end loop;
end BUBBLE_SORT;
```

In Chapter 7, where we present procedures and functions, we rework this program so that the programming style is more structured and thus more readable.

We now return to Program 5.1-1 and, using the bubble-sort method, add alphabetizing to the program. Comparisons of the type $<$, $<=$, $/=$, $>$, $>=$ are applicable to objects of type character, and the uppercase letters are less than the lowercase letters.

PROGRAM 5.1-4

```
with TEXT_IO; use TEXT_IO;
procedure ALPHABETIZE is
        type NAME is array(1..100,1..20) of CHARACTER;
        type ROW is array(1..20) of CHARACTER;
                              N: NAME;
                              R: ROW;
        SIZE,J,OUTER_COUNT,I: INTEGER;
                           CHAR: CHARACTER;
                           B,T: BOOLEAN;
begin
        --We initialize the two dimensional array to blanks
        for ROW in 1..100 loop
             for COLUMN in 1..20 loop
                  N(ROW,COLUMN):=' ';
             end loop;
        end loop;
        put("How many names will be alphabetized: ");
        get(SIZE);
        put_line(" ");
        --We input the list of names
        for I in 1..SIZE loop
             put("Enter name "); put(I);
             put(". Terminate name with '/-->");
             get(CHAR);
             J:=0;
             while CHAR /= '/' loop
```

```
                    J:=J+1;
                    N(I,J):=CHAR;
                    get(CHAR);
                    exit when J=20;   --A name cannot have more than 20
                                      --characters
              end loop;
              put_line(" ");
      end loop;                       --This is where Program 5.1-1 ends
      --We begin the bubble-sort
      OUTER_COUNT:=1;
      loop
              B:=FALSE;
              I:=0;
              loop
                    I:=I+1;
                    --We compare the Ith row with the (I+1)th row
                    J:=0;
                    loop
                            J:=J+1;
                            if N(I+1,J) < N(I,J) then
                                    T:=TRUE;
                            else
                                    T:=FALSE;
                            end if;
                            exit when (N(I+1,J) /= N(I,J)) or (J=20);
                    end loop;
                    if T then          --We interchange row I with row I+1
                            --We copy the (I+1)th row into array R as a temporary
                            --array
                            for K in 1..20 loop
                                    R(K):=N(I,K);
                            end loop;
                            for K in 1..20 loop
                                    N(I,K):=N(I+1,K);
                                    N(I+1,K):=R(K);
                            end loop;
                            B:=TRUE;
                            --We are not done sorting because we performed an
                            --interchange
                    end if;
                    exit when I=SIZE-OUTER_COUNT;
              end loop;
              OUTER_COUNT:=OUTER_COUNT+1;
              exit when (OUTER_COUNT=SIZE) or (not B);
      end loop;
      --We output the alphabetized list
```

```
        put_line(" ");
        put_line("The alphabetized list");
        put_line("---------------");
        for ROW in 1..SIZE loop
             for COLUMN in 1..20 loop
                  CHAR:=N(ROW,COLUMN);
                  put(CHAR);
             end loop;
             put_line(" ");
        end loop;
end ALPHABETIZE;
```

Program 5.1-4 is difficult to read because it lacks structure. We rework this program in Chapter 7, where we introduce procedures, functions, and structured programming. You may have noticed loops deeply nested within loops in Program 5.1-4. Have you taken careful notice of the indentation style used? Program 5.1-4 allows you to review the loop constructs of Chapter 4. Walk your way through Program 5.1-4 using as name 1, Wiener, and as name 2, Sincovec.

5.1.2 Another Prime Example

Before introducing additional array constructs, we return to the problem of generating prime numbers. In Chapter 4 we presented a program for generating prime integers (Program 4.5-2). Now we will rework that program using arrays. We will save each prime integer generated in an array. Then instead of generating divisors that consist of all the odd integers up to the square root of the candidate, we will generate divisors consisting only of previously obtained prime integers up to the square root of the candidate. This should speed up the computation significantly.

PROGRAM 5.1-5

```
--In this program, successive prime numbers are stored in an array called
--PRIME_NUMBER. To test whether a candidate integer is prime, it is divided by
--the previously obtained prime numbers that are equal to or less than the square
--root of the candidate.
with TEXT_IO; use TEXT_IO;
procedure FASTER_PRIME_NUMBERS is
        type INTEGER_ARRAY is array(1..1000) of INTEGER;
             CANDIDATE: INTEGER:=5;
        DIVISOR,INDEX,I: INTEGER;
                  PRIME: BOOLEAN;
        PRIME_NUMBER: INTEGER_ARRAY;   --Array of prime numbers
begin
        put_line("This program generates all the prime numbers up to 1999");
        put_line("------------------------------------");
```

```
put_line(" ");
put("2");           --The smallest prime number
put_line(" ");
put("3");           --The second smallest prime number
put_line(" ");
put("5");           --At this rate, this will be a long program!
put_line(" ");
PRIME_NUMBER(1):=3;
PRIME_NUMBER(2):=5;
INDEX:=2;
loop
        DIVISOR:=PRIME_NUMBER(1);
        CANDIDATE:=CANDIDATE+2;   --CANDIDATE was initialized to be 5
        PRIME:=TRUE;   --PRIME may have only the "values" TRUE or FALSE
                        --We assume that the candidate is prime
        I:=0;
        while DIVISOR*DIVISOR <= CANDIDATE loop
                I:=I+1;
                DIVISOR:=PRIME_NUMBER(I);
                if CANDIDATE mod DIVISOR = 0 then
                        PRIME:=FALSE;
                        exit;   --No need to keep testing with more divisors
                end if;
        end loop;
        if PRIME then
                put(CANDIDATE);
                put_line(" ");
                INDEX:=INDEX+1;
                PRIME_NUMBER(INDEX):=CANDIDATE;
        end if;
        exit when CANDIDATE=1999;
    end loop;
end FASTER_PRIME_NUMBERS;
```

5.1.3 Array Assignment Statements

Ada allows us two aggregate methods for assigning values into an array. The first is by position, the second is by value. We illustrate each of the two methods below.

Assignment by Position

```
type RARRAY is array(1..3) of FLOAT;
A,B: RARRAY:=(1.5,2.6,7.1);
  C: RARRAY;
begin
      C:=(4.0,0.0,-2.5);
```

The arrays A and B have both been initialized to the values 1.5, 2.6, and 7.1 in slots 1, 2, and 3, respectively. The array C has been assigned the values C(1)=4.0, C(2)=0.0, and C(3)=−2.5.

For positional assignments, the association between array components and array values is determined by their respective positions in a list.

Assignment by Value

```
type IARRAY is array(1..6) of INTEGER;
A,B: IARRAY:=(1..4=>61, 5=>−3, 6=>0);
  C: IARRAY;
begin
      C:=(1..2=>0, 3..5=>17, 6=>−14);
```

The arrays A and B have the value 61 in slots 1 through 4, the value −3 in slot 5, and the value 0 in slot 6. The array C has the value 0 in slots 1 and 2, the value 17 in slots 3, 4, and 5, and the value −14 in slot 6. For value assignments, the association between the array position and the value to be assigned to that position must be specified. The index or array positions do not need to be specified in order. The key word "others" may also be used but it must appear last. For example,

```
C:= (6=>−14, 1..2=>0, others=>17);
```

5.1.4 Array Equality and Array Constants

Ada allows one array to be set equal to another as an aggregate. The array assignment A:=B is legal only if A and B are of the same type and size. In fact, assignment and equality testing are defined for all Ada types except limited private types. This matter is further discussed in Chapter 13.

An array may be declared to be a constant provided its value is specified. For example, one way to define a 3 × 3 identity matrix is:

```
type MATRIX is array (1..3,1..3) of INTEGER;
IDENTITY: constant MATRIX:= (1=> (1=>1, 2=>0, 3=>0),
                             2=> (1=>0, 2=>1, 3=>0),
                             3=> (1=>0, 2=>0, 3=>1));
```

Another way would be:

```
IDENTITY: constant MATRIX:= (1=> (1, 0, 0),
                             2=> (0, 1, 0),
                             3=> (0, 0, 1));
```

5.1.5   Array Slices

We illustrate array slicing for single and multidimensional arrays in the following program segment.

```
A,B: array(1..10) of INTEGER;
  C: array(1..5,1..10) of INTEGER;
begin

A(4..9):= (4,5,6,7,8,9);
A(1..3):= A(7..9);
A(10):= A(5);
        ––Assume that the two dimensional array C has been defined

B(1..10):= C(4)(1..10);
        ––The array B is assigned the fourth row of matrix C

A(2..6):= C(2)(1..5);
        –– The elements in array A, slots 2 to 6 are assigned values
        –– equal to the elements in matrix C, row 2, elements 1 to 5
```

There is no mechanism for taking a slice of a column of a two dimensional array. For multidimensional arrays, the slice can be only over the leftmost index.

In Program 5.1-6 we illustrate some of the constructs just presented. In this program we allow the user to enter up to 50 grades for three different examinations for 50 students. Then we compute the average for each student over the three examinations and the average over all the students for each examination.

PROGRAM 5.1-6

```
with TEXT_IO; use TEXT_IO;
procedure GRADES_FOR_CLASS is
      type GRADES is array(1..50,1..3) of FLOAT;
          G: GRADES;
          H: array(1..3) of FLOAT;
      R,SUM: FLOAT;
begin
      --We input the grades
      for ROW in 1..50 loop
          for COLUMN in 1..3 loop
                put("Enter grade "); put(COLUMN);
                put(" for student "); put(ROW);
                get(R);
                put_line(" ");
                G(ROW,COLUMN):=R;
          end loop;
      end loop;
      --We average each student's grades
      for ROW in 1..50 loop
          --We take a slice of row ROW of matrix G
          H(1..3):=G(ROW)(1..3);
          SUM:=0.0;
          for I in 1..3 loop
                SUM:=SUM+H(I);
          end loop;
          put("The average for student ");
          put(ROW);
          put("=");
          put(SUM/3.0);
          put_line(" ");
      end loop;
      --We compute the average for each examination
      for COLUMN in 1..3 loop
          SUM:=0.0;
          for ROW in 1..50 loop
                SUM:=SUM+G(ROW,COLUMN);
```

```
    end loop;
    put("The average for examination");
    put(COLUMN);
    put("=");
    put(SUM/50.0);
    put_line(" ");
  end loop;
end GRADES_FOR_CLASS;
```

5.2   UNCONSTRAINED ARRAYS

Ada allows us to specify an array type without specifying the limits or range of the dimensions of the array. For an array of this type to be used, it must be dimensioned when an object of that type is declared (or when used as an actual parameter).

The syntax for an unconstrained array is as follows.

```
type USER_DEFINED_NAME is array(TYPE range <>) of [data type];
```

We illustrate the use of an unconstrained array type in Program 5.2-1, where we compute the sum of the elements in an array.

PROGRAM 5.2-1

```
with TEXT_IO; use TEXT_IO;
procedure UNCONSTRAINED_ARRAY is
    type IARRAY is array(INTEGER range <>) of INTEGER;
    SUM: INTEGER:=0;
        T: INTEGER;
        S: IARRAY(1..20);   --Memory is allocated
begin
    for I in 1..20 loop
        put("Enter element "); put(I); put(": ");
        get(T);
        put_line(" ");
        S(I):=T;
        SUM:=SUM+S(I);
```

```
          end loop;
          put_line(" ");
          put_line("The sum of the elements in the array is ");
          put(SUM);
     end UNCONSTRAINED_ARRAY;
```

To display the real power of unconstrained arrays, we need to define subprograms that accept as a parameter an unconstrained array. We do this in Chapter 7 when we discuss subprograms and present programs that display the use of unconstrained arrays in the proper context.

5.3 ATTRIBUTES ASSOCIATED WITH ARRAYS

An attribute is a predefined characteristic of a named entity. Ada allows us to refer to various attributes of arrays, which are as follows.

ATTRIBUTES FOR ONE DIMENSIONAL ARRAYS (VECTORS)

```
type VECTOR is array (INTEGER range <>) of FLOAT;
type MATRIX is array (INTEGER range <>, INTEGER range <>) of FLOAT;
V: VECTOR;
M: MATRIX;
```

VECTOR'FIRST	--Lower bound of index
VECTOR'LAST	--Upper bound of index
VECTOR'LENGTH	--Number of components in array
V'FIRST	--Lower bound of index for object V
V'LAST	--Upper bound of index for object V
V'RANGE	--The range, V'FIRST..V'LAST

ATTRIBUTES FOR MULTIDIMENSIONAL ARRAYS (MATRICES)

MATRIX'FIRST(I)	--Lower bound of Ith index of MATRIX type
MATRIX'LAST(I)	--Upper bound of Ith index of MATRIX type
MATRIX'LENGTH(I)	--Length of Ith index of MATRIX type
M'FIRST(I)	--Lower bound of Ith index of matrix object
M'LAST(I)	--Upper bound of Ith index of matrix object
M'LENGTH(I)	--Length of Ith index of matrix object
M'RANGE(I)	--The range, M'FIRST(I)..M'LAST(I)

We illustrate these array attributes in later chapters.

5.4 SUMMARY

- Array data structures are user defined using the key word "array". They may be of anonymous type, or a type name may be used.
- An array may have one, two, or more dimensions. All components of the array are of the same type.
- Aggregate array assignment can be by position or by value, but these two kinds of assignment cannot be mixed.
- A variety of array operations is permitted, including array assignment, testing for equality, and array slices. Assignment requires that the number of components in each dimension be equal, but the index bounds may be different.
- Unconstrained array types permit the definition of arrays in which the range constraints for the indices are not specified until objects of the array type are declared.
- Various array attributes are available that are useful in developing general purpose flexible software.

Exercises for Chapter 5

1. Write a program that allows the user to input an array of characters. Then the program should compute the number of vowels in the array.

2. Write a program that allows the user to input an array of floating point numbers. Then the program should compute the median value in the array.

3. Write a program that allows the user to input two arrays, A and B, each an array of floating point numbers containing the same number of elements. Then the program must compare the two arrays, element by element, and print out how many elements in array A are greater than the corresponding elements in array B.

4. Write a program that merges the two arrays created in Problem 3 into one ordered array C.

5. Write a program that sorts floating point numbers using an algorithm different from the two presented in this chapter.

6. Write a program that sorts an array of integers into descending order.

7. Write a program that determines all the duplicates in an array of integers.

8. Write a program that allows the user to input a two dimensional array of floating point numbers. Then the program should find the row and column of the component of the array with the maximum absolute value. Use attributes.

9. The Boolean operators "and", "or", "xor", and "not" are applicable to one dimensional Boolean arrays with the restriction that for binary operators the two operands have the same number of components. Write a program that creates Boolean arrays, performs these operations, and outputs the results.

10. Consider the following type declarations.

    type VECTOR **is array** (9..100) **of** INTEGER;
    type MATRIX **is array** (0..20,−25..30) **of** INTEGER;
    V: VECTOR;
    M: MATRIX;

    Compute all the attributes given in Section 5.3.

Chapter 6

TYPES

Ada is a strongly typed language. This means that every identifier must have its type declared before it can be used. In Chapter 2, we described the predefined data types of integer, float, Boolean, character, and string and gave examples illustrating their use. However, most problems can be more naturally described and more easily understood in terms of the actual data objects that arise within the definition of the problem. One of the powerful features of Ada is that it permits the programmer to define his or her own data types or objects, to specify the permissible set of values for the data types, and to restrict the set of operations applicable to the objects of the data types. Carefully defined data types that are especially tailored to the application or problem at hand simplify program understanding, readability, and maintainability.

The data description features of Ada are inherited from Pascal and are a significant improvement over the essentially nonexistent capabilities for describing data in Fortran. The features of Ada that permit original data definitions are described in detail in this chapter.

6.1 TYPES IN ADA

The common properties of the objects required in an Ada program may be defined using data type definitions. To change the properties, the data type definition needs to be revised. Program maintainability is enhanced if all the data type definitions are collected together in one place in the program.

A data type definition gives structure to objects or variables that are declared to be of that type. A type may be characterized as a set of values and a

75

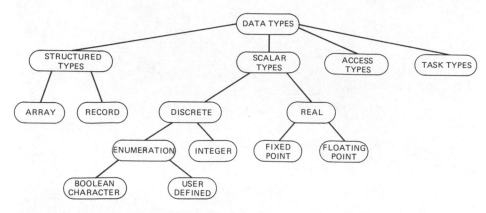

Figure 6.1 Classification of types in Ada.

set of operations that apply to objects of that type. All operations performed on an object must be an allowable operation and all values assigned to the object must be an allowable value. The compiler distinguishes objects of different types and enforces the rules that are applicable.

In Ada, equality testing and assignment are defined for all types except limited private types, which are discussed in Chapter 13.

There are three classes of data types in Ada: scalar types, whose values have no components, structured types, whose values have indexed or explicitly named components, and access types, which permit instances of the type to be dynamically allocated during execution. The two basic structured types are arrays and records. We encountered arrays in Chapter 5, record types are discussed in Chapter 8, and access types are the topic of Chapter 12. In this chapter we restrict our attention to scalar types. Figure 6.1 illustrates the classification of types in Ada.

Scalar types are characterized as data objects with no components. Scalar types are categorized as either discrete or real. Discrete types can take on values from an ordered set of values that has a lower bound and an upper bound. Since the set of values is ordered, any value other than the upper bound has a unique successor. Discrete types may be used as an iteration range of a "for" loop or as an index set of an array. Discrete types include integers, Boolean types, character types, and enumeration types. Real types include floating point types with a specified number of significant digits and fixed point types with a specified maximum error. That is, floating point types have relative accuracy specified and fixed point types have absolute accuracy specified.

6.1.1 Predefined Types

Several predefined scalar types in Ada are INTEGER, FLOAT, BOOLEAN, and CHARACTER. They may be used by simply declaring objects or identifiers to be of the desired type. The set of values that may be assigned to objects declared to be of a predefined type and the allowable operations that may be performed on the objects are determined by the system. These data types have been extensively used in the preceding chapters, but we illustrate them here in the following examples.

```
I,J,K: INTEGER;    --Declare I, J, K to be integer variables
X,Y,Z: FLOAT;      --Declare X, Y, Z to be floating point variables
P,Q: BOOLEAN;      --Declare P and Q to be Boolean variables
C: CHARACTER;      --Declare C to be a character variable
```

We may also initialize the identifiers in the declare statement as follows:

```
I,J: INTEGER:=0;          --I and J are integer variables with an initial value of
                          --0
X: FLOAT:=10.0;           --X is a floating point variable with an initial value of
                          --10.0
B,YES: BOOLEAN:=TRUE;     --B and YES are Boolean variables with an initial
                          --value of TRUE
CHAR: CHARACTER:='c';     --CHAR is a character variable with an initial value
                          --of 'c'
```

A constant may be declared by using the key word "constant" after the colon. For numeric constants, the numeric type may be omitted. For example,

```
PI: constant FLOAT:=3.141594;
```

or

```
PI: constant:=3.141594;
```

The mixing of objects of different types is illegal. For example, if I and J are of type INTEGER and X is of type FLOAT, the following expressions would be illegal.

```
I:=10.0;       --Illegal because the floating point literal 10.0 cannot be assigned
               --to an integer variable
I:=X;          --Illegal because a floating point variable cannot be assigned to an
               --integer variable
X:=10.0 + I;   --Illegal because a floating point number can cannot be added to
               --an integer variable
I:=10.0 * 10;  --Illegal because a floating point number cannot be multiplied by
               --an integer number
```

All the preceding errors would be detected by the compiler. Since Ada is a strongly typed language, the type of every variable and every expression can be determined by the compiler and checked for compatibility at compile time. This imposes stringent type compatibility restrictions.

The statements "X:=X+10.0;" and "I:=I+10;" both contain an addition operator "+". The two occurrences of "+" are logically distinct operators with different meanings, since the first statement involves the addition of floating point numbers and the second involves the addition of integers. The symbol "+" is said to be overloaded; that is, it has more than one meaning. The compiler determines the meaning of the operator symbol by examining the number and type of the associated operands. The overloading of operators is discussed in more detail in Chapter 7.

6.1.2 Type Declaration

Ada allows the programmer to define data objects with distinct names and properties. Carefully chosen descriptive names enhance the readability of the resulting program and often result in more expedient program development and verification. The syntax for defining a data type is:

type TYPE_NAME **is** TYPE_DEFINITION;

The data object type defined by such a declaration is referred to as the base or parent type in the sections that follow. A type characterizes a set of values and a set of operations applicable to those values. The TYPE DEFINITION is illustrated in the examples that appear in this chapter and it may contain a constraint that restricts the set of possible values without changing the set of applicable operations.

An example of a type definition and its use to declare objects of that type is:

type VECTOR **is array** (1..7) **of** INTEGER;
X,Y: VECTOR;
  Z: VECTOR:=(20,0,33,−12,89,−21,0);

This defines a VECTOR to be an array of seven integers. X and Y are declared to be of type VECTOR. Z is a VECTOR initialized to the seven values indicated.

Our second example is an enumeration type, which is discussed in more detail later in this chapter.

type DAY **is** (MON, TUE, WED, THU, FRI, SAT, SUN);

This introduces a user-defined type called DAY; there are only seven values that variables of this type can be assigned.

6.1.3 Subtype Declaration

Subtypes are simply a subset of some base or parent type. Subtypes are used to restrict the set of allowable values that identifiers of the subtype can be assigned. Subtype definitions are useful when specific constraints on the possible values of data objects are needed or desirable in the program.

The allowable operations defined for the base type carry over to the subtype. Assignment statements may freely assign values of subtypes to data objects or identifiers of the base type. However, assignment statements that assign values of the base type to the subtype are valid only if the constraint of the subtype is obeyed. Proper subtype definitions can help detect programming errors by preventing variables from being assigned inappropriate values. Only unconstrained arrays may have subtypes.

The syntax for defining subtypes is:

subtype SUBTYPE_NAME **is** TYPE_NAME **range** CONSTRAINT;

The "range (CONSTRAINT)" portion of the subtype syntax may be an accuracy constraint, an index constraint, or a discriminant constraint. The use of the accuracy constraint is considered in Section 6.3. The other constraints are discussed in later chapters in the proper context.

The following example illustrates subtype declarations.

```
type COLOR is (RED, AMBER, GREEN, BLUE, BROWN, BLACK);
type DAY is (MON, TUE, WED, THU, FRI, SAT, SUN);
subtype LIGHT is COLOR range RED. . GREEN;
subtype WEEKDAY is DAY range MON. . FRI;
subtype WEEKEND is DAY range SAT. . SUN;
     PEN: COLOR:=RED
SIGNAL: LIGHT:=GREEN;
  WORK: WEEKDAY;
   PLAY: WEEKEND;
```

In this example, COLOR and DAY are enumeration types with the set of possible values given. LIGHT is a subtype of the base type COLOR, and the variable SIGNAL can take on the values RED, AMBER, or GREEN. The variable PLAY can take on the values SAT and SUN.

Another example of subtypes involving integers with a constrained range is the following.

PROGRAM 6.1-1

```
––This exciting program has no output!
procedure SUBTYPES is
     subtype SMALL is INTEGER range −500. .500;
       I,J: SMALL:=0;
       P,Q: INTEGER:=0;
begin
       I:=150;     ––Legal
       I:=I+300;   ––Requires a check at execution time to verify that the constraint
                   ––is satisfied
       P:=I;       ––Always legal
       I:=P;       ––Requires a check at execution time to verify that P is in the
                   ––range of SMALL
       I:=Q+J;     ––Legal but also requires checking
end SUBTYPES;
```

Program 6.1-1 illustrates that constraints may be checked at compile time, or they may require checking at execution time. Note also that the mixing of subtypes from the same parent type is permitted. Expressions involving subtypes are evaluated as if the variables involved were all of the parent type, but the subsequent assignment statement may require a range check.

6.1.4 Derived Types and Conversion

A derived type is a new instance of a given type that derives its characteristics from the existing type or parent type. The syntax for derived types is:

type DERIVED_TYPE **is new** PARENT_TYPE [constraint];

The constraint is optional. It may be a range, accuracy, index, or discriminant constraint.

Derived types are useful in those applications where the mixing of types needs to be prevented. The set of values that the derived type can assume is identical to the set of values that the parent type can take on. Any constraints that apply to the parent type also apply to the derived type. The derived type inherits all the operations of the parent type. Since the derived type is distinct from the parent type, expressions can involve only the derived type or the parent type unless explicit conversion between types is specified. Explicit conversion between types and the tree structure of related types that the programmer can build via derived types is illustrated in the next example.

PROGRAM 6.1-2

```
with TEXT_IO; use TEXT_IO;
procedure DERIVED_TYPES_AND_CONVERSION is
      type WEIGHT is new INTEGER;
      type VOLUME is new INTEGER;
      type CARGO_WEIGHT is new WEIGHT;
      type TRUCK_WEIGHT is new WEIGHT;
      type DRIVER_WEIGHT is new WEIGHT;
          CARGO: CARGO_WEIGHT:=6000;
          TRUCK: TRUCK_WEIGHT:=10000;
          DRIVER: DRIVER_WEIGHT:=200;
      CUBIC_FEET: VOLUME:=0;
              W: WEIGHT:=0;
          L1,L2: INTEGER:=10;
            L3: INTEGER:=30;
            N: INTEGER;
begin
      W:=WEIGHT(CARGO)+WEIGHT(TRUCK)+WEIGHT(DRIVER);
      put(W);                                   ——16200 is printed
      CUBIC_FEET:=INTEGER(L1*L2*L3);
      put(CUBIC_FEET);                          ——3000 is printed
      W:=WEIGHT(INTEGER(CUBIC_FEET));           ——Conversion of volume
                                                ——type to weight type
      put(W);                                   ——3000 is printed
      CARGO:=CARGO_WEIGHT(WEIGHT(DRIVER));      ——Conversion of
                                                ——driver_weight type to
                                                ——cargo_weight type
      put(CARGO);                               ——200 is printed
end DERIVED_TYPES_AND_CONVERSION;
```

The tree structure of derived types defined in Program 6.1-2 is illustrated in Figure 6.2. Here type conversions are automatically defined between adjacent nodes of the tree but must be explicitly specified. Examples of explicit conversion between types are indicated in Program 6.1-2. To further illustrate this concept we present a few statements that if inserted into Program 6.1-2 would be illegal.

```
W:=CARGO+TRUCK+DRIVER;         ——Illegal because CARGO, TRUCK, and DRIVER
                              ——are all of different types
CUBIC_FEET:=L1*L2*L3;          ——Illegal because the product of L1, L2, and L3
                              ——is of type INTEGER, which cannot be assigned
                              ——to an identifier of type VOLUME
```

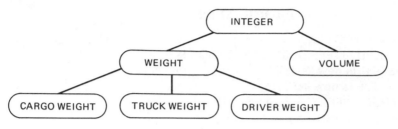

Figure 6.2   Tree structure of derived types for Program 6.1-2.

6.2 DISCRETE TYPES

6.2.1 Integer Types

The integer type is predefined in the implementation of Ada. The allowable range of integer values is dependent on the particular computer. For example, on a computer with 16-bit integers there are 65535 integers ($2^{16}-1$) that can be represented in the range from -32767 to $+32767$. On this 16-bit computer the predefined integer type is

type INTEGER **is range** $-32767 . . 32767$;

The natural numbers are a subtype of the type integer and are predefined in unit STANDARD as follows.

subtype NATURAL **is** INTEGER **range** $0 . . $INTEGER'LAST;

where the attribute INTEGER'LAST represents the largest integer that can be represented on the computer.

The subtype NATURAL permits the user to define the set of natural numbers available on the computer independent of the computer that the program will actually execute on. Of course, if the range of natural numbers required in the algorithm is greater than INTEGER'LAST, serious errors may result unless the programmer checks and accounts for such a possibility in the program.

Integer literals are strings of digits possibly separated by an underscore. Thus 5_112_336 and 51_1233_6 both represent the integer 5112336. Ada also permits based integer literals for any base between 2 and 16. A based integer with n base-b digits is given by

$$b\#a(n)a(n-1)a(n-2)\cdots a(0)\#$$

where $2 <= b <= 16$ and $0 <= a(i) <= b - 1$ for $i = 0, \ldots, n$. The decimal value of this base integer is given by

$$(\cdots ((a(n) * b + a(n - 1)) * b + a(n - 2)) * b + \cdots + a(1)) * b + a(0)$$

For a base greater than 10, the letters A through F are used to represent the numbers 10 through 15, respectively.

The operations that are applicable to integer types are listed in order of decreasing precedence.

**	--Exponentiation
*, /, **mod**, **rem**	--Multiplication and division operators
+, −	--Unary operators
+, −	--Addition and subtraction operators
=, /=, <, <=, >, >=	--Relational operators
abs	--Absolute value

The exponentiation operator must have a nonnegative integer exponent. The division operator truncates the result. The **rem** and **mod** functions were described in Chapter 2.

Program 6.2-1 illustrates operations with integer types and conversion.

PROGRAM 6.2-1

```
with TEXT_IO; use TEXT_IO;
procedure INTEGER_TYPES is
        type NUMBER is new INTEGER;
        type HEIGHT is new INTEGER;
        type PEAK is new HEIGHT;
        type HUMAN is new HEIGHT;
            I: INTEGER;
        VALUE: NUMBER;
            H: HEIGHT:=10;
          MTN: PEAK:=14110;
          MAN: HUMAN:=6;
begin
        VALUE:=2#1101#;
        put("Value="); put(VALUE);        --13 is printed
        put_line(" ");
        VALUE:=16#1_101#;
        put("Value="); put(VALUE);        --4353 is printed
        put_line(" ");
        VALUE:=10#1101#;
        put("Value="); put(VALUE);        --1101 is printed
        put_line(" ");
        H:=H+2;
```

```
    put("H="); put(H);                  ——12 is printed
    put_line(" ");
    H:=HEIGHT(MTN);                     ——Type conversion
    put("H="); put(H);                  ——14110 is printed
    put_line(" ");
    H:=HEIGHT(MAN) + HEIGHT(MTN);       ——Type conversion
    put("H="); put(H);                  ——14116 is printed
    put_line(" ");
end  INTEGER_TYPES;
```

All the following statements would be illegal in Program 6.2-1.

```
H:=MTN + MAN;            ——H, MTN, and MAN are of different
                        ——types
I:=H;                   ——I and H are of different types
MAN:=MTN;               ——MAN and MTN are of different types
VALUE:=HEIGHT(MAN);     ——Illegal conversion between nonadja-
                        ——cent types
```

The derived type tree structure defined in Program 6.2-1 can be illustrated in Figure 6.3. Here we can specify conversion between adjacent types. For example, we can convert INTEGER types to HEIGHT or NUMBER types, and we can convert HEIGHT types to PEAK or HUMAN types. We cannot convert NUMBER type to HEIGHT type directly because they are not adjacent, but we can still perform the conversion by HEIGHT(INTEGER(NUM)), where NUM is declared to be of type NUMBER. This converts a NUMBER type to INTEGER type and then converts an INTEGER type to HEIGHT type.

An implementation of Ada may also contain (implementation dependent) other predefined types such as SHORT_INTEGER and LONG_INTEGER in addition to the type INTEGER (see package STANDARD in Appendix C). On the computer described earlier in this section, we could not manipulate integers with a magnitude larger than 32767. In this case, the application would require the use of LONG_INTEGER. However, if we move our software to a computer where type INTEGER is represented as 32 bits rather than 16, using type

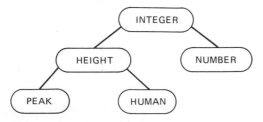

Figure 6.3   Tree structure of derived types for Program 6.2-1.

LONG_INTEGER would clearly be extravagant. How can we write portable software in Ada? If we write

type INTEGER_REQUIRED **is range** −5E4..5E4;

the implementation will choose the smallest appropriate type at compilation time. On the 16-bit computer, the type LONG_INTEGER would be chosen and the preceding type definition would be equivalent to

type INTEGER_REQUIRED **is new** LONG_INTEGER **range** −5E4..5E4;

whereas on the 32-bit computer the type INTEGER would be chosen and the type definition would be equivalent to

type INTEGER_REQUIRED **is new** INTEGER **range** −5E4..5E4;

6.2.2   Enumeration Types

Enumeration types use the syntax specified in Section 6.1.2 with the type definition consisting of a finite, ordered set of values that the identifiers of that type can take on. The Ada operations that are applicable to enumeration types are as follows.

```
:=                      --Assignment
=, /=                   --Test for equality
<, <=, >, >=            --Test for ordering
in, not in              --Test for whether a value is in the set of values for the
                        --type or subtype
```

All operations are valid only if the operands are of the same type or if the operation has been previously defined for the type of operands that the programmer is attempting to use. The type declarations provide sufficient information to the compiler so that only the operations that satisfy this criterion are permitted.

Examples of enumeration types have been given earlier in this chapter. Here is another.

```
type CURRENCY is (PENNY,NICKLE,DIME,QUARTER,HALF_DOLLAR,
                  ONE_DOLLAR,
                  FIVE_DOLLARS,TEN_DOLLARS,TWENTY_DOLLARS,
                  FIFTY_DOLLARS);
subtype COIN is CURRENCY range PENNY..HALF_DOLLAR;
```

Such an enumeration type or subtype might be useful in, say, a program designed to make change for the purchase of an item or items with a specified amount tendered.

The package TEXT_IO that we have been using contains provisions for obtaining input and output for user-defined enumeration types provided the programmer performs a "generic instantiation" of package ENUMERATION_IO, referenced in Appendix B. The subject of generics and generic instantiation is covered in Chapter 15. In many of the programs in this book, we assume that the appropriate generic instantiation has been performed, thus allowing us to use "get" and "put" statements for enumeration types.

As another example, consider the following simple program.

PROGRAM 6.2-2

```
with  TEXT_IO; use TEXT_IO;
procedure ENUMERATION_TYPES is
      type LIGHT is (RED, AMBER, GREEN);
      type DAY is (MON, TUE, WED, THU, FRI, SAT, SUN);
      SIGNAL: LIGHT;
       TODAY: DAY;
begin
      put("Input color of signal: ");
      get(SIGNAL);
      if SIGNAL=RED then
            put("Stop");
      elsif SIGNAL=AMBER then
            put("Slow down and prepare to stop");
      else
            put("Go");
      end if;
      put_line(" ");
      put("Input day of week: ");
      get(TODAY);
      if (TODAY /= SAT) and (TODAY /= SUN) then
            put("Go to work");
      else
            put("Relax and have fun");
      end if;
end ENUMERATION_TYPES;
```

In Program 6.2-2, the assignment statement TODAY:=RED would be illegal, since RED is not in the set of values for the variable TODAY, which is of type DAY. This statement would result in a compile time error.

The next example illustrates iteration over enumeration types and the use of enumeration types as index sets for arrays.

PROGRAM 6.2-3

```
with TEXT_IO; use TEXT_IO;
procedure USER_DEFINED_ENUMERATION_TYPES is
      types MONTHS is (JAN,FEB,MAR,APR,MAY,JUN,JUL,AUG,SEP,OCT,NOV,
      DEC);
      subtype DAYNUMBER is INTEGER range 1..31;
      type WEATHER_RECORD is array(MONTHS,DAYNUMBER) of INTEGER;
      LOTEMP,HITEMP: WEATHER_RECORD;
            DAY,DAYS: DAYNUMBER;
      T_LOW,T_HIGH: INTEGER;
            ANSWER: CHARACTER;
            MONTH: MONTHS;
--This program creates a table containing the lowest and highest temperature
--recorded for each day of the month for one year. After the table is completed, the
--user can query the table by specifying a month and a day.
begin
      for M in MONTHS loop
            case M is
                  when SEP|APR|JUN|NOV => DAYS:=30;
                  when FEB               => DAYS:=28;   --We ignore leap
                  when others            => DAYS:=31;   --years!
            end case;
            for D in 1..DAYS loop
                  put("Enter lowest temperature for ");
                  put(M); put(" "); put(D);
                  get(T_LOW);
                  LOTEMP(M,D):=T_LOW;
                  put_line(" ");
                  put("Enter highest temperature for ");
                  put(M); put(" "); put(D);
                  get(T_HIGH);
                  HITEMP(M,D):=T_HIGH;
            end loop;
      end loop;
```

```
put_line(" ");
put("Do you wish to fetch information from table(y/n)? ");
get(ANSWER);
while (ANSWER='Y') or (ANSWER='y') loop
        put("Enter month: ");
        get(MONTH);
        put_line(" ");
        put("Enter day of month: ");
        get(DAY);
        put_line(" ");
        T_LOW:=LOTEMP(MONTH,DAY);
        T_HIGH:=HITEMP(MONTH,DAY);
        put("Low temperature=");   put(T_LOW);   put_line(" ");
        put("High temperature=");   put(T_HIGH);   put_line(" ");
        put("Do you wish to fetch more information from table(y/n)? ");
        get(ANSWER);
    end loop;
end USER_DEFINED_ENUMERATION_TYPES;
```

It is possible to create ambiguity when using enumeration types with the same set of values or a subset of values. For example, consider the following declarations:

```
type COLOR is (WHITE, RED, BLUE, AMBER, GREEN, BLACK);
type SIGNAL is (RED, AMBER, GREEN);
```

and suppose that in the program the following statement appears:

```
for I in RED..GREEN loop;
```

This statement is ambiguous because it could mean (RED, BLUE, AMBER, GREEN) of type COLOR or (RED, AMBER, GREEN) of type SIGNAL. To resolve this ambiguity, we can use a qualified expression of the form:

```
type'(expression)
```

where "type" refers to the named type or named subtype and "expression" is any legal expression involving the named type. The preceding ambiguity can be resolved using any of the following, depending on what is desired.

```
for I in SIGNAL loop;
for I in COLOR range RED..GREEN loop;
for I in COLOR'(RED)..COLOR'(GREEN) loop;
for I in COLOR'(RED)..GREEN loop;
```

In the last example, GREEN does not need to be qualified because RED is established to be a COLOR and so GREEN must also be a COLOR.

The attributes FIRST and LAST also apply to enumeration types. For example, COLOR'FIRST=WHITE and COLOR'LAST=BLACK. Other attributes that are applicable to enumeration types are presented in Chapter 9.

6.2.3 Boolean Types

The predefined type BOOLEAN is an enumeration type with the two literals, TRUE and FALSE. The type declaration may be considered to have the following form.

```
type BOOLEAN is (FALSE,TRUE);
```

Hence, FALSE<TRUE.

There are two tests for membership that apply to all scalar types. These tests, **in** and **not in**, allow us to test whether a value lies within a given range. Some examples are:

```
T: BOOLEAN;
J: INTEGER;
K: CHARACTER;
T: =J not in range 3..23;  ——T is either true or false
T: =J in NATURAL;          ——T is true if J in range 0..INTEGER'LAST
T: =K in range 'B'..'L';   ——T is either true or false
```

The predefined logical operations on Boolean types are **not** (negation), **and** (conjunction), **or** (inclusive disjunction), and **xor** (exclusive disjunction).

In Boolean expressions, **not** has a higher precedence than **and, or,** and **xor,** which all have the same precedence. The three binary Boolean operators have a lower precedence than the relational operators. This means that the expression

```
I=J or X<Y;
```

is permitted, whereas in Pascal, parentheses are required. However, the expression

A **or** B **and** C;

is illegal Ada unless parentheses are used to emphasize the intended meaning of the expression. For example,

(A **or** B) **and** C;   or   A **or** (B **and** C);

Since **not** has a higher precedence than the binary Boolean operators, the Boolean expression

not A **and** B;

means

(**not** A) **and** B;

6.2.4 Character Types

The predefined type CHARACTER may be regarded as an enumeration type with the standard 128 ordered ASCII character literals. The type declaration may be considered to have the following form.

type CHARACTER **is**

(*nul*,	*soh*,	*stx*,	*etx*,	*eot*,	*enq*,	*ack*,	*bel*,
bs,	*ht*,	*lf*,	*vt*,	*ff*,	*cr*,	*so*,	*si*,
dle,	*dc1*,	*dc2*,	*dc3*,	*dc4*,	*nak*,	*syn*,	*etb*,
can,	*em*,	*sub*,	*esc*,	*fs*,	*gs*,	*rs*,	*us*,
' ',	'!',	'"',	'#',	'$',	'%',	'&',	''',
'(',	')',	'*',	'+',	',',	'−',	'.',	'/',
'0',	'1',	'2',	'3',	'4',	'5',	'6',	'7',
'8',	'9',	':',	';',	'<',	'=',	'>',	'?',
'@',	'A',	'B',	'C',	'D',	'E',	'F',	'G',
'H',	'I',	'J',	'K',	'L',	'M',	'N',	'O',
'P',	'Q',	'R',	'S',	'T',	'U',	'V',	'W',
'X',	'Y',	'Z',	'[',	'\',	']',	'^',	'_',
',	'a',	'b',	'c',	'd',	'e',	'f',	'g',
'h',	'i',	'j',	'k',	'l',	'm',	'n',	'o',
'p',	'q',	'r',	's',	't',	'u',	'v',	'w',
'x',	'y',	'z',	'{',	'|'	'}',	'~',	*del*);

It is useful to remember in sorting problems that letters appear after digits and that all the capital letters appear before the lowercase letters.

6.3 REAL TYPES

Real types consist of floating point numbers and fixed point numbers. Ada distinguishes between relative accuracy and absolute accuracy. If we specify the number of decimal digits of precision, we have specified a floating point number with a designated number of significant digits. If we specify the magnitude of the error, we have specified a fixed point number with a designated absolute error.

6.3.1 Floating Point Types

In Ada there is a predefined type FLOAT with a precision and range determined by the computer. The programmer can control the precision by using the key word "digits" in the type definition portion of a type declaration. For floating point types, "digits" refers to the relative precision, which is equivalent to the number of significant decimal digits in the mantissa. An optional range constraint can also be specified. If it is omitted, the range will default to the range of floating point numbers permitted on the host computer. The syntax for a floating point type declaration is:

type FLOATING_POINT_NAME **is digits** D **range** L..U;

where D, L, and U are static expressions. An example of a floating point type declaration is:

type NEW_FLOAT **is digits** 7 **range** −1.0E30..1.0E30;

Floating point literals consist of a number literal with a decimal point followed by an optional exponent or an integer followed by an exponent. An exponent is the symbol "E" or "e" and an integer optionally preceded by a + or − sign. Examples of floating point literals are 5.0, 7.2e−2, 5.0E2, 3.0e−10, 0.567E+4, and 0.3e9.

The operations that are permitted on floating point types include all operations on integers except for "mod" and "rem". The precedence of operations is the same as that for integers. No mixed mode is permitted in floating point operations. Exponentiation may involve either positive or negative integers as the exponents but may not involve a floating point number as an exponent.

In subtype and derived type declarations that involve floating point types, the digits constraint cannot be larger than that of the parent type and the range constraint must be within the range constraint of the parent type. These features permit us to constrain the precision or the range of floating point numbers. Some examples:

```
type NEW_FLOAT is digits 7 range −1.0E30..1.0E30;
subtype SMALL_FLOAT is NEW_FLOAT digits 3;
      ——Range constraint is assumed to be the same as the parent type
subtype NORMAL is NEW_FLOAT range −1.0..1.0;
      ——Digit constraint is assumed to be the same as the parent type
subtype WRONG is NEW_FLOAT digits 10;
      ——Illegal because digits constraint cannot be larger than that of the parent
      ——type
type DERIVED_FLOAT is new NEW_FLOAT digits 6;
      ——Range constraint is assumed to be the same as the parent type
type DERIVED_WRONG is new NEW_FLOAT digits 8 range 0.0..1.0E50;
      ——Illegal because digits constraint cannot be larger than that of the parent
      ——type and range constraint must be within that of the parent type
```

The predefined type FLOAT has a system-defined precision and range determined by the computer hardware. The precision and range may be constrained via type, subtype, and derived type declarations. For example,

```
type WEIGHT is new FLOAT digits 4 range 0.0..1.0E20;
type F is digits 5;
type G is digits 6 range 0.0..100.0;
subtype SMALL is FLOAT digits 3 range −1.0E10..1.0E10;
```

All the preceding examples assume that the predefined type FLOAT has a precision and a range sufficiently large that these type declarations are legal. A number of attributes are available for determining the characteristics of floating point types. These are described in Chapter 9.

The precision and range specified in a floating point type declaration should be carefully chosen to satisfy the requirements of the problem that is being solved. The actual precision and range limits will be determined by the hardware characteristics of the host computer and may exceed those required in the problem specification. For example, the floating point type declaration

```
type NEW_FLOAT is digits 7 range −1.0E30..1.0E30;
```

requires at least 28 bits for the mantissa and 8 bits for the exponent. If the host computer has 36-bit words, this declaration can be efficiently implemented on the computer. However, if the host computer has a 32-bit word the implementation of this type would require two words.

One of the frustrating experiences in moving scientific software from one computer to another has been switching back and forth from single to double precision depending on the word length of the host computer. If one is careful in Ada most of these portability problems can be eliminated. We now describe both the incorrect and correct ways to specify floating point types for portability. First, consider the following type declaration.

type FLOAT_REQUIRED **is new** FLOAT **digits** 8 **range** −1.0E30 . . 1.0E30;

This declaration requires that the predefined type FLOAT have at least the precision and range specified. If FLOAT does not, then this declaration is illegal. However, now consider the declaration

type FLOAT_REQUIRED **is digits** 8 **range** −1.0E30 . . 1.0E30;

This declaration is guaranteed to be portable because it is a programmer-defined type that is implemented by the compiler to satisfy the constraints. To preserve portability, all subtypes and derived types should in turn be declared in terms of the programmer-defined type. For example, the derived type

type NEW_FLOAT **is new** FLOAT_REQUIRED **digits** 6 **range** −1.0E20 . . 1.0E20;

is portable, whereas the derived type

type NEW_FLOAT **is new** FLOAT **digits** 6 **range** −1.0E20 . . 1.0E20;

may not be portable.

As with types SHORT_INTEGER and LONG_INTEGER, some implementations of Ada support types SHORT_FLOAT and LONG_FLOAT. These are used in a manner similar to types SHORT_INTEGER and LONG_INTEGER.

We assume that most readers are familiar with floating point operations, so Program 6.3-1 primarily emphasizes type conversion.

PROGRAM 6.3-1

```
with TEXT_IO; use TEXT_IO;
procedure FLOAT_TYPES is
      type NEW_FLOAT is new FLOAT digits 4 range −1.0E15..1.0E15;
      A,B,C: NEW_FLOAT:=2.0;
      X,Y,Z: FLOAT:=3.0;
          I,J: INTEGER:=15;
begin
      X:=Y*FLOAT(I);
      put(X); put_line(" ");
      A:=5.0*A*B;
      put(A); put_line(" ");
      C:=1.3e−3*A**3;
      put(C); put_line(" ");
      Z:=Y+7.2*FLOAT(B);
      put(Z); put_line(" ");
      C:=16.3E−2*NEW_FLOAT(X)/NEW_FLOAT(J)−3.6*(A+NEW_FLOAT(Z));
      put(C); put_line(" ");
end FLOAT_TYPES;
```

6.3.2 Fixed Point Types

Fixed point types are real numbers with an absolute accuracy specification rather than a relative accuracy specification. The accuracy is specified by using the key word "delta" in the type definition portion of a type declaration. A range constraint is also required to be part of the type definition. Thus the syntax for a fixed point type declaration is:

type FIXED_POINT_NAME **is delta** D **range** L..U;

where D, L, and U are static expressions. There are no predefined fixed point types in Ada, so explicit declaration is necessary. An example of a fixed point type declaration is:

type FIXED **is delta** 0.01 **range** −100.0..100.0;

If X is declared to be of type FIXED, then X can take on any value in the set $\{-100.00, -99.99, -99.98, \ldots, 0.00, 0.01, \ldots, 99.99, 100.00\}$. This set has 20001 elements.

The operations that are permitted on fixed point types are the same as those for floating point types. In addition, fixed point types permit mixed mode multiplication and division by an integer. The result is a fixed point number. This is in contrast to floating point, where an explicit conversion is required to multiply or divide a floating point number by an integer. For example, if X is declared to be of type FIXED, the expression X/5+7*X is legal.

In subtype declarations that involve fixed point types, the delta of the constraint in the subtype cannot be smaller than the delta of the constraint in the parent type. Also the range constraint values of the subtype must be within the range constraint values of the parent type. For example, consider the following declarations.

```
type FIXED is delta 0.01 range −100.0..100.0;
subtype NEW_FIXED is FIXED delta 0.1;
        ——Legal with the range constraint assumed to be the same as the parent
        ——type
subtype SMALL_FIXED is FIXED delta 0.001;
        ——Illegal because delta of subtype is smaller than delta of the parent type
subtype BIG_FIXED is FIXED delta 0.1 range −1000.0..1000.0;
        ——Illegal because the range has been increased
```

A derived type declaration with a delta of 0.1 can be specified by:

```
type FIXED is delta 0.01 range −100.0..100.0;
type DERIVED_FIXED is new FIXED delta 0.1;
        ——Range constraint is assumed to be the same as the type from which it is
        ——derived
```

It is also permissible to specify the precision and range in two stages, as follows.

```
type FIXED is delta 0.01;
X,Y: FIXED range −100.0..100.0;
```

The use of fixed point types guarantees that the numbers will be represented to at least the accuracy specified by the delta. For example, consider the type:

```
type FIXED is delta 0.01 range −100.0..100.0;
```

If we assume that the computer has 16-bit words and uses two's complement arithmetic, the implemented range would be to the next power of 2; that is, the implemented range is −128..127. This means that 7 bits are required above the decimal point. Similarly, the implementation of the delta of .01 requires 7 bits below the decimal point, since $1/128 = 2\#0000000.0000001\# = .0078125$, which is less than .01. One bit is required for the sign, and so 15 bits are required to satisfy the specification of FIXED. There is one spare bit at the bottom of the word. If the delta were changed to .001 and the range left unchanged, 10 bits would be required below the decimal point for a total of 18 bits. On this computer this would probably require two words in the computer implementation.

Accuracy can be lost in fixed point calculations if the numbers calculated are smaller or larger than expected or if small errors accumulate as a result of the computer representation. Fixed point types guarantee that numbers will be represented to at least the accuracy specified by the delta; the numbers are not guaranteed to be stored in the computer exactly. For example, consider Program 6.3-2.

PROGRAM 6.3-2

```
with TEXT_IO; use TEXT_IO;
procedure FIXED_ERROR is
        type FIXED is delta 0.01 range −100.0..100.0;
        X,Y: FIXED;
begin
        X:=1.01+2.01+3.01;   −−Value of 6.02 is printed
        put(X);
        put_line(" ");
        Y:=0.04;
        X:=Y/100.0;
        put(X);                        −−Value of 0.00 is printed
        put_line(" ");
        Y:=70.0+80.0;
        put(Y);                        −−Value of 50.0 is printed
end FIXED_ERROR;
```

In Program 6.3-2, the value 6.02 is obtained because the internal representation of 1.01 is $2\#0000001.0000001\# = 1.0078125$, for 2.01 it is 2.0078125, and for 3.01 it is 3.0078125. The sum is 6.0234375, which is printed as 6.02. The second output of 0.00 represents underflow, and the final output of 50.0 represents fixed point overflow where the most significant digit is lost. This may also raise a numeric error exception.

As a final example on fixed point types, consider Program 6.3-3.

PROGRAM 6.3-3

```
with TEXT_IO; use TEXT_IO;
procedure FIXED_POINT_TYPES is
        type FIXED is delta 0.01 range −100.0..100.0;
        type DERIVED_FIXED is new FIXED delta 0.1;
        subtype NEW_FIXED is FIXED delta 0.1;
        X: FIXED:=1.01;
        Y: DERIVED_FIXED:=5.5;
        Z: NEW_FIXED:=2.2;
        I: INTEGER:=7;
begin
        X:=X*FIXED(Y);   −−Explicit conversion of Y to type FIXED before
                         −−multiplication
        put(X);          −−5.55 is printed
        put_line(" ");
        Z:=Z*I;          −−Legal because no conversion is necessary
        put(Z);          −−15.4 is printed
        put_line(" ");
        Z:=Z+X;          −−Legal but loss of accuracy
        put(Z);          −−16.4 is printed
        put_line(" ");
end FIXED_POINT_TYPES;
```

6.4 OTHER TYPES

6.4.1 The Natural Numbers

The natural numbers are a predefined type in Ada. They are a subtype of the type INTEGER and are defined by the following subtype definition:

subtype NATURAL **is** INTEGER **range** 0..INTEGER'LAST;

where INTEGER'LAST is an attribute whose value is the largest integer represented on the host computer. The positive numbers are predefined as: **subtype** POSITIVE **is** INTEGER **range** 1..INTEGER'LAST;

6.4.2 Strings

The predefined type STRING denotes one dimensional arrays of the predefined type CHARACTER indexed by values of the predefined subtype POSITIVE. The type definition is given by:

type STRING **is array** (POSITIVE **range** <>) **of** CHARACTER;

The operator "&" catenates two strings. The resulting string must not exceed the index constraint defined for the string. For example, "abc"&"defg"= "abcdefg". The null string is the string with no elements.

The "&" operator is also defined when one operand is a string and the other operand is a character. For example, "abc"&'d'="abcd".

6.5 SUMMARY

- Ada is a strongly typed language. Each type definition introduces a distinct type. The data abstraction features of Ada are inherited from Pascal and are essentially nonexistent in Fortran.
- Carefully defined data types permit problems to be described in terms of the actual data objects that arise in the problem definition. This permits the problem to be more naturally described and the resulting software to be more readable and easier to maintain.
- Subtypes restrict the set of allowable values that identifiers of the subtype can be assigned. The allowable operations of the base type carry over to the subtype.
- Derived types are a new instance of a given type that are useful when the mixing of types needs to be prevented.
- Enumeration types are user-defined discrete types that permit the definition of variables that range over a finite set of values (e.g., colors, weekdays, months, directions).
- Integer floating point types are predefined with an allowable range of values dependent on the computer implementation.
- Floating point types permit the programmer to control the precision and range for floating point numbers. Careful definition of subtypes and derived types enhances program portability.
- Fixed point types are real numbers with an absolute accuracy specification. There are no predefined fixed point types in Ada.
- Mixed mode arithmetic is not permitted, nor is the mixing of different types in an expression; however, features exist in Ada that permit type conversion.

Exercises for Chapter 6

1. Write declarations for each of the following.
   (a) A real variable X giving it an initial value of zero.
   (b) Integer constants ONE, TWO, and THREE with the corresponding values.
   (c) The planets in the solar system.
   (d) The constants T and F having the values TRUE and FALSE.
   (e) The four directions NORTH, EAST, SOUTH, and WEST.

2. Consider the following program segment.

   ```
   type SIGNAL is (RED, AMBER, GREEN);
   DANGER: BOOLEAN;
     LIGHT: SIGNAL;
   if LIGHT = RED then
         DANGER := TRUE;
   else
         DANGER := FALSE;
   end if;
   ```

   Write down an alternative assignment statement that assigns DANGER the appropriate value determined by the value of LIGHT.

3. Evaluate (A **xor** B) = (A = B) for all combinations of Boolean variables A and B.

4. What is the value of each of the following?
   (a) 16#E1E#E1
   (b) 2#101#e1
   (c) 8#727#E2

5. Define a two dimensional array and associated types so that the array contains values of a type color. The row index is over the months of the year, and the column index spans the years 1983 through 2000.

6. Write declarations for each of the following subtypes.
   (a) Fall, winter, spring, and summer as a subset of the months of the year.
   (b) Integers with a range of 1 through 100 as a subset of INTEGER and NATURAL, and POSITIVE.
   (c) Floating point numbers with a range of −1.0 through 1.0.
   (d) Floating point numbers with a range of −100.0 through 100.0 with three significant digits.

7. Write derived type declarations for each of the following.
   (a) AGE that can take on the values from 0 to 125.
   (b) UNDER_AGE derived from AGE and restricted to the values 0 through 18.
   (c) AREA that can take on values from 0 to 1.0E16.
   (d) LENGTH that can take on the values from 0 to 1.0E16.

8. Derive types APPLES and ORANGES from type INTEGER. Then show how to use type conversion to add apples and oranges. (You may also try to add APPLES and TRS 80s!)

9. Suppose that computer A implements INTEGER using 16 bits and type LONG_INTEGER using 32 bits, and that computer B implements type INTEGER using 24 bits, type SHORT_INTEGER using 12 bits, and type LONG_INTEGER using 48 bits. What types are used on computers A and B to represent each of the following declarations?

type R **is range** −2000 . . +2000;
type S **is range** 1 . . 32767;
type T **is range** −1E10 . . 1E10;
type U **is range** −32768 . . 32768;

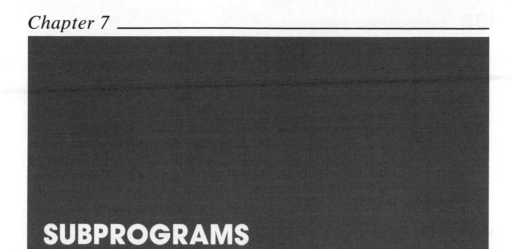

SUBPROGRAMS

In this chapter we introduce Ada constructs that support the writing of structured programs and the use of top-down methodology in program design. We discuss the various methods of transferring information in and out of subprograms. We discuss local and global variables.

In a sense, Chapter 7 represents a transition from concern about the details of local program control to concern about global program structure. We pursue the subject of program structure in Chapters 8, 10, 12, 13, 14, and 16. In Chapter 16 we show how Ada program structure lends itself to software engineering.

7.1 PROCEDURES WITHOUT PARAMETERS; LOCAL AND GLOBAL VARIABLES

We have already seen programs in which many different tasks are performed sequentially. Although comments inserted by the programmer may contribute to the readability of such programs, the sheer size of unstructured programs (e.g., Program 5.1-4) makes them cumbersome to read and maintain. Ada allows blocks of code to be packaged together in logical units. One important logical unit is the procedure. We illustrate next the essential concept of global program control via procedures by showing an example of a very simple program structure that uses procedures without parameters.

```
procedure GLOBAL_PROGRAM_CONTROL is
--Global type and variable declarations

        procedure LOGICAL_UNIT_1 is
        --Local type and variable declarations
        begin
              executable statement(s);
                      --These perform operations of unit 1
        end LOGICAL_UNIT_1;

        procedure LOGICAL_UNIT_2 is
        --Local type and variable declarations
        begin
               executable statement(s);
                      --These perform operations of unit 2
        end LOGICAL_UNIT_2

        procedure LOGICAL_UNIT_3 is
        --Local type and variable declarations
        begin
              executable statement(s);
                      --These perform operations of unit 3
        end LOGICAL_UNIT_3;

begin   --Main program
      executable statement(s);
      LOGICAL_UNIT_1;
      LOGICAL_UNIT_2;
      LOGICAL_UNIT_3;
      executable statement(s);
end GLOBAL_PROGRAM_CONTROL;
```

When the statement "LOGICAL_UNIT_1" is encountered during program execution, control will pass to the body of code between the "begin" and "end" statements of procedure LOGICAL_UNIT_1. Then, control will revert to the line below where "LOGICAL_UNIT_1" was called.

Packaging all the code associated with unit 1 in a procedure with a descriptive user-defined name at the front of it, and packaging similarly for units 2 and 3 makes it much easier to read and maintain the software. For example, if later in the life cycle of the program, a new programmer wishes to improve the performance of unit 3, only procedure LOGICAL_UNIT_3 must be rewritten, without concern about undesirable "fallout" effects on the rest of the program, assuming that no global variables are reassigned in this subprogram.

The procedure construct of Ada allows program development to be easily undertaken by a team. Programmer 1 may be assigned to write the code for procedure LOGICAL_UNIT_1, programmer 2 for LOGICAL_UNIT_2, and so forth. Because of the insulation of variables provided by local variables, as discussed below, this division of labor may be easily accomplished without much concern for interface problems.

We illustrate some of these ideas with a very trivial program. In Program 7.1-1 we have two procedures, INPUT and OUTPUT. User-defined procedure names may be created like any other identifiers.

PROGRAM 7.1-1

```
with TEXT_IO; use TEXT_IO;
procedure TRIVIAL_PROGRAM is
      A: array(1..10) of INTEGER;
      I: INTEGER;

      procedure INPUT is
            I: INTEGER;
            T: INTEGER;
      begin
            I:=0;
            loop
                  I:=I+1;
                  put("Enter A(");
                  put(I);
                  put("): ");
                  get(T);
                  A(I):=T;
                  exit when I=10;
            end loop;
      end INPUT;

      procedure OUTPUT is
            T,I: INTEGER:=20;
      begin
            for I in 1..10 loop    --The "I" in this loop has a separate identity
                  put("A(");        --from the local variable I
                  put(I);
                  put(")=");
                  T:=A(I);
                  put(T);
                  put_line(" ");
            end loop,
            put(I);                 --The value 20 is printed
      end OUTPUT;
```

```
begin                    ––Main program
    put("Enter an integer: ");
    get(I);
    put_line("We will now enter an array of integers");
    INPUT;
    put_line(" ");
    put_line("We will now output the array of integers");
    OUTPUT;
    put_line(" ");
    put("The value of the integer inputed earlier is ");
    put(I);
end TRIVIAL_PROGRAM;
```

Suppose that in response to the first line of Program 7.1-1, the user inputs the integer 5. What will be the last output of the main program, "The value of the integer inputed earlier is "? The answer is 5. Since the variable "I" has been declared as a local variable in procedure INPUT, any changes in assignment that may occur within procedure INPUT will not be coupled either to the main program or to any other procedure outside the scope of procedure INPUT (e.g., OUTPUT). That is, the local variable "I" has the same name as the global variable also called "I", but the local "I" is functionally separate from the global "I". In fact, the local "I" may be declared to be of a different type than the global "I" ("Aye, aye," you say).

What would happen, in Program 7.1-1, if the local declaration "I:INTEGER" were removed from procedure INPUT? The answer: the final output in the main program would be 10. This follows because in procedure INPUT, "I" is assigned values from 1 to 10 and the "I" used in INPUT is the same "I" as in the main program. By declaring a local variable "I" in procedure INPUT, the global variable "I" is hidden in procedure INPUT.

The procedure OUTPUT does not influence the value that global variable "I" or the local variable "I" assumes because any implicit loop variable acts like a constant for each excursion of the loop.

We present another illustrative program to contrast local and global variables.

PROGRAM 7.1-2

```
with TEXT_IO; use TEXT_IO;
procedure LOCAL_VERSUS_GLOBAL_VARIABLES is
        A,B,C,D: FLOAT;
          E,F,G,H: INTEGER;

        procedure P1 is
                A,B,C: CHARACTER;
              D,E,F,G: INTEGER;
```

```
        begin
                put_line("We have just entered procedure P1");
                put_line(" ");
                A:='A';
                B:='D';
                C:='A';
                D:=2;
                E:=1;
                F:=2;
                G:=3;
                H:=4;
                put(A); put(B); put(C);
                put_line(" ");
                put("D="); put(D);
                put(" E="); put(E);
                put(" F="); put(F);
                put(" G="); put(G);
                put(" H="); put(H);
                put_line(" ");
                put_line("We have just left procedure P1");
        end P1;

begin   --Main program
        A:=11.0;
        B:=12.0;
        C:=13.0;
        D:=14.0;
        E:=21;
        F:=22;
        G:=23;
        H:=24;
        P1;                         --This transfers control to procedure P1
        put_line(" ");
        put("A=");    put(A);
        put(" B="); put(B);
        put(" C="); put(C);
        put(" D="); put(D);
        put(" E="); put(E);
        put(" F="); put(F);
        put(" G="); put(G);
        put(" H="); put(H);
        put_line(" ");
end LOCAL_VERSUS_GLOBAL_VARIABLES;
```

OUTPUT OF PROGRAM 7.1-2

We have just entered procedure P1

ADA
D=2 E=1 F=2 G=3 H=4

We have just left procedure P1

A= 1.100000E1 B= 1.200000E1 C=1.300000E1 D=1.400000E1 E=21 F=22 G=23

H=4 (This would be printed on the previous line)

7.2 TRANSFER OF PARAMETERS IN AND OUT OF PROCEDURES; BINDING MODES

The specification of a subprogram (a procedure or function contained within a program) indicates the flow direction (binding mode) and type of formal parameters that the subprogram requires. We have three possible flow directions for Ada subprogram parameters: **in**, **in out**, and **out**. A typical procedure specification illustrating all three flow directions is:

procedure SAMPLE(A: **in** FLOAT; B: **in out** FLOAT; C: **out** BOOLEAN);

7.2.1 Flow Direction "In"

When a parameter is transferred using flow direction "in", this implies that the body of the procedure uses the formal parameter like a local constant. A value for the parameter must be supplied when the procedure is called. For example, if one specifies a procedure

procedure EXAMPLE(A,B: **in** INTEGER; C: **in** FLOAT);

a typical call to the procedure might be EXAMPLE(4,7,1.5). Another possible call to the procedure might be EXAMPLE(C,D,E), where C and D are integer variables and E is a floating point variable; the values of C, D, and E are presumed to have been established before the call to EXAMPLE.

An expression may be used in the calling statement of a procedure when a parameter of flow direction "in" is being used. Thus, the following construct would be permissible.

HOPE_IT_WORKS(X*X+3);

Here it is assumed that X is an integer variable and the parameter in the subprogram HOPE_IT_WORKS is specified as an integer.

The absence of a flow direction specification implies a default to the "in" direction.

7.2.2 Flow Direction "In Out"

When a parameter is transferred using binding mode "in out", this implies a linkage in memory between the parameter in the subprogram and the variable used in the subprogram call. For example, if a subprogram is specified

procedure ANOTHER_EXAMPLE(C: **in out** INTEGER);

a typical call might be ANOTHER_EXAMPLE(H). The variable H is assumed to be an integer variable (otherwise a compile time error will be generated). If parameter C is modified in the procedure ANOTHER_EXAMPLE, the calling variable H will also be modified so that H always equals C, since they share the same memory location. The initial value of parameter C corresponds to the value of variable H when the procedure call is made. Thus a value has been taken "in" and possibly another value has been returned.

7.2.3 Flow Direction "Out"

The flow direction "out" operates very much like the flow direction "in out" inasmuch as a linkage is established between the "out" parameter of the subprogram and the calling variable. The basic difference is that when the flow direction is "out", no initial value may be transferred to the subprogram. If the calling variable has some value, this value will be ignored by the subprogram.

We illustrate these ideas in Program 7.2-1.

PROGRAM 7.2-1

```
with TEXT_IO; use TEXT_IO;
procedure PARAMETER_FLOW_DIRECTION is
     A,B: INTEGER;
       C: FLOAT;
       D: CHARACTER;

     procedure P1(E,F: in INTEGER; G: in out FLOAT; H: out CHARACTER) is
          L,M: INTEGER;
```

```
     begin
            put("E="); put(E);
            put_line(" ");
            put("F="); put(F);
            put_line(" ");
            put("G="); put(G);
            put_line(" ");
            put("H="); put(H);   ——This should be interesting
            put_line(" ");
             L:=2*E;
            M:=2*F;
            G:=2.0*G;
            H:='Z';
     end P1;

begin   ——Main program
       A:=1;
       B:=1;
       C:=1.0;
       D:='A';
       P1(A,B,C,D);
       put("A=");  put(A);
       put_line(" ");
       put("B=");  put(B);
       put_line(" ");
       put("C=");  put(C);
       put_line(" ");
       put("D=");  put(D);
end PARAMETER_FLOW_DIRECTION;
```

OUTPUT OF PROGRAM 7.2-1

```
E=1
F=1
G=1.000000
H=                            ——The value of D sent in is ignored by P1
A=1
B=1
C=2.000000
D=Z
```

A parameter of flow direction ''in'' may receive either a value, an expression, or a calling variable. Parameters of flow direction ''in out'' or ''out'' may receive only a calling variable. This follows because for ''in out'' or ''out'' parameters, a linkage is created to a memory location. One cannot link to a value!

7.3 SUBPROGRAM PARAMETER TYPES

Parameters that have been declared to be of any formal type may be used in the specification of a subprogram. For example,

procedure MATRIX_MULT(A,B: MATRIX; C: **out** MATRIX);

It is assumed that MATRIX has been declared in some type declaration such as: **type** MATRIX **is array**(1..100,1..100) **of** FLOAT. Another example is

procedure COLOR_CHART(G: **in out** COLOR);

where

type COLOR **is** (RED,BLUE,ORANGE, GREEN);

has been declared.

In Chapter 16, we show how procedure specifications and bodies can be compiled separately.

Program 7.3-1 illustrates subprogram parameter types.

PROGRAM 7.3-1

```
with TEXT_IO; use TEXT_IO;
procedure SUBPROGRAM_PARAMETER_TYPES is
     type COLOR is (RED,BLUE,ORANGE,GREEN,BLACK,YELLOW);
     C: COLOR;

procedure CHANGE_COLOR(G: in out COLOR) is
begin
     if G=RED then
          G:=BLACK;
     elsif G=GREEN then
          G:=YELLOW;
     elsif G=BLUE then
          G:=ORANGE;
     else
          G:=RED;
     end if;
end CHANGE_COLOR;
```

```
begin
      C:=GREEN;
      CHANGE_COLOR(C);
      case C is
            when RED        => put("C is red");
            when BLUE       => put("C is blue");
            when ORANGE     => put("C is orange");
            when GREEN      => put("C is green");
            when BLACK      => put("C is black");
            when YELLOW     => put("C is yellow");
      end case;
end SUBPROGRAM_PARAMETER_TYPES;
```

7.4   TRANSFERRING PARAMETERS TO SUBPROGRAMS BY NAME; DEFAULT VALUES

7.4.1   Transferring Parameters by Name

Ada allows explicit naming of formal subprogram parameters in a subprogram call, thus relaxing the constraint that the order of variables in the subprogram call match the order of formal parameters in the subprogram specification. For example, suppose a subprogram specification is:

PROCEDURE ILLUSTRATION(A,B: INTEGER; C: **in out** FLOAT; D: CHAR);

We may call this subprogram typically in the following ways:

```
ILLUSTRATION(D=>'R', B=>3, C=>R, A=>1);     --R is of type FLOAT
ILLUSTRATION(3, 6, R, 'U');
ILLUSTRATION(A=>I-L, B=>3, D=>'Q', C=>R);
```

As another example, suppose we have a subprogram with the specification:

procedure ANOTHER_ILLUSTRATION(A:VECTOR; N:INTEGER);

Suppose that VECTOR has been declared, **type** VECTOR **is array**(1..5) **of** CHARACTER. Then a legitimate call to the subprogram might be

```
ANOTHER_ILLUSTRATION(A=>('A','E','I','O','U'),5);
```

7.4.2 Default Values for Parameters in Subprograms

In some applications, one or more parameters with binding mode "in" may have the same value for many subprogram calls. Ada allows a default mode in which we can indicate a default value or values in the subprogram specification and then omit it or them from the subprogram call.

As an example, suppose the procedure WEATHER has the three "in" parameters, BAR_PRESSURE, WIND_SPEED, and SUNNY, and is specified as follows.

```
procedure WEATHER(BAR_PRESSURE,WIND_SPEED: FLOAT;
                  SUNNY:BOOLEAN:=TRUE);
```

The parameter SUNNY has an indicated default value of TRUE. Some legal and typical calls to subprogram WEATHER are as follows.

```
WEATHER(23.4,8.7,FALSE);
WEATHER(24.5,4.6);          ––SUNNY defaults to TRUE
WEATHER(23.6,5.5,TRUE);    ––It is legal to respecify the default value
WEATHER(WIND_SPEED=>3.8,BAR_PRESSURE=>25.0); ––SUNNY defaults to
                                              ––TRUE
```

Default parameters cannot be given for overloaded function operators. Default values are evaluated when the subprogram is declared. Each call to the subprogram invokes the same default values.

As another illustration of default values, consider the following subprogram specification.

```
procedure DEFAULT_EXAMPLE(A: FLOAT:=4.5; B: INTEGER:=6; C:
                          INTEGER:=8);
```

Following are some possible legal calls to procedure DEFAULT_EXAMPLE.

```
DEFAULT_EXAMPLE;                    ––All parameters take on their default
                                   ––values
DEFAULT_EXAMPLE(B=>4,A=>2.0);  ––Parameter C defaults to 8
DEFAULT_EXAMPLE(6.7,C=>0);         ––Mixture of positional and named transfer;
                                   ––B defaults to 6
```

7.5 FUNCTION SUBPROGRAMS

Function subprograms return values that may be used as an operand in an expression or in an output statement outside the scope of the function subprogram.

The syntax for Ada functions is as follows.

function USER_DEFINED_IDENTIFIER(FORMAL PARAMETERS) **return** DATA_TYPE;

All the formal parameters of a function are of type "in". Binding modes "in out" and "out" are not allowed for parameters of functions. Ada allows structured data types such as arrays and records to be returned by a function. This capability is not available in Fortran or Pascal, which restrict functions to return scalar data types.

Functions and procedures may call themselves recursively. We defer discussion about recursion until Chapter 12.

Program 7.5-1 illustrates some of the concepts discussed above. In this simple program we print a table of values for the mathematical function $f(x) = 3*x**3 + 2*x**2 + x + 1$.

PROGRAM 7.5-1

```
with TEXT_IO; use TEXT_IO;
procedure MATHEMATICAL_FUNCTION_EVALUATION is
     T: FLOAT;

function F(X: FLOAT) return FLOAT is
     TEMP: FLOAT;
begin
     TEMP := 3.0*X**3 + 2.0*X**2 + 1.0*X + 1.0;
     return TEMP;  --Could use "return 3.0*x**3+2.0*x**2+1.0*x+1.0;"
end F;

begin   --Main program
     put_line(" ");
     put_line("X                                        F(X)");
     put_line("--------------------------------------------");
     T:=0.0;
     while T <= 10.0 loop
          T:=T+1.0;
          put(T); put("              ");
          put(F(T));
          put_line(" ");
     end loop;
end MATHEMATICAL_FUNCTION_EVALUATION;
```

To illustrate how a function may return a more complex data type, Program 7.5-2 uses a function that computes the maximum and minimum values of an array of integers and returns the values in the form of a vector with two components. We use unconstrained arrays here. You may wish to briefly review Section 5.2.

PROGRAM 7.5-2

```
with TEXT_IO; use TEXT_IO;
procedure MAXIMUM_MINIMUM is
      type VECTOR is array(INTEGER range <>) of INTEGER;
      type SOLN is array(1..2) of INTEGER;
      G: VECTOR(1..75);   ——Memory allocation for G occurs at this point
   TEMP: INTEGER;
ANSWER: SOLN;

function MAX_MIN(A:VECTOR) return SOLN is
            X: SOLN;
      MAX,MIN: INTEGER;
begin
      MAX:=A(A'FIRST);
      MIN:=A(A'FIRST);
      for I in A'RANGE loop
            if A(I) > MAX then
                  MAX:=A(I);
            else
                  if A(I) < MIN then
                        MIN:=A(I);
                  end if;
            end if;
      end loop;
      X(1):=MAX;
      X(2):=MIN;
      return X;   ——We return a data structure of type SOLN
end MAX_MIN;

procedure INPUT(L: out VECTOR) is
      T: INTEGER;
```

```
begin
      for I in L'RANGE loop
            put("Enter value ");
            put(I);
            put(": ");
            get(T);
            L(I):=T;
            put_line(" ");
      end loop;
end INPUT;

begin   --Main program
      INPUT(G);
      --The procedure INPUT returns the array G
      ANSWER := MAX_MIN(G);
      --We call the function MAX_MIN with input G
      TEMP := ANSWER(1);
      put("Maximum value in array=");
      put(TEMP);
      put_line(" ");
      TEMP := ANSWER(2);
      put("Minimum value in array=");
      put(TEMP);
end MAXIMUM_MINIMUM;
```

7.6 OVERLOADING OF FUNCTION OPERATORS AND SUBPROGRAMS

Whenever the same symbol is used for distinct meanings in a given context, that symbol is said to be overloaded. Ada allows operator symbols to be overloaded. That is, they can be defined for operands other than the scalar data types float, integer, Boolean, and character, for which they are predefined in the language. This powerful feature of Ada allows you to extend the predefined features of the language in many important areas and contributes greatly to the creation of software libraries. With appropriate operator definitions, a calculus-like language can be created within Ada.

The operators that may be overloaded are the following.

abs, and, or, xor, not, mod, rem, =, <, <=, >, >=, +, −, *, /, **, &

We give three examples of functions that overload operators.

EXAMPLE 1 OF OPERATOR OVERLOADING: DOT PRODUCT OF VECTORS

```
type VECTOR is array(INTEGER range <>) of INTEGER;
```

```
function "*" (A,B: VECTOR) return INTEGER is
      SUM: INTEGER:=0;
begin
      for I in VECTOR'RANGE loop
            SUM:=SUM+A(I)*B(I);   --The symbol "*" means integer multiply
      end loop;
      return SUM;
end "*";
```

With the function above defined, we have extended the domain of the multiplication symbol to include the dot product of vectors. Thus, if two variables of type VECTOR, such as X and Y, are declared in a program, it would be legal to write

```
I:=X*Y;
```

where I is an integer variable.

EXAMPLE 2 OF OPERATOR OVERLOADING: ADDITION AND MULTIPLICATION OF MATRICES

```
type MATRIX is array(INTEGER range <>,INTEGER range <>) of FLOAT;

function "+" (A,B: MATRIX) return MATRIX is
      C: MATRIX;
begin
      for ROW in A'RANGE(1) loop
            for COLUMN in B'RANGE(2) loop
                  C(ROW,COLUMN):=A(ROW,COLUMN)+B(ROW,COLUMN);
            end loop;
      end loop;
      return C;
end "+";

function "*" (A,B: MATRIX) return MATRIX is
      C: MATRIX;
      SUM: FLOAT;
begin
      for ROW in A'RANGE(1) loop
            for COLUMN in B'RANGE(2) loop
                  SUM:=0.0;
                  for ELEMENT in A'RANGE(2) loop
                        SUM:=SUM +A(ROW,ELEMENT)*B(ELEMENT,COLUMN);
                  end loop;
```

```
                        C(ROW,COLUMN):=SUM;
              end loop;
         end loop;
         return C;
end "*";
```

With the operator functions above, we could perform matrix arithmetic as follows (we assume that A, B, C, and D are of type MATRIX).

D:=A*B+C;

EXAMPLE 3 OF OPERATOR OVERLOADING: COMPARISON OF STRINGS

```
type WORD is array(1..10) of CHARACTER;
function "<" (A,B: WORD) return BOOLEAN is
      T: BOOLEAN;
begin
      T:=FALSE;
      for I in 1..10 loop
            if A(I) < B(I) then
                  T:=TRUE;
                  exit;
            end if;
            if A(I) > B(I) then
                  exit;
            end if;
      end loop;
      return T;   --In the event A equals B, T will come out FALSE
end "<";

function ">" (A,B: WORD) return BOOLEAN is
      T: BOOLEAN;
begin
      T:=FALSE;
      for I in 1..10 loop
            if A(I) > B(I) then
                  T:=TRUE;
                  exit;
            end if;
            if A(I) < B(I) then
                  exit;
            end if;
      end loop;
      return T;
end ">";
```

The establishment of these overloaded operator functions means that the programmer has effectively added string comparisons to the Ada language. This added capability might be useful in alphabetizing names. We could use statements such as

if X<Y **then** INTERCHANGE(X,Y);

where X and Y are assumed to be of type WORD and procedure INTER-CHANGE is suitably defined.

The identifiers used for subprograms may also be overloaded. The compiler distinguishes overloaded subprograms by examining the number, position, and type of parameters called, and in the case of a function, the type of parameter returned. Consider the three function specifications that follow.

function ADD(A,B: FLOAT) **return** INTEGER **is**
function ADD(A,B: FLOAT) **return** FLOAT **is**
function ADD(A,B: INTEGER) **return** INTEGER **is**

Suppose that variable R is declared to be of type FLOAT and variable J is declared to be of type INTEGER. Then the following function calls would be legal.

R: =ADD(4.0,5.0);
J: =ADD(4.0,5.0);
J: =ADD(4,5);

The compiler can distinguish each of the three ADD functions from the context of the function call.

The "put" command that you have been using for output is an overloaded subprogram. The "put" procedure that is defined for writing integers differs from that for writing strings.

The ability to overload the names of subprograms allows an Ada programmer to employ greater clarity of expression. It also allows different teams of programmers to use the same identifiers for their respective subprogram names without any interface problems occurring later.

7.7 SOME PROGRAMS RESTRUCTURED

In this section we rework two previously presented programs and improve their structure. Compare against the older versions the readability of the new versions that employ subprograms and better program structure. Program 7.7-1 is a new version of Program 5.1-2, Exchange Sort.

PROGRAM 7.7-1

```
with TEXT_IO; use TEXT_IO;
procedure EXCHANGE_SORT_REWORKED is
    type IARRAY is array(1..5000) of INTEGER;
    A: IARRAY;
    SIZE,INDEX,POS: INTEGER;

    procedure INPUT(N: INTEGER; Z: out IARRAY) is
        TEMP: INTEGER;
    begin
        for I in 1..N loop
            put("Enter Z(");
            put(I);
            put("): ");
            get(TEMP);
            Z(I):=TEMP;
        end loop;
    end INPUT;

    function MAX(A: IARRAY; UPPER: INTEGER) return INTEGER is
        MAX,POSITION: INTEGER;
    begin
        MAX:=A(1);
        POSITION:=1;
        for I in 1..UPPER loop
            if A(I) >= MAX then
                MAX:=A(I);
                POSITION:=I;
            end if;
        end loop;
        return POSITION;
    end MAX;

    procedure EXCHANGE(X,Y: INTEGER) is
        TEMP: INTEGER;
    begin
        TEMP:=A(X);
        A(X) :=A(Y);
        A(Y) :=TEMP;
    end EXCHANGE;

    procedure OUTPUT(N: INTEGER; A: IARRAY) is
        TEMP: INTEGER;
```

```
begin
        put_line(" ");
        put_line("The sorted integers");
        put_line("------------");
        for I in 1..N loop
            TEMP:=A(I);
            put(TEMP);
            put_line(" ");
        end loop;
    end OUTPUT;

begin   --Main program
    put("How many integers will be sorted: ");
    get(SIZE);
    --We input the array to be sorted
    INPUT(SIZE,A);
    put_line(" ");
    INDEX:=SIZE+1;
    --We start the exchange sort algorithm
    loop
        INDEX:=INDEX-1;
        --We find the maximum in the array A from 1 to INDEX
        POS:=MAX(A,INDEX);
        --Exchange the items in array positions POS, INDEX
        EXCHANGE(POS,INDEX);
        exit when INDEX=2;
    end loop;
    --We output the sorted array of integers
    OUTPUT(SIZE,A);
end EXCHANGE_SORT_REWORKED;
```

By comparing Programs 5.1-2 and 7.7-1, you can observe how many of the tasks (e.g., input, maximum of array of integers, exchange, and output) have been packaged as subprograms in Program 7.7-1. It is possible to read and comprehend the main program (in Program 7.7-1) without getting bogged down in the fine details of how the various subprograms are implemented. The general flow of the algorithm is made evident in the main program. The use of subprograms here has made Program 7.7-1 easier to maintain. To modify the technique for performing any of the subprograms, only that isolated portion of the program must be changed.

Program 7.7-2 is a reworked version of Program 5.1-4, Alphabetize.

PROGRAM 7.7-2

```
with TEXT_IO; use TEXT_IO;
procedure ALPHABETIZE_REWORKED is
      type NAME is array(1..100,1..20) of CHARACTER;
         N: NAME;
      SIZE: INTEGER;

procedure INITIALIZE is
begin
      for ROW in 1..100 loop
            for COLUMN in 1..20 loop
                  N(ROW,COLUMN):=' ';
            end loop;
      end loop;
end INITIALIZE;

procedure INPUT(SIZE: INTEGER; N: out NAME) is
         J: INTEGER;
      CH: CHARACTER;
begin
      for I in 1..SIZE loop
            put ("Enter name "); put(I);
            put(". Terminate name with '/'-->");
            get(CH);
            J:=0;
            while CH /= '/' loop
                  J:=J+1;
                  N(I,J):=CH;
                  get(CH);
                  exit when J=20;   --A name cannot have more than 20
                                    --characters
            end loop;
            put_line(" ");
      end loop;
end INPUT;

procedure BUBBLE_SORT(SIZE: INTEGER; N: out NAME) is
      type ROW is array(1..20) of CHARACTER;
      OUTER_COUNT,I,J: INTEGER;
                  B,T: BOOLEAN;
             R1,R2,R: ROW;
--We overload the operator "<"
function "<" (A,B: ROW) return BOOLEAN is
      T: BOOLEAN;
```

```
begin
      T:=FALSE;
      for I in 1..20 loop
            if A(I) < B(I) then
                  T:=TRUE;
                  exit;
            end if;
            if A(I) > B(I) then
                  exit;
            end if;
      end loop;
      return T;
end "<";

procedure INTERCHANGE(X,Y: INTEGER) is
begin
      R:=N(X)(1..20);   --Temporary array
      N(X)(1..20):=N(Y)(1..20);
      N(Y)(1..20):=R;
end INTERCHANGE;

begin   --Bubble sort
      OUTER_COUNT:=1;
      loop
            B:=FALSE;
            I:=0;
            loop
                  I:=I+1;
                  --We slice the Ith row of matrix N
                  R1:=N(I)(1..20);
                  R2:=N(I+1)(1..20);
                  --We interchange row I with row I+1
                  if R2 < R1 then
                        INTERCHANGE(I,I+1);
                        --Not through sorting, because we have performed an
                        --interchange
                        B:TRUE;
                  end if;
                  exit when I=SIZE_OUTER_COUNT;
            end loop;
            OUTER_COUNT:=OUTER_COUNT+1;
            exit when (OUTER_COUNT=SIZE) or (not B);
      end loop;
end BUBBLE_SORT;

procedure OUTPUT(SIZE: INTEGER; N: NAME) is
      CH: CHARACTER;
```

```
begin
      put_line(" ");
      put_line("The alphabetized list");
      put_line("--------------");
      for ROW in 1..SIZE loop
            for COLUMN in 1..20 loop
                  CH:=N(ROW,COLUMN);
                  put(CH);
            end loop;
            put_line(" ");
      end loop;
end OUTPUT;

begin --Main program
      --We initialize the two dimensional array to blanks
      INITIALIZE;
      put("How many names will be alphabetized: ");
      get(SIZE);
      put_line(" ");
      --We input the names to be alphabetized
      INPUT(SIZE,N);
      BUBBLE_SORT(SIZE,N);
      --We output the alphabetized names
      OUTPUT(SIZE,N);
end ALPHABETIZE_REWORKED;
```

Have you compared Program 5.1-4 with Program 7.7-2? In Program 7.7-2 we embedded a function "<" and a procedure INTERCHANGE within subprogram BUBBLE_SORT. These two computational resources are required only by subprogram BUBBLE_SORT. They are invisible to the portions of the program outside the scope of procedure BUBBLE_SORT. In Chapter 14 we discuss at much greater length the visibility and scope of Ada units and variables.

7.8 MORE ADA PROGRAMS

We now present a series of programs that use important subprograms. We believe that it is desirable to see the subprogram constructs introduced above demonstrated in a realistic context. Some of the subprograms developed in this section are used later in connection with packages and compilation units.

7.8.1 Procedures and Functions on Strings

Some versions of Pascal, for example University of California, San Diego (UCSD)™ Pascal, provide string utilities for the user as part of the compiler. Ada requires that the programmer write his or her own string utilities. In Program 7.8-1 we present Ada procedures and functions that include all the Pascal string capabilities that are built into the UCSD version of Pascal that is used on a Western Digital Microengine computer. The following chart below summarizes the various procedures and functions contained in Program 7.8-1 and their respective purposes.

Utilities Contained in Program 7.8-1 and Their Purpose

1. **function** COPY(SOURCE: SUB_STRING; START_AT,NUMBER _CHAR: INTEGER);
   This function returns a portion of SOURCE starting at START_AT, containing NUMBER_CHAR characters. For example,
   COPY("This is a string",6,2) returns "is"

2. **procedure** INSERT(INSERTION: SUB_STRING; SOURCE: **in out** SUB _STRING; START_AT: INTEGER);
   This procedure inserts INSERTION into SOURCE starting at START _AT. For example,
   INSERT(A,B,6) where A is "is better than", where B is "To be or not to be" produces "To be is better than or not to be"

3. **procedure** DELETE(SOURCE: **in out** SUB_STRING; START_AT, NUMBER_CHAR:INTEGER);
   DELETE(A,22,3) where A is "To be is better than or not to be" produces "To be is better than not to be".

PROGRAM 7.8-1

```
with TEXT_IO; use TEXT_IO;
procedure STRING_UTILITIES is
        --We limit strings to one line of text
        subtype SUB_ST is STRING(1..80);
        subtype INDEX is INTEGER range 1..80;
                S1,S2: SUB_ST;
        START,NUMCHAR: INDEX;
                CH: CHARACTER;

procedure INSERT (INSERTION: SUB_ST; SOURCE: in out SUB_ST; START_AT:
                INDEX) is
        LENGTH_SOURCE,LENGTH_INSERTION,I: INTEGER;
```

```
begin
        --We use an attribute of strings in the next statement
        LENGTH_INSERTION := INSERTION'LENGTH;
        LENGTH_SOURCE := SOURCE'LENGTH;
        if LENGTH_SOURCE+LENGTH_INSERTION <= 80 then
                for K in reverse START_AT..LENGTH_SOURCE loop
                        SOURCE(K+LENGTH_INSERTION) := SOURCE(K);
                end loop;
                I:=START_AT;
                for J in 1..LENGTH_INSERTION loop
                        SOURCE(I) := INSERTION(J);
                        I:=I+1;
                end loop;
        else
                put_line("Void insertion.");
        end if;
end INSERT;

procedure DELETE(SOURCE: in out SUB_ST; START_AT,NUMBER_CHAR:
                INTEGER) is
        SOURCE_LENGTH: INTEGER;
begin
        SOURCE_LENGTH := SOURCE'LENGTH;
        if NUMBER_CHAR <= SOURCE_LENGTH then
                for I in START_AT..SOURCE_LENGTH-NUMBER_CHAR loop
                        SOURCE(I) := SOURCE(I+NUMBER_CHAR);
                end loop;
        else
                put_line("Void deletion.");
        end if;
end DELETE;

function COPY(SOURCE: SUB_ST; START_AT,NUMBER_CHAR: INTEGER)
        return SUB_ST is
        S: SUB_ST;
        I: INTEGER:=START_AT;
begin
        if START_AT + NUMBER_CHAR <= SOURCE'LENGTH then
                for K in 1..NUMBER_CHAR loop
                        S(K):=SOURCE(I+K-1);
                end loop;
                return S;
        else
                put_line("Void copy.");
                return " ";
        end if;
end COPY;
```

```
procedure SKIF_LINE(N:INTEGER range 1..24) is
begin
        for I in 1..N loop
                put_line(" ");
        end loop;
end SKIP_LINE;


procedure MENU is
CHOICE:INTEGER;
begin
        SKIP_LINE(4);
        put_line("------------------------------------------------------------");
        put_line(S1);
        put_line(" ");
        put_line("1-->Insert in string");
        put_line(" ");
        put_line("2-->Delete from string");
        put_line(" ");
        put_line("3-->Copy from string");
        put_line(" ");
        put("Enter choice: ");
        get(CHOICE);
        case CHOICE is
                when 1=>put_line(" ");
                        put_line("Enter string to insert");
                        get(S2);
                        put_line(" ");
                        put("Where should insertion start: ");
                        get(START);
                        put_line(" ");
                        INSERT(S2,S1,START);
                        put_line(" ");
                        put_line(S1);
                when 2=>put_line(" ");
                        put("Where should deletion begin: ");
                        get(START);
                        put_line(" ");
                        put("How many characters should be deleted: ");
                        get(NUMCHAR);
                        DELETE(S1,START,NUMCHAR);
                        put_line(" ");
                        put_line(S1);
                when 3=>put_line(" ");
                        put("Start copying from where: ");
                        get(START);
```

```
                        put_line(" ");
                        put("How many characters do you wish to copy: ");
                        get(NUMCHAR);
                        S2:=COPY(S1,START,NUMCHAR);
                        put_line(" ");
                        put_line(S2);
              when others=> MENU;
        end case;
end MENU;

        begin   --Main program
        put_line("  ");
        put_line("Enter a string on the next line");
        get(S1);
        put_line(" ");
        MENU;
end STRING_UTILITIES;
```

We suggest that you walk your way through Program 7.8-1 so that you understand every function and procedure used.

7.8.2   Solving Simultaneous Equations

The problem of solving N linear simultaneous equations in N unknowns is an important one. Its solution provides an important cornerstone for a numerical analysis software package, since many important numerical analysis problems require, as a subproblem, the solution of N simultaneous equations.

In this section we present a stand-alone Ada program that solves N simultaneous equations in N unknowns. Embedded in this program are subprograms that will be included in a linear systems package in Chapter 13.

We assume that the reader either is familiar with or has access to works on Gaussian elimination. An excellent reference, among many, is *Introduction to Numerical Computations* by James S. Vandergraft (Reference 5, pp. 162–188). In Program 7.8-2, Gaussian elimination is implemented by performing an "LU-decomposition" of the given matrix of coefficients. This transforms the given ($N \times N$) matrix of coefficients into a lower and upper (LU) triangular ($N \times N$) matrix that allows the N equations to be solved by "forward" and "backward" substitution. If the theory supporting Program 7.8-2 is not familiar to you, please consult an appropriate reference.

PROGRAM 7.8-2

--This program will solve up to 100 simultaneous equations in 100 unknowns

```ada
with TEXT_IO; use TEXT_IO;
procedure SOLUTION_OF_N_SIMULTANEOUS_EQUATIONS is
      MAXSIZE: constant INTEGER:=100;
      subtype INDEX is INTEGER range 1..MAXSIZE;
      type RMATRIX is array(INDEX,INDEX) of FLOAT;
      type RARRAY is array(INDEX) of FLOAT;
      type IARRAY is array(INDEX) of INTEGER:
      SUB: IARRAY;
      SIZE: INTEGER;
      A:    RMATRIX;
      X,B:  RARRAY:
      T:    FLOAT:
--LU_FACTOR destroys the input matrix A and converts it to a lower-upper
--triangular matrix. If the programmer wishes to preserve the input matrix, copy it
--first, before calling LU_FACTOR

procedure LU_FACTOR(N: in INTEGER; A: in out RMATRIX) is
      INDX,J:            INTEGER;
      PIVOT,MAX,AB,T: FLOAT;

procedure ERROR is
begin
      put_line(" ");
      put_line(" ");
      put_line("The matrix of coefficients is singular");
      put_line(" ");
      put_line("Cannnot continue processing");
      put_line(" ");
end ERROR;

begin   --LU_FACTOR
      if N > MAXSIZE then
            put_line(" ");
            put("Can solve up to only ");
            put(MAXSIZE);
            put_line(" simultaneous equations.");
            put_line(" ");
      else
            for I in 1..N loop
                  SUB(I):=I;                --We initialize subscript array
            end loop;
```

```
            for K in 1..N-1 loop
                    MAX:=0.0;
                    for I in K..N loop
                    T:=A(SUB(I),K);
                    AB:=ABS(T);
                            if AB > MAX then
                                    MAX:=AB;
                                    INDX:=I;
                            end if;
                    end loop;
                    if MAX<=1.0E-7 then
                            ERROR;
                    end if;
                    J:=SUB(K);
                    SUB(K):=SUB(INDX);
                    SUB(INDX):=J;
                    PIVOT:=A(SUB(K),K);
                    for I in K+1..N loop
                            A(SUB(I),K):=-A(SUB(I),K)/PIVOT;
                            for J in K+1..N loop
                                    A(SUB(I),J):=A(SUB(I),J)+A(SUB(I),K)*A(SUB(K),J);
                            end loop;
                    end loop;
            end loop;
            for I in 1..N loop
                    if A(SUB(I),I)=0.0 then
                            ERROR;
                    end if;
            end loop;
      end if;
end LU_FACTOR;

--The matrix A in SOLVE is assumed to be an upper-lower triangular produced by
--LU_SOLVE

procedure SOLVE(N: in INTEGER; A:in RMATRIX; C:in RARRAY; X:out RARRAY) is
      K:INTEGER;
begin
      if N=1 then
              X(1):=C(1)/A(1,1);
      else
              X(1):=C(SUB(1));
              for K in 2..N loop
                      X(K):=C(SUB(K));
```

```
            for I in 1..K-1 loop
                    X(K):=X(K)+A(SUB(K),I)*X(I);
            end loop;
        end loop;
        X(N):=X(N)/A(SUB(N),N);
        K:=N;
        loop
            K:=K-1;
            for I in K+1..N loop
                    X(K):=X(K)-A(SUB(K),I)*X(I);
            end loop;
            X(K):=X(K)/A(SUB(K),K);
            exit when K=1;
        end loop;
    end if;
end SOLVE;

procedure MESSAGE is
begin
    put_line("We solve N simultaneous equations of the form");
    put_line(" ");
    put_line("               A*X=B");
    put_line(" ");
    put_line("where A is an n × n matrix of coefficients and B");
    put_line("is a column vector of coefficients.");
    put_line(" ");
end MESSAGE;

procedure INPUT is
begin
    put("Enter the number of equations to be solved: ");
    get(SIZE);
    if SIZE > MAXSIZE then
        put_line(" ");
        put("Cannot solve more than ");
        put(MAXSIZE);
        put_line(" equations.");
        put_line(" ");
        INPUT;
    end if;
    put_line(" ");
```

```
        for I in 1..SIZE loop
            for J in 1..SIZE loop
                put("Enter A("); put (I); put(","); put(J); put("): ");
                get(T);
                A(I,J):=T;
            end loop;
        end loop;
        put_line(" ");
        for K in 1..SIZE loop
            put("Enter B("); put(K); put("): ");
            get(T);
            B(K):=T;
        end loop;
end INPUT:

procedure OUTPUT is
        T:  FLOAT;
begin
        put_line(" ");
        put_line("The solution");
        put_line("--------");
        for I in 1..SIZE loop
            T:=X(I);
            put(T);
            put_line(" ");
        end loop;
end OUTPUT;

begin --Main program
        MESSAGE;
        INPUT;
        LU_FACTOR(SIZE,A);   --The matrix A will be changed by this procedure
        SOLVE(SIZE,A,B,X);
        OUTPUT;
end SOLUTION_OF_N_SIMULTANEOUS_EQUATIONS;
```

7.9 SUMMARY

• Subprograms can greatly enhance program readability and maintainability.
As logical units, subprograms should perform some well-defined task. The
subprogram name should describe the purpose of the task being performed.
Subprograms often have nested within them other subprograms that perform
subsidiary tasks necessary to accomplish the main task of the outermost
subprogram. These internal subprograms are invisible (inaccessible) to logical
units outside the boundary of the outermost subprogram.

- In allocating jobs for programming teams in a large software development project, subprogram specifications are often provided to development teams with the charge to write the code (bottom-up development) for each specified subprogram.

- Subprograms communicate with their respective host programs by way of formal parameters of binding modes "in", "in out", and "out". If the variables used in the subprogram are local to the subprogram, the subprogram becomes an autonomous entity that may be transported from one host program to another. In writing code for a subprogram, an attempt should be made to make the subprogram a self-contained software entity. It should be as independent as possible from the host program containing it.

- Functions must return a data type that is given in the function specification.

- Default values in a subprogram are evaluated when a subprogram is declared, not when it is called.

- Scalar parameters are copied. The mechanism for arrays and records is not specified in Ada.

- Parameters may be transferred to a subprogram either by position or by name. If a mixed mode transfer is desired, the positional parameters must be indicated before any named parameters.

- Subprogram identifiers may be overloaded. The compiler resolves subprogram calls by examining the position and type of parameters in the calling statement as well as the type of parameter returned in the case of a function.

- When operator functions are overloaded, the operator must be defined in quotes. The operations in the Ada language, in effect, may be extended through the use of overloaded operators.

Exercises for Chapter 7

1. Write a procedure for taking the cube root of a number.
2. What is the output of the following program?

```
procedure QUESTION2 is
    I,J:INTEGER;
    G:FLOAT;

procedure P1(A,B:INTEGER;C:FLOAT) is
    I,J,K:INTEGER;
begin
    I:=4*A;
    J:=5*B;
    K:=I*J;
end P1;
```

```
procedure P2(I:FLOAT) is
        J:FLOAT;
begin
        J:=I*2.0;
        put(J); put_line(" ");
end P2;

begin   --Main program
        I:=1;
        J:=2;
        G:=1.0;
        P1(J,I,G);
        put(I); put_line(" ");
        put(J); put_line(" ");
        P2(G);
end;
```

3. Walk through Program 7.8-1 testing each of the string utilities.
4. Walk through Program 7.8-2 by solving the following set of equations.

$$2*X + 3*Y = 5$$
$$3*X + 5*Y = 8$$

5. Write a small descriptive statistics program that does each of the following.

   (a) Allows the user to enter an array of data.
   (b) Computes the sample mean of the data.
   (c) Computes the sample median of the data.
   (d) Computes any percentile of the data.
   (e) Computes the variance of the data.

6. Overload the operators "*" and "+" and then determine whether precedence is maintained by calculating:

$$A + B * C$$

   Is the result $(A+B)*C$ or $A+(B*C)$?

7. Write a function CONVERT that allows a Roman numeral of up to eight characters to be entered and returns the floating point equivalent to the Roman numeral.

8. Write an overloaded function ">" that compares the numerical value of two Roman numerals, each containing at most eight characters.

Chapter 8

ON THE RECORD

In Chapter 5 we introduced our first structured data type, the array. A limitation of the array structure is the requirement that all elements in an array be of the same type. That is, if one declares "type EXAMPLE is array(1 . . 100) of INTEGER", every element in the array EXAMPLE must be an integer.

Ada supports a data structure called a "record," which allows different data types to be grouped together under the umbrella of a single data unit. This powerful feature of Ada supports the creation of other important data structures (e.g., stacks, queues, trees, graphs). The "record" type also makes Ada an important language for the development of data base management software.

In this chapter we introduce the various "record" constructs and illustrate them in the context of Ada programs.

8.1 THE RECORD TYPE

Record types are constructed as follows.

```
type USER_DEFINED_IDENTIFIER is record
      identifier_1: DATA_TYPE_1;
      identifier_2: DATA_TYPE_2;
      identifier_3: DATA_TYPE_3;
      identifier_N: DATA_TYPE_N;
end record;
```

133

A record declaration, like an array declaration, defines a "template" from which data objects may be created by object declarations. Consider the following example.

```
type DAYS is (MON, TUES, WED, THURS, FRI, SAT, SUN);
subtype HOURS is INTEGER range 1..24;
type KIND_OF_DAY is (CLEAR, CLOUDY, STORMY);
type WEATHER_RECORD is
        record
                K: KIND_OF_DAY;
                TEMP: array(HOURS) of INTEGER;
        end record;
W: array(DAYS) of WEATHER_RECORD;
```

We have created a user-defined data structure W, which is an array of objects called WEATHER_RECORD. Each of the objects, WEATHER_RECORD, has two fields. The first is KIND_OF_DAY and the second is an array of integers, each integer representing a temperature for each hour of the day.

The operations of equality testing and assignment are predefined for records as they are for any type other than a limited private type.

How can we access information from a record?

8.1.1 Sign on the Dotted Line: Dot Notation for Record Access

To access any field of a record we use the name of the object that has been declared to be a record followed by a dot, ".", followed by the name of the object we wish to access. For example, for the record structure defined above, some typical access statements might be as follows.

```
I:=W(TUES).TEMP(20);    --We access the temperature on Tues at hour 20
J:=W(THURS).K;          --We access the kind of day for Thurs
```

We assume that "I" has been declared to be an integer and "J" has been declared to be of type KIND_OF_DAY.

Can we have records within records? For the record, we say yes. For example, suppose we modify the WEATHER_RECORD presented above as follows.

```
type WEATHER_ATTRIBUTE is record
        TEMPERATURE,BAROMETRIC_PRESSURE,WIND_VELOCITY: INTEGER;
end record;
```

```
type WEATHER_RECORD is
    record
            K: KIND_OF_DAY;
            DATA: array(HOURS) of WEATHER_ATTRIBUTE;
    end record;

W: array(DAYS) of WEATHER_RECORD;
```

A typical access to this data structure might be

```
I: - W(MON).DATA(10).WIND_VELOCITY;
```

where "I" has been declared to be an integer. "W(MON)" fetches the data object (a WEATHER_RECORD) in position MON. ".DATA(10)" fetches the field "DATA" from this record and gets the tenth data object in the DATA array, corresponding to the tenth hour of Monday. ".WIND_VELOCITY" fetches the field WIND_VELOCITY from the record WEATHER_ATTRIBUTE. Confusing?

We illustrate these concepts in Program 8.1-1.

PROGRAM 8.1-1

```
with TEXT_IO; use TEXT_IO;
procedure WEATHER_RECORDS is
    type DAYS is (MON, TUES, WED, THURS, FRI, SAT, SUN);
    subtype HOURS is INTEGER range 1..24;
    type KIND_OF_DAY is (CLEAR, CLOUDY, STORMY);
    type WEATHER_ATTRIBUTE is
        record
                TEMPERATURE, BAROMETRIC_PRESSURE, WIND_VELOCITY:
                INTEGER;
        end record;
    type WEATHER_RECORD is
        record
                K: KIND_OF_DAY;
                DATA: array(HOURS) of WEATHER_ATTRIBUTE;
        end record;
    W: array(DAYS) of WEATHER_RECORD;

procedure CREATE_RECORD is
    subtype CHOICE is INTEGER range 1..3;
    KOD: CHOICE;
        T: INTEGER;
```

```
begin
    for D in MON..SUN loop
        put("Enter the kind of day (1-->CLEAR, 2-->CLOUDY,
        3-->STORMY): ");
        get(KOD);
        put_line(" ");
        case KOD is
            when 1 => W(D).K:= CLEAR;
            when 2 => W(D).K:= CLOUDY;
            when 3 => W(D).K:= STORMY;
        end case;
        for I in 1..24 loop
            put("Enter the temperature for hour ");
            put(I); put(": ");
            get(T);
            W(D).DATA(I).TEMPERATURE:=  T;
            put_line(" ");
            put("Enter the barometric pressure for hour ");
            put(I); put(": ");
            get(T);
            W(D).DATA(I).BAROMETRIC_PRESSURE:=  T;
            put_line(" ");
            put("Enter the wind velocity for hour ");
            put(I); put(": ");
            get(T);
            W(D).DATA(I).WIND_VELOCITY:=T;
            put_line(" ");
        end loop;
    end loop;
end CREATE_RECORD;
begin
    CREATE_RECORD;
    --Once a weather record has been created, one may wish to add
    --procedures for accessing and modifying information
end WEATHER_RECORDS;
```

8.1.2 Initialization of Records

Ada allows you to provide initial conditions in a record specification. We
illustrate this with two type specifications.

```
type STUDENT is
      record
              HEIGHT: INTEGER: =60;
              WEIGHT: INTEGER;
      end record;
type INDIVIDUAL is
      record
              NAME:   STRING(1..15):=(NAME'RANGE=>' ');
              SCORE: INTEGER;
      end record;
HENRY: INDIVIDUAL;
```

We could write:

```
HENRY.NAME(1..5):=  "HENRY";
```

8.1.3   Positional and Nonpositional Assignments to Records

One may assign values to a variable of a record type in a manner similar to that
for an array variable. The following example illustrates this.

```
type DAY_MONTH is
      record
              DAY: INTEGER  range 1..31;
              MONTH: (JAN,FEB,MAR,APR,MAY,JUN,JUL,AUG,SEP,OCT,NOV,DEC);
      end record;
A,B,C,D: DAY_MONTH;
begin
      A:= (25,FEB);   ――The order of assignment follows the order of the fields in
                      ――the record declaration
      B:= (MONTH=> MAR, DAY=> 15);   ――Nonpositional assignment
      C.DAY:= 14;
      C.MONTH:= APR;
      D:= A;          ――We may assign one record to another
end;
```

8.1.4   Records as Formal Subprogram Parameters

.One can pass records or arrays of records to a subprogram if the subprogram
contains one or more formal parameters declared to be of record type. In
Program 8.1-1 the procedure "CREATE_RECORD" could be changed to

"CREATE_RECORD(W: out WRECORDS)" if "type WRECORDS is array (DAYS) of WEATHER_RECORD" is declared above the procedure "CREATE_RECORD".

Functions can return records, as in the following example.

```
function EXAMPLE(A: INTEGER) return WRECORDS is
begin
      executable statement(s);
end EXAMPLE;
```

8.1.5 Vector Addition Example to Illustrate Records

Program 8.1-2 allows two vectors, given in polar form, to be added together. Only the magnitude of the resultant vector is computed. We assume that the library unit MATH_LIB contains the functions sine and cosine.

PROGRAM 8.1-2

```
with MATH_LIB,TEXT_IO; use MATH_LIB,TEXT_IO;
procedure VECTOR_ADDITION_MAGNITUDE is
      type VECTOR is              --Polar representation of vector
          record
              MAG:FLOAT;        --Magnitude of vector
              ANGLE:FLOAT;    --Angle of vector in radians
          end record;
      A,B: VECTOR;
        T: FLOAT;

procedure INPUT(C: out VECTOR) is
begin
      put("Enter magnitude of vector: ");
      get(T);
      put_line(" ");
      C.MAG:= T;
      put("Enter angle of vector: ");
      get(T);
      put_line(" ");
      C.ANGLE:= T;
end INPUT;
```

```
function ADD_MAG(A,B: VECTOR) return FLOAT is
      H,V,R: FLOAT,
begin
      H:= A.MAG*COS(A.ANGLE) + B.MAG*COS(B.ANGLE);
      V:= A.MAG*SIN(A.ANGLE) + B.MAG*SIN(B.ANGLE);
      R:= SQRT(H*H + V*V);
      return R;
end ADD;

begin   --Main program
      INPUT(A);
      INPUT(B);
      T:= ADD_MAG(A,B);
      put("The magnitude of the resultant is ");
      put(T);
end VECTOR_ADDITION_MAGNITUDE;
```

8.1.6 Record Structure Using Linked List

In this section, as an application of record types, we demonstrate efficient list maintenance. This fundamental concern in computer science is part of the basic subject matter of data structures.

Suppose we wish to build and maintain an alphabetized list of records, using the last name of each person for the alphabetizing. How can we add new records while maintaining order? How can we delete records and maintain order?

A naive method would be the following: create an array of records and alphabetize it using an algorithm such as bubble sort (see Program 5.1-3). Whenever a record must be deleted, search for the appropriate array location and purge the record in that location. Then close the gap that has been created by moving all records in locations greater than the deleted record's location one position. The resulting array of records will be compact and will contain one less record. Whenever a record must be added, search for the appropriate location. Then move every record whose locations are equal or greater than the position for the insertion one position. This will create a hole into which the new record may be inserted.

Although the logic of the foregoing method for list insertion and deletion is correct, the process is most inefficient. When the list is large (the array has many records), the process of shifting records up or down is expensive. Indeed, in the worst case, $N - 1$ records may have to be shifted per insertion or deletion operation, where N is the size of the list.

Another approach is to maintain a linked list of records. Then the process of list insertion or deletion becomes size independent and thus very efficient. Suppose that each record in the array of records has an additional integer field that "points" to the array location of the next record's array position. In addition, suppose that there exists an integer variable that "points" to the array position containing the first record in the list. Thus we have created a chain. Each record in this chain has a link pointing to the next element in the chain. Each time we add a new record to the list, we automatically add the record to the first available array position and take proper account of the new record's position in the alphabetized list by modifying the link of the record just preceding the new record and having the "pointer" of the new record point to the record immediately following the new record. Thus the alphabetized list can be maintained without the need for any record shifting. Deletion of records can proceed in a similar manner. Only one pointer (in the record immediately preceding the record to be deleted) must be changed to bypass the deleted record's position.

We illustrate this linked-list data structure that uses records in Program 8.1-3. Garbage collection (the process of conserving memory space by either returning or reusing memory space after a deletion) is performed in this program. This process is implemented by keeping a linked list of unused space.

PROGRAM 8.1-3

```
with TEXT_IO; use TEXT_IO;
procedure LINKED_LISTS_USING_ARRAY_OF_RECORDS is
        MAX: constant INTEGER:=500;
        subtype STRING20 is string(1..20);
        type NODE is
            record
                    KEY: STRING20;    --This is a last name
                    INFO: STRING20;
                    LINK: INTEGER;    --This field points to the position of the next
                                      --record
            end record;
        type LINKED_LIST is array(1..MAX) of NODE;
                R: LINKED_LIST;
            FIRST: INTEGER;        --Points to the position of the first record
        AVAILABLE: INTEGER;        --Points to the position of the first available
                                   --record
                I: INTEGER;
                OVER: BOOLEAN;
--This procedure traverses the linked list and prints out the data contained in the
--list

procedure PRINT_OUT is
        NEXT: INTEGER;
            C: CHARACTER;
```

```
begin
      if FIRST=0 then
            put_line(" ");
            put_line("No records are available.");
      else
            NEXT:=. FIRST;
            while (NEXT /= 0) loop
                  put_line(" ");
                  --We output a record
                  for I in 1..20 loop
                        C:= R(NEXT).KEY(I);
                        put(C);
                  end loop;
                  put_line(" ");
                  for I in 1..20 loop
                        C:=R(NEXT).INFO(I);
                        put(C);
                  end loop;
                  NEXT:= R(NEXT).LINK;
            end loop;
      end if;
end PRINT_OUT;

--This procedure compares two strings and returns TRUE if they are equal

function EQUAL(S1,S2: STRING20) return BOOLEAN is
      T: BOOLEAN;
      I: INTEGER;
begin
      I:= 0;
      T:= TRUE;
      loop
            I:=I+1;
            if S1(I) /= S2(I) then
                  T:= FALSE;
                  exit;
            end if;
            exit when I=20;
      end loop;
      return T;
end EQUAL;
```

—This procedure determines whether string S1 precedes string S2

```
function PRECEDENCE(S1,S2: STRING20) return BOOLEAN is
      T: BOOLEAN;
      I: INTEGER;
begin
      I:= 0;
      T:= TRUE;
      loop
            I:= I+1;
            if S1(I) > S2(I) then
                  T:= FALSE;
                  exit;
            end if;
            if S1(I) < S2(I) then
                  exit;
            end if;
            exit when I=20;
      end loop;
      return T;
end PRECEDENCE;

procedure INPUT(SLOT: in INTEGER) is
      POS: INTEGER;
         C: CHARACTER;
begin
      put_line(" ");
      put("Enter last name (end with /): ");
      POS:= 1;
      get(C);
      while (C /= '/') and (POS <= 20) loop
            R(SLOT).KEY(POS):= C;
            get(C);
            POS:= POS+1;
      end loop;
      --We fill up the remaining elements of the string KEY with blanks
      while POS <= 20 loop
            R(SLOT).KEY(POS):= ' ';
            POS:=POS+1;
      end loop;
```

```
    put_line(" ");
    put_line("Enter information (end with /): ");
    POS:= 1;
    get(C);
    while (C /= '/') and (POS <= 20) loop
        R(SLOT).INFO(POS):=C;
        get(C);
        POS:= POS+1;
    end loop;
    --We fill up the remaining elements of the string INFO with blanks
    while POS <= 20 loop
        R(SLOT).INFO(POS):= ' ';
        POS:= POS+1;
    end loop;
    put_line(" ");
end INPUT;

--This procedure enables us to delete a record from the list

procedure DELETE is
    PREVIOUS,OLD,POS: INTEGER;
            NAME: STRING20;
                C: CHARACTER;
begin
    --We enter the name of the person whose record we wish to delete
    put_line(" ");
    put("Enter last name (end with /): ");
    POS:= 1;
    get(C);
    while (C /= '/') and (POS <= 20) loop
        NAME(POS):= C;
        get(C);
        POS:= POS+1;
    end loop;
    --We fill up the remaining elements of the string NAME with blanks
    while POS <= 20 loop
        NAME(POS):= ' ';
        POS:= POS+1;
    end loop;
    put_line(" ");
    --We look for a matchup between NAME and a similar name in list
    OLD:= FIRST;
    while (OLD /= 0) and (not EQUAL(R(OLD).KEY,NAME)) loop
        PREVIOUS:= OLD;
        OLD:= R(OLD).LINK;
    end loop;
```

```
        if OLD=0 then            --No matchup exists
            put_line(" ");
            put_line("No matchup exits.");
    else
            --We realign the link structure to allow deletion
            if FIRST=OLD then
                FIRST:= R(OLD).LINK;
            else
                R(PREVIOUS).LINK:= R(OLD).LINK;
            end if;
        --We do garbage collection
        R(OLD).LINK:= AVAILABLE;
        AVAILABLE:= OLD;   --The first available position is the position of the
                           --record removed. Its position has been linked to the
                           --linked list of available positions.
        end if;
end DELETE;
```

--This procedure enables us to add a record to the list

```
procedure ADD is
        NEWW,PREVIOUS,NEXT: INTEGER;
        --Since NEW is a reserved word, we use NEWW
 begin
        if AVAILABLE = 0 then
            put_line(" ");
            put_line("Available Space Gone. Cannot Add New Record.");
            put_line(" ");
    else
            NEWW:= AVAILABLE;
            --We have a linked list of available space
            AVAILABLE:= R(AVAILABLE).LINK;
            --We input a new record
            INPUT(NEWW);
            --Test to see whether new record goes first in the list
            if (FIRST = 0) or PRECEDENCE(R(NEWW).KEY,R(FIRST).KEY) then
                R(NEWW).LINK:= FIRST;
                FIRST:= NEWW;
        else
                --New node not the first in the list
                PREVIOUS:= FIRST;
                NEXT:= R(FIRST).LINK;
                while (NEXT /= 0) and
                (PRECEDENCE(R(NEXT).KEY,R(NEWW).KEY)) loop
                    PREVIOUS:= NEXT;
                    NEXT:= R(NEXT).LINK;
                end loop;
```

```
                        --Adjust the links to make the insertion
                        R(PREVIOUS).LINK:= NEWW;
                        R(NEWW).LINK:= NEXT;
                end if;
        end if;
end ADD;

procedure MENU is
        CHOICE: INTEGER;
begin
        put_line(" ");
        put_line(" ")'
        put_line("1--> Add new record");
        put_line(" ");
        put_line("2--> Delete a record");
        put_line(" ");
        put_line("3--> Printout all records");
        --In practice, one would probably desire to print out only a single record
        put_line(" ");
        put_line("4--> Exit from program");
        put_line(" ");
        put("Enter choice: ");
        get(CHOICE);
        put_line(" ");
        case CHOICE is
                when 1 => ADD;
                when 2 => DELETE;
                when 3 => PRINT_OUT;
                when 4 => OVER:= TRUE;
        end case;
end MENU;

begin   --Main program
        AVAILABLE:= 1;
        FIRST:= 0;
        --We initially link up all the available array positions
        for I in 1..MAX-1 loop
                R(I).LINK:= I+1;
        end loop;
        R(MAX).LINK:= 0;
        OVER:= FALSE;
        loop
                MENU;
                exit when OVER;
        end loop;
end LINKED_LISTS_USING_ARRAY_OF_RECORDS;
```

In Program 8.1-3 we have created several important software modules in the form of subprograms, namely, procedure INPUT and functions PRECE-DENCE and EQUAL. These software resources may be reused in other contexts with perhaps only minor changes.

8.1.7 Tree Structure Using Records

In Program 8.1-4 we illustrate a powerful data structure, the tree structure; it is constructed using a record type. Suppose that we wish to determine all the duplicates in a file of numbers. We assume that the numbers have been placed into an array.

Our strategy will be to form a special type of binary tree (please consult any text on data structures for additional theory, e.g., Reference 4) that has the property that each node's left offspring has a value that is less than the value of the parent node. Furthermore, the value of the right offspring is greater than the value of its parent.

We insert the numbers sequentially into the binary tree as follows. The first number input becomes the root of the tree. The second number is compared to the root. If it is smaller, it becomes the left offspring of the root. If it is larger, it becomes the right offspring of the root. If it is equal to the root, it is listed as a duplicate. Then the third number is input. It is first compared to the root. If less than the root, we move down the left branch of the tree. If greater than the root, we move down the right branch. In fact, we continue to move down the tree either to the left or the right, as we encounter each node, by comparing the number to each node. We move to the left if the number is less than the node, to the right if the number is greater than the node. Whenever we encounter a tie, we print out the duplicate. If we get to the bottom of the existing tree, we add the number (as a node) to the tree in the appropriate location.

Study Program 8.1-4 to see how we implement the foregoing concept.

PROGRAM 8.1-4

```
with TEXT_IO; use TEXT_IO;
procedure DUPLICATES is
      MAX: constant INTEGER:=1000;
      subtype NODEPTR is INTEGER range 0..MAX;
      type NODETYPE is
          record
                INFO:  INTEGER;    --Each node will represent a number
                LEFT:  NODEPTR;    --Pointer to left offspring of the node
                RIGHT: NODEPTR;    --Pointer to right offspring of the node
          end record;
```

```
    NODE: array(0..MAX) of NODETYPE;
    N: NODEPTR;        --The size of the list of numbers
    A: array(1..MAX) of INTEGER;
    TREE,P,Q,T,AVAIL: NODEPTR;
```

--This procedure creates a tree root with no offspring
procedure MAKETREE(X: INTEGER; P: **out** NODEPTR) **is**
begin
```
    P:= AVAIL;
    AVAIL:= AVAIL+1;
    NODE(P).INFO:= X;
    NODE(P).LEFT:= 0;     --A leaf node has both offspring equal to zero
    NODE(P).RIGHT:= 0;
```
end MAKETREE;

--This procedure adds a new node as the left offspring of P
procedure SETLEFT(P: **in out** NODEPTR; X: INTEGER) **is**
```
    Q: NODEPTR;
```
begin
```
    if NODE(P).LEFT /= 0 then
        put_line("Illegal setleft operation.");
    else
        MAKETREE(X,Q);
        NODE(P).LEFT:= Q;
    end if;
```
end SETLEFT;

--This procedure adds a new node as the right offspring of P
procedure SETRIGHT(P: **in out** NODEPTR; X: INTEGER) **is**
```
    Q: NODEPTR;
```
begin
```
    if NODE(P).RIGHT /= 0 then
        put_line("Illegal setright operation.");
    else
        MAKETREE(X,Q);
        NODE(P).RIGHT:= Q;
    end if;
```
end SETRIGHT;

procedure INPUT **is**
```
    I,T: INTEGER;
```

```
begin
      put_line(" ");
      put("How many integers will be loaded: ");
      get(N);
      put_line(" ");
      for I in 1..N loop
            put("Enter integer ");
            put(I); put(":");
            get(T);
            A(I):= T;
      end loop;
end INPUT;

begin   --Main program
      AVAIL:= 1;
      INPUT;
      put_line(" ");
      MAKETREE(A(1),TREE);   --TREE is the root of the binary tree
      for J in 2..N loop
            Q:= TREE;
            P:= TREE;
            while (A(J) /= NODE(P).INFO) and (Q /= 0) loop
                  P:=Q;
                  if A(J) < NODE(P).INFO then
                        Q:= NODE(P).LEFT;
                  else
                        Q:= NODE(P).RIGHT;
                  end if;
            end loop;
            if A(J) = NODE(P).INFO then
                  T:=A(J);
                  put(T);
                  put(" is a duplicate.");
                  put_line(" ");
            else
                  if A(J) < NODE(P).INFO then
                        SETLEFT(P,A(J));
                  else
                        SETRIGHT(P,A(J));
                  end if;
            end if;
      end loop;
end DUPLICATES;
```

8.2   **VARIANT RECORDS**

Records, in Ada, may be defined in a manner to allow variations in size or structure. In this section we examine both possibilities.

8.2.1   **Record Types of Varying Size**

We illustrate a record declaration of varying size.

```
type VARYING_SIZE (SIZE: INTEGER range 1..50) is
        record
                IARRAY: array(1..SIZE) of INTEGER;
                NUMBER: FLOAT;
        end record;
R: VARYING_SIZE (20);   --In this declaration, size is set to 20
```

The parameter SIZE is called the discriminant. Once the discriminant has been fixed, the record structure is fully defined and the discriminant cannot be changed. The discriminant or discriminants of a record type are collected in a manner similar to a list of subprogram parameters. Discriminants must be discrete. If we attempt a complete assignment that changes the value of a discriminant, a CONSTRAINT_ERROR exception will be raised (see Chapter 10).

We illustrate both object declarations and assignments to a record of varying size in the following example.

```
R1: VARYING_SIZE:=(5,  (4,2,-4,1,0),  5.6);   --Positional assignment
R2: VARYING_SIZE:=(SIZE=>3,  IARRAY=>(6, 7, 8), NUMBER=>1.1);
R2:= (3,(-5,-2,1),1.5);         -- Assignment to a varying record
R2.IARRAY(3):= 12;              -- Assignment to a component of a record
R1.IARRAY:= (1, 2, 3, 4, 5);   -- Assignment of one field of a record
```

Ada allows default values to be specified for the discriminants of a record. When default values are given for a discriminant, their values may be overridden by a record declaration. As before, once a discriminant value has been assigned, it cannot be changed. If a variable is declared without a discriminant value, the default value is assumed.

If default values are given, they must be given for all discriminants. That is, one may not discriminate against discriminants! If default values are given for the discriminants of a record type, any data objects that are declared to be of that type must have all constraints supplied or none supplied (in which case the default values will prevail).

As an example of a record type with default values for its discriminants, consider the following.

```
type DEFAULT_VALUES(A:INTEGER range 0..100:=5,B:INTEGER range
                        2..20:=7) is
    record
            W: array(0..A) of FLOAT;
            Z: array(-20..B) of INTEGER;
    end record;
    H,R,Q: DEFAULT_VALUES;          --A will equal 5, B will equal 7
        P: DEFAULT_VALUES(96,19);   --A will equal 96, B will equal 19
        Q: DEFAULT_VALUES(40,15);   --Once set, these values cannot change
```

8.2.2 Record Types of Varying Structure

We illustrate record types with varying structure with the following example:

```
type SEX is (M, F);
type STUDENT(GENDER: SEX) is
    record
            case GENDER is
                    when F=>    MATH_SCORE: INTEGER range 1..100;
                    when M=> VERBAL_SCORE: INTEGER range 1..100;
            end case;
    end record;
```

We illustrate how objects and assignments to these objects may be accomplished for records of varying structure.

```
R1: STUDENT:= (M, 88);
R2: STUDENT:= (F, 89);
R3: STUDENT;
R4: STUDENT(M);         --Constrained record with unmodifiable discriminant
R3:= (F, 85);           --Complete record assignment
R3.VERBAL_SCORE:=99;    --Assignment to component of record
R2:= R3;                --Complete record assignment
R4:= (M, 56);           --Complete record assignment
```

8.3 **SUMMARY**

- A record type declaration establishes a template. Data objects may then be declared to be of the given record type.
- The fields of a record may contain any previously declared data structures, including other records.
- To access the field of a record, we require the name of the data object, followed by a dot, followed by the name of the field in the record. The name of the record is not used.
- The data objects declared within a record may be assigned initial values.
- Both size and structure discriminants may be used in defining a record type. Once the discriminant value or values have been set, they may not be changed. If one discriminant declared within a record is given a default value, all discriminants within the record must also be given default values. If default values are overridden, they must all be overridden.
- The combination of arrays and records allows the programmer to create powerful data structures.

Exercises for Chapter 8

1. Write a set of subprograms that perform complex number addition, subtraction, multiplication, and division using a record structure to represent complex numbers.

2. Add an additional menu item (and associated subprogram) to Program 8.1-3 that enables you to search for and print out any given record using the last name as a key.

3. Modify Program 8.1-4 so that it can search for all duplicate words in a text.

4. Indicate any statements in the following program that are illegal.

```
procedure SOME_STATEMENTS_ARE_ILLEGAL is
    type QUESTIONABLE(SIZE: INTEGER range 1..N) is
        record
            A: array(1..SIZE) of INTEGER;
            SEX: (M,F);
            case SEX is
                when M=> B: INTEGER;
                when F=> C: INTEGER;
            end case;
        end record;
```

```
            R1: QUESTIONABLE:=(2,(1,2,3,),M,3));
            R2: QUESTIONABLE;
            R3: QUESTIONABLE:=(4,(1,2,3,4,),F,2);
            R4: QUESTIONABLE(3,M);
    begin
        R2:= (SEX=>M, SIZE=>2, (1,2), 4);
        R4:= R2;
        R4:= (3,M,(1,2,3,),F,5);
    end;
```

5. Write an Ada program, with a full explanation of what its function is, which·
   uses the following record type.

   type RECTANGULAR (ROW, COLUMN) **is**
      record
           RECT_MATRIX: **array** (1..ROW,1..COLUMN) **of** FLOAT;
      end record;

6. For the data type RECTANGULAR, defined in Exercise 5, tell whether
   the subtype

   subtype COL_12 **is** RECTANGULAR (COLUMN=> 12)

   produces the equivalent of

   type COL_12 (ROW: POSITIVE) **is**
     record
         MATRIX: **array** (1..ROW,1..12) **of** FLOAT;
     end record;

   Explain. If the two are not equivalent, can you modify subtype COL_12 so
   that it is equivalent to type COL_12? Explain.

Chapter 9

ATTRIBUTES

An attribute is a predefined characteristic or quality of a named data type. It may be useful to the programmer during the course of a computation and can be accessed by an attribute inquiry. An attribute inquiry consists of a type or object name followed by a single quote mark and an attribute name. An attribute is a read-only variable that provides a value that the programmer may find useful in controlling the course of a computation. The careful use of attributes can lead to more versatile software and improved program portability. A variety of attributes are predefined in Ada; there are no user-defined attributes in the language.

In this chapter we describe the attributes that are available in Ada. Because the material in Sections 9.2 and 9.3 is highly technical and detailed, the reader may wish to skip to the summary at the end of the chapter before reading these sections.

Rather than present a list of attributes, we illustrate their function by means of a sequence of examples.

9.1 SCALAR TYPE AND DISCRETE TYPE ATTRIBUTES

Program 9.1-1 introduces the scalar and discrete type attributes.

153

PROGRAM 9.1-1

```
with TEXT_IO; use TEXT_IO;
procedure SCALAR_AND_DISCRETE_ATTRIBUTES is
      type COLOR is (RED, AMBER, GREEN, BLUE, BROWN, BLACK);
      subtype NEW_INTEGER is INTEGER range 1..1000;
      I: NEW_INTEGER;
begin
      put(COLOR'FIRST);                        --RED is printed; the minimum value
                                               --in COLOR

      put_line(" ");
      put(COLOR'LAST);                         --BLACK is printed; the maximum
                                               --value in COLOR

      put_line(" ");
      put(NEW_INTEGER'FIRST);                  --1 is printed; the minimum value in
                                               --NEW_INTEGER

      put_line(" ");
      put(NEW_INTEGER'LAST);                   --1000 is printed; the maximum value
                                               --in NEW_INTEGER

      put_line(" ");
      put(COLOR'IMAGE(BLUE));                  --BLUE is printed; a string
                                               --representing BLUE

      put_line(" ");
      I:=150;
      put(NEW_INTEGER'IMAGE(I));               --150 is printed; a string representing
                                               --I

      put_line(" ");
      put(COLOR'VALUE("BLUE"));                --BLUE is printed; BLUE is the value
                                               --in COLOR that can be represented
                                               --by the string "BLUE"

      put_line(" ");
      put(NEW_INTEGER'VALUE("199"));           --199 is printed; 199 is the value in
                                               --NEW_INTEGER that can be
                                               --represented by the string "199"

      put_line(" ");
      put(COLOR'POS(BLUE));                    --3 is printed; the position of BLUE in
                                               --COLOR

      put_line(" ");
      put(NEW_INTEGER'POS(NEW_INTEGER'FIRST));
                                               --1 is printed; the position of
                                               --NEW_INTEGER'FIRST is itself

      put_line(" ");
      put(COLOR'VAL(4));                       --BROWN is printed because it is in
                                               --the fourth position of COLOR

      put_line(" ");
```

```
    put(COLOR'PRED(BLUE));            --GREEN is printed because it is the
                                      --preceding value of BLUE
    put_line(" ");
    put(NEW_INTEGER'PRED(100));       --99 is printed because it is the
                                      --preceding value of 100
    put_line(" ");
    put(COLOR'SUCC(BLUE));            --BROWN is printed because it is the
                                      --succeeding value of BLUE
    put_line(" ");
    put(NEW_INTEGER'SUCC(100));       --101 is printed because it is the
                                      --succeeding value of 100
    end SCALAR_AND_DISCRETE_ATTRIBUTES;
```

The comments that appear in Program 9.1-1 should explain the attributes presented. However, several of the attributes presented can generate exceptions, which are the topic of Chapter 10. For example, if the attribute VALUE is used with a string that does not denote any possible value in the type, the DATA_ERROR exception will be raised. If the value lies outside the range of the type, the CONSTRAINT_ERROR exception will be raised. The CONSTRAINT_ERROR exception will also be raised with the attribute VAL if no such value exists, with the attribute PRED if no preceding value exists (i.e., we are already at the first value of the type), and with the attribute SUCC if no succeeding value exists (i.e., we are already at the last value of the type).

9.2 FIXED POINT ATTRIBUTES

To illustrate the fixed point attributes that are available, we consider the following fixed point type definition.

type NEW_FIXED **is delta** 0.01 **range** −100.0..100.0;

If the computer is a 16-bit computer that uses two's complement arithmetic, the implemented range would be the next power of 2, or 7 bits above the binary point. That is, with 6 bits we can represent numbers in the range −64..63, which does not satisfy our type definition. However with 7 bits, we can represent numbers in the range −128..127. Similarly 7 bits are required below the binary point to satisfy the delta of 0.01 in the type definition. Hence, 15 bits are required: one for the sign, 7 above the binary point, and 7 below the binary point. This means that there is one spare bit that we can consider to be a fortuitous guard bit.

A declaration of real type demands a specified accuracy. The implementation will usually use a greater accuracy than that requested. "Model numbers" refers to the set of numbers that corresponds to the accuracy requested and are exactly represented. Since the implemented accuracy is usually greater than the specified accuracy, the implementation will contain other values. If a value is a model number, the model interval is the model number; otherwise, the model interval is the interval defined by the two model numbers on each side of the value. This idea of model numbers and model intervals is related to the attributes for floating point and fixed point numbers.

For fixed point types, the error bound is specified by an absolute value called the "delta" of the fixed point type. The model numbers of a fixed point type consist of consecutive integer multiples of a certain number called actual_delta. Actual_delta is positive and less than or equal to the "delta" that is specified. The multipliers comprise all integers in the range $-(2**N) + 1$ to $(2**N) - 1$ for some positive integer N that is chosen so that the model numbers cover the specified range.

For every fixed point type of subtype T, the following attributes are defined.

T'DELTA   = the requested delta
T'ACTUAL_DELTA = the actual_delta
T'BITS   = the integer N
T'LARGE   = the largest model number whose value is $(2**T'BITS - 1) * T'ACTUAL\_DELTA$

Program 9.2-1 illustrates the values of these attributes for a particular fixed point definition.

PROGRAM 9.2-1

```
with TEXT_IO; use TEXT_IO;
procedure FIXED_POINT_ATTRIBUTES is
     type NEW_FIXED is delta 0.01 range −100.0..100.0;
begin
     put(NEW_FIXED'DELTA);              −−0.01 is printed; the delta
                                        −−specified in the declaration of
                                        −−NEW_FIXED
     put(NEW_FIXED'ACTUAL_DELTA);       −−0.0078125 is printed; this is
                                        −−1/128, which represents the delta
                                        −−of the numbers actually used to
                                        −−satisfy the type definition
     put(NEW_FIXED'BITS);               −−14 is printed; the number of bits
                                        −−required to represent the
                                        −−unsigned integer K where the
                                        −−model numbers of NEW_FIXED
                                        −−are expressed as
                                        −−K*NEW_FIXED'ACTUAL_DELTA
                                        −−Note: K is the same as N defined
                                        −−above
```

put(NEW_FIXED'LARGE);   ——127.9921875 is printed; the
                                            — largest number representable in
                                            ——the implementation of
                                            ——NEW_FIXED (i.e.,
                                            ——2#1111111.1111111#)
put(NEW_FIXED'MACHINE_ROUNDS);   ——TRUE is printed if the computer
                                            ——rounds to the nearest even value
                                            ——when computing values of type
                                            ——NEW_FIXED. FALSE is printed
                                            ——otherwise
    end FIXED_POINT_ATTRIBUTES;

9.3 ATTRIBUTES FOR FLOATING POINT TYPES

In this section we illustrate the attributes that are available for floating point types or subtypes of floating point types. Many of these attributes depend on the underlying machine representation of floating point numbers.

For example, consider a computer that uses 32-bit words to represent floating point numbers, with 1 bit for the sign, 7 bits for the exponent, and 24 bits for the mantissa. Any floating point number except zero is always represented in normalized form, which means that the first bit of the mantissa is 1. If it is not 1, the exponent is adjusted accordingly. For example, $2\#.01\#e0 = 2\#.10\#e\text{-}1$. The relative precision of this computer is $2**(-23)$, which implies that the number of significant digits is 6.92, or almost 7.

Recall from Chapter 6 that for floating point types, the error bound is specified as a relative precision by giving the minimum required number of decimal digits for the decimal mantissa. This required number of digits, D, is specified by the value of a static expression following the key word "digits". It must be positive and of some integer type. The value of D determines a corresponding minimum number, B, of binary digits for the binary mantissa such that the relative precision of the binary form is no less than that specified for the decimal form. In particular, B must satisfy the following.

$$B - 1 < \frac{D*\ln(10)}{\ln(2)} < B$$

The model numbers of the type consist of zero plus all numbers of the form:

sign * binary_mantissa * (2 ** exponent)

where sign is +1 or −1
    $0.5 <= $ binary_mantissa < 1.0
    $-4*B <= $ exponent $<=4*B$
and the binary_mantissa has exactly B digits after the binary point when expressed in base two. The range of the exponent was chosen rather arbitrarily

after an examination of ranges provided by contemporary computer architectures.

For every floating point type or subtype T with digits specification D, the attributes EMAX, SMALL, LARGE, and EPSILON are related to the attribute MANTISSA, which in turn is related to DIGITS by the following formulas.

T'DIGITS	= D
T'MANTISSA	= B
T'EMAX	= 4 * T'MANTISSA
T'SMALL	= 2.0 ** (−T'EMAX − 1)
T'LARGE	= 2.0 ** (T'EMAX) * (1.0 − 2.0 ** (−T'MANTISSA))
T'EPSILON	= 2.0 ** (−T'MANTISSA + 1)

Program 9.3-1 illustrates the values of these attributes for a specific floating point type definition.

PROGRAM 9.3-1

```
with TEXT_IO; use TEXT_IO;
procedure FLOATING_POINT_ATTRIBUTES is
    type NEW_FLOAT is new FLOAT digits 4 range −1.0E16..1.0E16;
begin
    put(NEW_FLOAT'DIGITS);          --4 is printed; the number of
                                    --digits specified in the
                                    --declaration of NEW_FLOAT

    put(NEW_FLOAT'MANTISSA);        --14 is printed; the number of
                                    --bits in the mantissa for
                                    --model numbers of type
                                    --NEW_FLOAT

    put(NEW_FLOAT'EMAX);            --56 is printed; the largest
                                    --exponent value for model
                                    --numbers of type
                                    --NEW_FLOAT

    put(NEW_FLOAT'SMALL);           --6.9389E-18 is printed; the
                                    --smallest positive model
                                    --number of type
                                    --NEW_FLOAT

    put(NEW_FLOAT'LARGE);           --7.2053E16 is printed; the
                                    --largest positive model
                                    --number in the representation
                                    --of NEW_FLOAT

    put(NEW_FLOAT'EPSILON);         --6.1035E-5 is printed; the
                                    --relative precision of
                                    --numbers of type
```

	--NEW_FLOAT (i.e., --2**(−14))
put(NEW_FLOAT'MACHINE_RADIX);	--2 is printed; the radix of the --computer representation of --numbers of type --NEW_FLOAT is printed
put(NEW_FLOAT'MACHINE_MANTISSA);	--24 is printed; the number of --bits in the mantissa of the --computer representation of --numbers of type --NEW_FLOAT
put(NEW_FLOAT'MACHINE_EMAX);	--127 is printed; the largest --exponent value of the --computer representation of --NEW_FLOAT
put(NEW_FLOAT'MACHINE_EMIN);	-- −126 is printed; the --smallest exponent value of --the computer representation --of numbers of type --NEW_FLOAT
put(NEW_FLOAT'MACHINE_ROUNDS);	--TRUE is printed if the --computer rounds to the --nearest even value when --computing values of type --NEW_FLOAT. FALSE --otherwise
put(NEW_FLOAT'MACHINE_OVERFLOWS);	--TRUE is printed if the --exception --NUMERIC_ERROR is raised --when a value too large to be --represented by the --underlying computer --representation of --NEW_FLOAT is generated --FALSE otherwise

end FLOATING_POINT_ATTRIBUTES;

9.4   ATTRIBUTES FOR ARRAYS

Arrays are data structures in which all the components are of the same type. An individual component from an array can be selected by indexing. The declaration of array types and the accessing of components of arrays were discussed in Chapter 5. The attributes for array types include the lower and upper bounds for all indices and the number of elements for each index set. We give two examples in this section: the first merely indicates the array attributes that are available, whereas the second shows their use in a matrix–vector multiplication procedure.

PROGRAM 9.4-1

```
with TEXT_IO; use TEXT_IO;
procedure ARRAY_ATTRIBUTES is
        type VECTOR is array (1..100) of INTEGER;
        type MATRIX is array (0..20,−25..30) of INTEGER;
        A: MATRIX;
        X: VECTOR;
begin
        put(X'FIRST);          −−1 is printed.
        put(A'FIRST(1));       −−0 is printed.
        put(A'FIRST(2));       −− −25 is printed.
        put(X'LAST);           −−100 is printed.
        put(A'LAST(1));        −−20 is printed.
        put(A'LAST(2));        −−30 is printed.
        put(X'LENGTH);         −−100 is printed.
        put(A'LENGTH(1));      −−21 is printed.
        put(A'LENGTH(2));      −−56 is printed.
end ARRAY_ATTRIBUTES;
```

An additional array attribute is the RANGE attribute, which is useful in the specification of ranges for loops and for subtypes. For example, the attribute X'RANGE indicates the subtype X'FIRST..X'LAST, which would be the range 1..100 in Program 9.4-1. Similarly A'RANGE(1) indicates the range A'FIRST(1)..A'LAST(1) and A'RANGE(2) indicates the range A'FIRST-(2)..A'LAST(2). For Program 9.4-1 these are the ranges 0..20 and −25..30, respectively. In Program 9.4-2, we illustrate the use of this type of array attribute.

PROGRAM 9.4-2

```
with TEXT_IO; use TEXT_IO;
procedure MATRIX_VECTOR_MULT_MAIN is
        type NATURAL is range 1..INTEGER'LAST;
        type MATRIX is array (NATURAL range <>,NATURAL range <>) of FLOAT;
        type VECTOR is array (NATURAL range <>) of FLOAT;
        AA: MATRIX(1..50,1..5);
        XX: VECTOR(1..5);
        YY: VECTOR(1..50):=1.0;   −−All components initialized to 1.0
        I,J: INTEGER;
```

```
      procedure MATRIX_VECTOR_MULT(A: in MATRIX; X: in VECTOR;
                                       Y: out VECTOR) Is
           I,J: INTEGER;
begin
      if A'LENGTH(2) = X'LENGTH then
           --The number of columns of A must equal the number of rows of X
           for I in A'RANGE(1) loop
                Y(I):= 0.0;
                for J in A'RANGE(2) loop
                     Y(I):= Y(I) + A(I,J)*X(J);
                end loop;
           end loop;
      else
           put_line("Error: Number of columns of matrix is not equal");
           put_line(" to the number of rows of vector.");
      end If;
end MATRIX_VECTOR_MULT;

begin
      if (AA'LENGTH(2) = XX'LENGTH) and (AA'LENGTH(1) = YY'LENGTH) then
           for I in AA'FIRST(1)..AA'LAST(1) loop
                for J in AA'FIRST(2)..AA'LAST(2) loop
                     AA(I,J):= FLOAT(J);
                end loop;
           end loop;
           MATRIX_VECTOR_MULT(AA,XX,YY);
           for I in YY'RANGE loop
                put_line(" ");
                put(" YY(");
                put(I); put(")=");
                put(YY(I));
           end loop;
      else
           put_line("Error: Matrix and vector are not compatible to");
           put_line(" perform multiplication.").
      end if;
end MATRIX_VECTOR_MULT_MAIN;
```

9.5   OTHER ATTRIBUTES

In this section we describe most of the remaining attributes that are available in Ada. Rather than writing out complete programs to illustrate these attributes, we give only the definitions and a trivial example to show its use.

9.5.1 The ADDRESS Attribute

The ADDRESS attribute returns an integer corresponding to the location of the first storage cell of any object or subprogram. The computer memory must be linear. If X is any object or subprogram name, then X'ADDRESS is the starting location of X in the computer memory.

9.5.2 The SIZE Attribute

The SIZE attribute returns an integer giving the number of bits used to implement objects of the specified type or subtype. If X is a type or subtype, X'SIZE is the maximum number of bits used to implement objects of type X.

9.5.3 The BASE Attribute

The BASE attribute is used only in conjunction with other attributes so that further attributes of the base type may be obtained. If this attribute is applied to a subtype, it yields the base type. If it is applied to a type, it yields the type itself. The following examples clarify this.

type VECTOR **is array** (1..100) **of** INTEGER;

The attribute VECTOR'BASE'FIRST returns the value of 1.

type NEW_FLOAT **is new** FLOAT;
subtype SMALL_FLOAT **is** NEW_FLOAT **digits** 2;

If the computer implementation of FLOAT satisfies FLOAT'DIGITS = 7, then SMALL_FLOAT'DIGITS = 2 and SMALL_FLOAT'BASE'DIGITS = 7.

9.5.4 Record Attributes

The record attributes are POSITION, CONSTRAINED, FIRST_BIT, and LAST_BIT. The following record declaration illustrates these attributes.

type DATE **is**
    record
        DAY: INTEGER **range** 1..31;
        MONTH: (JAN,FEB,MAR,APR,MAY,JUN,JUL,AUG,SEP,OCT,NOV,DEC);
        YEAR: INTEGER **range** 0..1982;
    end record;

The attribute request YEAR'POSITION returns an integer value that indicates the number of storage units within the record before the first unit of storage occupied by YEAR. YEAR'FIRST_BIT returns an integer value indicating the offset from the start of YEAR'POSITION to the first bit used to hold the value of YEAR. YEAR'LAST_BIT returns an integer indicating the offset from the start of YEAR'POSITION of the last bit used to hold the value of YEAR. It is not necessary for YEAR'LAST_BIT to lie within the same storage unit as YEAR'FIRST_BIT.

The CONSTRAINED attribute is applicable only to record with discriminants, as discussed in Chapter 8. If R is an object of a record type with discriminant, then R'CONSTRAINED is TRUE if and only if the discriminant values of R cannot be modified.

9.5.5 Task Attributes

Tasks are described in Chapter 11. If T represents a task or an object of task type, the following task attributes are available: T'TERMINATED returns TRUE when the task T is terminated and FALSE otherwise; T'PRIORITY returns an integer value indicating the priority of T; T'FAILURE is an exception that may be raised by another task, thereby causing failure within T; finally, T'STORAGE_SIZE is an integer value that indicates the number of storage units allocated for the execution of T.

The COUNT attribute is used to obtain the number of calling tasks currently waiting on a specified entry type. For example, E'COUNT is the number of calling tasks currently waiting on E.

9.5.6 Access Type Attributes

Dynamic allocation and access types are the topic of Chapter 12. If P is an access type, then P'STORAGE_SIZE is the total number of storage units reserved for allocation for all objects of type P.

9.6 SUMMARY

- Attributes make available to the programmer characteristics of data types that may be useful in controlling the computation and may improve software portability.
- Enumeration type attributes are available to obtain the first and last value of the type, to give the successor or predecessor, and to give the position number of the enumeration value.
- Discrete type attributes provide the first and last value, the successor, the predecessor, and the position of the discrete value in the specified range for the discrete type.

- Floating point attributes give the number of decimal digits for predefined types or the number of digits specified in the accuracy constraint of a type definition, the length of the binary mantissa, the binary exponent range, the smallest and largest model numbers, and relative precision.

- Certain attributes of floating point types are machine dependent. Machine-dependent attributes are available to determine the machine radix, the size of the machine mantissa, the maximum exponent, the smallest exponent, how the machine treats an overflow, and whether the machine rounds. Numerical programs that use these attributes may exploit general machine properties, thereby resulting in robust portable mathematical software.

- Fixed point attributes are available that give the "delta" in the fixed point type definition, the actual delta used by the machine, a number related to the number of bits required to represent the model numbers, and the largest model number.

- Array attributes are available that give the lower and upper bounds of the indices, the range of the indices, and the length (number of values) of the indices.

- Attributes for records, tasks, and access types are also available.

Exercises for Chapter 9

1. Consider the declarations

   type REAL **is new** FLOAT;
   subtype SHORT **is** REAL **digits** 1;

   where FLOAT'DIGITS = 7. What are the values of the following attributes?
   (a) SHORT'DIGITS
   (b) SHORT'MANTISSA
   (c) SHORT'EMAX
   (d) SHORT'SMALL
   (e) SHORT'LARGE
   (f) SHORT'EPSILON
   (g) SHORT'BASE'DIGITS

2. For the declarations given in Exercise 1:
   (a) Plot the model numbers defined by SHORT near 1 and 0.
   (b) Indicate how many model numbers are defined by type SHORT.

3. Consider the following enumeration type declarations.

   type SUIT **is** (CLUBS, DIAMONDS, HEARTS, SPADES);
   subtype MAJOR **is** SUIT **range** HEARTS. . SPADES;

What are the values of the following attributes?

(a) SUIT'FIRST
(b) MAJOR'LAST
(c) SUIT'SUCC(DIAMONDS)
(d) MAJOR'PRED(HEARTS)
(e) SUIT'POS(SPADES)
(f) MAJOR'BASE'FIRST

4. Consider the following array declarations.

```
type COLOR is (WHITE, RED, YELLOW, GREEN, BLUE, BROWN, BLACK);
MIX   : array (COLOR range RED..BLUE) of BOOLEAN;
GRID  : array (−25..25, 0..100) of INTEGER;
```

What are the values of the following attributes?

(a) MIX'FIRST   **(b)** MIX'LAST
(c) MIX'LENGTH   **(d)** MIX'RANGE
(e) GRID'FIRST(I)   for I=1 and I=2
(f) GRID'LAST(I)   for I=1 and I=2
(g) GRID'LENGTH(I)   for I=1 and I=2
(h) GRID'RANGE(I)   for I=1 and I=2

5. For the declaration

```
type VOLT is delta 0.1 range 0.0..255.0;
```

determine the values of the following attributes (assume the computer is a 16-bit two's complement machine).

(a) VOLT'DELTA
(b) VOLT'ACTUAL_DELTA
(c) VOLT'BITS
(d) VOLT'LARGE

6. Determine the model interval that contains X after the following declarations.

```
type NEW_FLOAT is digits 4;   −−Derived from FLOAT that has 7 digits
A: NEW_FLOAT:=1.0;
B: NEW_FLOAT:=3.0;
X: NEW_FLOAT:=(A/B)*B;
```

7. For the following integer declarations

```
type PAGE is range 1..65;
subtype SMALL is INTEGER range −100..100;
```

Find the values for the following attributes.

(a) PAGE'FIRST   **(b)** SMALL'FIRST
(c) PAGE'SUCC(50)   **(d)** SMALL'PRED(−100)
(e) SMALL'POS(10)   **(f)** SMALL'VAL(10)
(g) PAGE'POS(PAGE'SUCC(50))   **(h)** PAGE'POS(PAGE'PRED(50))

Chapter 10

EXCEPTIONS TO THE RULE

Unexpected situations often arise in the execution of a program. These situations are called exceptions because they were not intended to appear during the normal course of the calculations. For normal operation to continue, however, any exceptions must be dealt with. In this chapter we define exceptions and describe how exception handling features can be developed in your programs. We also cover the predefined exceptions available within Ada.

Exceptions are especially important in real-time systems that must remain in continuous operation. Since any action might fail, the exception raised because of the failed action would probably attempt to define an alternative action that would replace the incompleted action in such a manner that normal program execution would be permitted to continue. The ability to handle such error situations is essential for the reliability of real-time systems.

There are two basic approaches to exception handling. In the first approach, when an exception occurs, normal program flow is interrupted and control is passed to the exception handler. After completion of the exception handling, control is returned to the point at which the exception occurred. This type of exception handling permits some repair actions to be performed and permits normal execution to continue thereafter. This is the type of exception handling defined in PL/1 and PL/C where exceptions are called "conditions."

The second approach to exception handling considers exceptions to be events that make the normal flow of the program impossible, hence should be considered to be terminating conditions. This means that when an exception occurs in a program unit, the unit will be terminated immediately upon completion of the exception handler. Control will not return to the point in the program where the exception occurred. This type of exception handling also allows the exception handler to redefine the conditions that caused the exception and then to reinvoke the program unit under the new conditions. Thus the second approach can be used to simulate the first approach but the programming style will be substantially different. This is the approach used in Ada.

10.1   DECLARATION OF EXCEPTIONS

User-defined exceptions are declared by specifying the name associated with the exception. The form of an exception declaration is exactly the same as for identifier declaration. The exception declaration is given by:

EXCEPTION_NAME: **exception**;

where EXCEPTION_NAME is the name assigned to the exception by the programmer.

More than one exception may be defined in one exception declaration by separating the exception names by commas. Some examples:

SINGULAR: **exception**;
STACK_OVERFLOW, STACK_EMPTY: **exception**;

The exception names can be used only in exception handlers and in raise statements. Exceptions may be viewed as constants, and so even in recursive procedures the exception declaration introduces only one exception. Exceptions cannot be overloaded.

Exceptions may not be used as procedure parameters because they are not data objects. The predefined exceptions (see Section 10.5) do not need to be declared because they *are* predefined in the Ada environment. Exception declarations may occur in a package specification (see Chapter 13).

10.2   HOW TO GET A RAISE?

Raising an exception refers to the action of indicating that there is an exceptional situation that prevents normal program flow from continuing. An exception may be explicitly raised by a raise statement, or it may be raised because of propagation of the exception from another program unit. The latter type of exception raising is discussed in Section 10.4. The principal form of the raise statement includes the reserved word "raise" along with the name of the exception that is being raised. Any number of raise statements can exist for any exception. The raise statement is

raise EXCEPTION_NAME;

and examples are as follows.

raise SINGULAR;
raise STACK_OVERFLOW;

The preceding examples show how to explicitly raise an exception. An exception can also be raised by a statement of the form

raise;

This type of statement can appear only in an exception handler. Its effect is to raise the same exception that caused the transfer to the exception handler. This permits the condition that raised the exception to be partially handled before passing it on to a more general handler, as illustrated in Section 10.4.

The predefined exceptions available in Ada are raised implicitly when the exception occurs during the course of execution of the program. That is, no raise statement needs to appear to raise the exception. The programmer can, however, explicitly raise a predefined exception by using the raise statement.

The raising of an exception disrupts the normal flow of the program. The execution of the current block is terminated and the exception handler is executed instead. In the next section, we describe exception handlers and present several illustrative examples.

10.3 HOW TO HANDLE AN EXCEPTION?

The part of the program to which control is passed when exceptions occur is called the exception handler. The exception handler contains instructions that specify the particular recovery actions that are desired before normal processing can continue. The exception handler may appear in any block of the program that is in the scope of the declaration for the exception. The exception handler always appears at the end of the block. Different handlers for the same exception can appear in different blocks.

The syntax for the exception handler is designed to accommodate several handlers for different exceptions that can be raised in the block. The alternatives are similar to the case statement, with exception names used as the selector. The exception handler construct is built as follows.

```
exception
      when EXCEPTION_1 =>
            executable statement(s);   ——Handler for EXCEPTION_1
      when EXCEPTION_2 =>
            executable statement(s);   ——Handler for EXCEPTION_2
      when others =>
            executable statement(s);   ——Handler for all other exceptions must
                                       ——be last
end;
```

In the preceding example, EXCEPTION_1 and EXCEPTION_2 are exception names that have previously been declared via an exception declaration; alternatively, they can be predefined exceptions (e.g., see Section 10.5). Each particular exception handler is prefixed by the reserved word "when". The executable statement(s) that appear after the "=>" define the specific actions that are to be taken when the exception is raised. A handler started by "when others" services all exceptions for which no explicit exception handler is defined in the same program unit. Since the "when others" exception handler will also handle all the predefined exceptions (see Section 10.5), it should be used with caution. If the same handler is desired for EXCEPTION_1 and EXCEPTION_2, then "when EXCEPTION_1|EXCEPTION_2 =>" is a valid construct for the exception handler. The "end" statement is the "end" corresponding to the end of the block. Since the exception construct must appear at the end of the block, it does not require an "end" statement.

The sequence of statements in an exception handler can include any statement that would be permissible in the current block. If the current block is a subprogram with parameters, the exception handler can refer to these parameters. If the current block is a function, the exception handler may very well contain a return statement. If the current block is an exception handler, the exception is handled as if it occurred in the block that contains the handler. A goto statement cannot transfer control from a block into its handler or from a handler back to the block that raised the exception, nor can it be used to transfer control from one exception handler to another.

We now present several examples to illustrate simple exception declarations, exception raising, and exception handling.

First we rework Program 4.5-3 for calculating the square root of a real number via Newton's algorithm.

PROGRAM 10.3-1

```
with TEXT_IO; use TEXT_IO;
procedure EXCEPTION_EXAMPLE is
      NUMBER: FLOAT;
```

```
function SQRT(N: in FLOAT) return FLOAT is
        X0,XOLD: FLOAT;
     CONVERGE: BOOLEAN;
          NMAX: INTEGER:=8;
            EPS: FLOAT:=0.000001;
     ZERO,NEGATIVE,ACCURACY: exception;
begin
     if N = 0.0 then
            raise ZERO;
     end if;
     if N < 0.0 then
            raise NEGATIVE;
     end if;
     X0:= N/2.0;
     XOLD:= X0;
     for I in 1..NMAX loop
          CONVERGE:= TRUE;
          exit when abs(X0*X0−N) < EPS*N;
          X0:= (X0*X0+N)/(2.0*X0);
          exit when abs(X0−XOLD) <= EPS*X0;
          XOLD:= X0;
          CONVERGE:= FALSE;
     end loop;
     if not CONVERGE then
            raise ACCURACY;
     end if;
     return X0;
exception
     when ZERO      =>
            return 0.0;
     when NEGATIVE =>
            put("The square root of the negative number ");
            put(N);
            put(" is not permitted.");
            put_line(" ");
            put("The square root of ");
            put(−N);
            put(" will be returned.");
            return SQRT(−N);
     when ACCURACY =>
            put("The iteration did not converge.");
            put_line(" ");
            put("The square root may not be accurate.");
            return X0;
end SQRT;
```

```
begin
        put("Enter a real number:");
        get(NUMBER);
        put_line(" .");
        put("The square root =");
        put(SQRT(NUMBER));
end EXCEPTION_EXAMPLE;
```

In Program 10.3-1, three exceptions are defined. The exception handler for ZERO returns the correct SQRT for an input of zero and also prevents a later divide by zero in the loop in the program. If we had not trapped the zero input, the predefined exception NUMERIC_ERROR would have been raised when the divide by zero was attempted. The raising of this exception would have aborted our program in the absence of an exception handler that permitted execution to continue. The handler for NEGATIVE traps the illegal value of N and recalls the function in which the exception was raised.

10.4 PROPAGATING EXCEPTIONS

When an exception is raised the normal flow of program execution is interrupted and a handler is sought for the exception. The first place to look for the exception handler is at the end of the current block that gave rise to the exception. For example, if the exception is named TROUBLE, we look in the exception portion of the block for "when TROUBLE =>". The executable statements that follow are then executed, instead of the remainder of the block. If no exception handler exists for TROUBLE but the statement "when others =>" appears, the executable statements that follow are executed.

However, there may not be an exception handler in the block for TROUBLE. In this case, execution of the block is terminated and an exception handler for TROUBLE would be sought in the block that dynamically encloses the current block (e.g., the block that called the current block). If none is found in this block, an exception handler is sought in the block two calls or levels removed from the current block. This unraveling is continued until the main program is reached. If no exception handler can be found, the program is terminated.

Another possibility is that the handler for TROUBLE might raise an exception. In this case the exception is propagated to the dynamically enclosing block. If the handler raises another exception, it is also propagated to the dynamically enclosing block.

Program 10.4-1 illustrates exception propagation.

PROGRAM 10.4-1

```
with TEXT_IO; use TEXT_IO;
procedure EXCEPTION_PROPAGATION is
      TROUBLE: exception;
              X: FLOAT;

      procedure ONE(X: in out FLOAT) is
      begin
              X:= X-1.0;
              if X=0.0 then
                      raise TROUBLE;
              end if;
      end ONE;

      procedure TWO(X: in out FLOAT) is
      begin
              X:= X+1.0;
              ONE(X);
              X:= 2.0*X;
      exception
              when TROUBLE =>
                      put("Exception handler in procedure TWO.");
                      put_line(" ");
                      X:= 1.0;
                      put("X="); put(X); put_line(" ");
      end TWO;

begin   --Main program
      X:= 0.0;
      TWO(X);
      ONE(X);
      put("X=");
      put(X);
      put_line(" ");
exception
      when TROUBLE =>
              put("Exception handler in main procedure.");
              put_line(" ");
              X:=2.0;
              put("X="); put(X); put_line(" ");
end EXCEPTION_PROPAGATION;
```

In Program 10.4-1, the procedure TWO is called with X=0.0. Procedure TWO then calls ONE with X=1.0. The calculation in ONE causes the exception TROUBLE to be raised. However there is no exception handler for trouble in ONE, so the exception is propagated back to TWO. In TWO an exception handler for TROUBLE is found and the statements that define the handler are executed. This results in X being set to 1.0. Control then returns to the next executable statement in the main program, which in this case is the call to ONE. During the execution of ONE the exception TROUBLE is raised again. Again since there is no exception handler in ONE for the exception TROUBLE, the exception is propagated to the calling program. In this case this is the main procedure, so the exception handler for TROUBLE in the main procedure is executed.

If we modify the exception handler for TROUBLE in TWO by adding the "raise" statement as the last executable statement, the exception TROUBLE is raised again and propagated to the exception handler for TROUBLE in the main procedure.

Exceptions can arise during the elaboration of the declaration part of a block because the evaluation of an expression might be specified for calculating a default value or an initial value. The resulting value might not be a possible value for the declared object. The declaration part of the block is considered to be a separate block from the executable portion of the block. So an exception that is raised in the declarative part is propagated back to the statement or declaration that called the block. This assures us that in any exception handler all the declarations of the block were successfully elaborated. We give an example of this in Program 10.4-2.

PROGRAM 10.4-2

```
with TEXT_IO; use TEXT_IO;
procedure EXCEPTION_DECLARATION is
    ERROR: exception;

    function SQUARE(N: in INTEGER) return INTEGER is
    begin
        if N>10 then
            raise ERROR;
        end if;
        return N*N;
    end SQUARE;

    procedure CALC(N: INTEGER) is
        C: constant INTEGER:=SQUARE(N);
        D: INTEGER:=C;
    begin
        --Executable statements that define CALC
        if D=25 then
            raise ERROR;
        end if;
```

```
            --Possibly more executable statements that define CALC
        exception
                when ERROR =>
                        put("Error handler in CALC"); put_line(" ");
            end CALC;

    begin   --Main program
            CALC(5);
            CALC(20);
    exception when ERROR =>
            put("Error handler in main procedure");
            put_line(" ");
    end EXCEPTION_DECLARATION;
```

Program 10.4-2 is an executable program. On the first call to CALC from the main procedure, the exception ERROR will eventually occur within procedure CALC. In this case the exception handler for ERROR in CALC will be executed. The second call of CALC in the main program will eventually give rise to the ERROR exception during the elaboration of the constant C. A handler for ERROR does not exist in SQUARE, so the exception is propagated back to CALC. However, since the exception occurred in the declaration portion of the block CALC, it is propagated back to the statement or declaration that called CALC. In this case, this is the main procedure; therefore the exception handler for ERROR is the one given in the main procedure.

The exception that occurs in the elaboration of the constant C in Program 10.4-2 results in D not being initialized.

Exceptions may arise in the specification part of a package (see Chapter 13). If no local exception handler is available, the exception is considered to have been raised in the declaration part of the package and so it is propagated back to the enclosing block. If the package exists as a separately compiled unit, the exception will cause termination. Exceptions can arise during tasking. We discuss exceptions and tasking in more detail in Chapter 11. In tasking, exceptions are not propagated. Instead the task is terminated and no other action is taken.

10.5 PREDEFINED EXCEPTIONS

The standard Ada language environment has five predefined or intrinsic exceptions: CONSTRAINT_ERROR, NUMERIC_ERROR, SELECT_ERROR, STORAGE_ERROR, and TASKING_ERROR. Each of these is implicitly raised when the corresponding exception occurs; however, the programmer can also explicitly raise these exceptions. We briefly describe each of the predefined exceptions and give some examples.

10.5.1 **CONSTRAINT_ERROR**

The exception CONSTRAINT_ERROR is raised whenever the current value is inconsistent with the current requirement. For example, this exception is raised if an assignment statement attempts to assign a value to an identifier that is out of the range for the identifier. It is also raised if an array component is referenced with an index value that is out of the range of the array component. An attempt to reference a record component with a field selector for the wrong variant will also give rise to this exception. In addition, it can be raised by referencing an access type object with an access value of "null" (see Chapter 12) or by improper matching of subprogram parameters. As an example, if we are given the following declarations:

```
type COLOR is (RED, BLUE, ORANGE, GREEN, BLACK, YELLOW);
type VECTOR is array (1..10) of INTEGER;
subtype SMALL is range 1..5;
B: BOOLEAN;
C: COLOR;
V: VECTOR;
S: SMALL;
```

then all the following assignment statements will raise the CONSTRAINT_ERROR exception.

```
B:= CORRECT;
C:= BROWN;
V(12):= 5;
S:= 7;
```

10.5.2 **NUMERIC_ERROR**

The NUMERIC_ERROR exception is raised whenever the current numerical value is not within the implemented range. A divide by zero will raise this exception, as would a divide by a small number that results in an answer with a magnitude beyond the range of that implemented on the computer. The product of two numbers, whether floating point or integer, can also produce a number beyond the range of the computer. If one were to develop mathematical functions for SQRT, LN, and EXP, then in the implementation the programmer could raise NUMERIC_ERROR if the parameter of SQRT or LN were negative or if the parameter to EXP were too large (so that a number beyond the range of the computer would result).

The next example demonstrates how the programmer can protect a program when the NUMERIC_ERROR is implicitly raised in the course of the calculations.

```
function FUN(X: FLOAT) return FLOAT;
      CON: FLOAT;
begin
      CON:=X*X;
      return CON*EXP(CON);
exception
      when NUMERIC_ERROR =>
            return FLOAT'LAST;
end FUN;
```

Here, FLOAT'LAST is an attribute that has a value corresponding to the largest floating point number available on the computer.

10.5.3 SELECT_ERROR

The SELECT_ERROR exception is raised whenever execution is blocked by a select statement. This exception is useful in conjunction with tasks (see Chapter 11) and is raised if a select statement is met with all its select alternatives closed and no "else" option exists. In such a situation, the statement can never complete its execution.

10.5.4 STORAGE_ERROR

If the program requires more computer memory storage space than is available on the computer, the STORAGE_EXCEPTION error is raised. The exception can occur because of array storage requests that are too large, recursive procedures that call themselves too many times, dynamic allocation of too much storage, or the execution of an allocator in a task.

10.5.5 TASKING_ERROR

The TASKING_ERROR exception is raised when an entry call to a task is satisfied but the corresponding accept statement is terminated before it can accept the entry (see Chapter 11).

10.6 SUPPRESSING EXCEPTIONS

The detection and subsequent raising of exceptions can be suppressed within a unit by a pragma of the following form.

pragma *suppress* (EXCEPTION_NAME);

This pragma indicates to the compiler that no run time checks need to be performed for the designated exception or exceptions. Regardless of whether the compiler obeys, the pragma may be implementation dependent. That is, if the exception is detected by special hardware, inhibiting the check may be too costly.

As described in Section 10.5, there are events that may cause a predefined exception to be raised. Ada permits portions of some of these predefined exceptions to be suppressed. For example, DIVISION_CHECK, which checks for a divide-by-zero error and raises the NUMERIC_ERROR exception, may be suppressed. The portions of predefined exceptions that may be suppressed are the following.

NUMERIC_ERROR	DIVISION_CHECK, OVERFLOW_CHECK
CONSTRAINT_ERROR	ACCESS_CHECK, DISCRIMINANT_CHECK, INDEX_CHECK, LENGTH_CHECK, RANGE_CHECK
STORAGE_ERROR	STORAGE_CHECK

The interested reader may wish to consult the Language Reference Manual (Reference 2) for additional details.

10.7 SOFTWARE ENGINEERING AND EXCEPTIONS

In software engineering one approach to proving programs correct is to use assertions. The careful selection of assertions is usually the first step. Assertions are based on the premise that as a program executes, certain relationships between variables in the problem or system remain true even though the individual values of the variables change. If certain relationships are no longer true, the program probably should be terminated.

The exception feature of Ada permits you to define your own assertions by specifying the following procedure in your program.

```
ASSERT_ERROR: exception;
procedure ASSERT(CONDITION: BOOLEAN) is
      begin
            if not CONDITION then
                  raise ASSERT_ERROR;
            end if;
end ASSERT;
```

With the preceding procedure, assertions of the following form become legal statements in the program.

```
ASSERT(BANK_BALANCE > 0.0);
ASSERT(A**2 + B**2 = C**2);
ASSERT(X+Y < Z);
```

Assertions are particularly useful for checking whether certain relationships exist for "in" parameters of a procedure call, for determining whether a loop was suitably completed, for checking whether certain relationships exist for "out" parameters before returning to the calling program, and for checking whether certain relationships are valid after the performance of a sequence of statements or a set of alternatives.

Exceptions facilitate fault-tolerant computing in that they permit a recovery to a normal condition after a fault. This permits the programmer to consider actions that might fail, to assess the seriousness of the failure, and to define an appropriate action. Of course a fault is usually a symptom of a more serious problem; thus fault-tolerant computing requires careful consideration of conditions that can produce a fault and equally careful consideration of how to handle the fault.

10.8   AN EXAMPLE USING STACKS AND EXCEPTIONS

As the final example of this chapter, we develop several procedures for performing operations on stacks. A stack is an ordered list in which all insertions and deletions are made at one end called the top. Thus the last element added to the stack becomes the first element to be removed. We define several exceptions that are raised if we try to remove an element from an empty stack or insert an element onto a full stack.

PROGRAM 10.8-1

```
with TEXT_IO; use TEXT_IO;
procedure STACK_EXAMPLE is
    SIZE: constant INTEGER:=10;
    STACK: array (1..SIZE) of STRING(1..80);
    ITEM: STRING(1..80);
    TOP: INTEGER:=0;
    YES: BOOLEAN;
    STACK_OVERFLOW, STACK_UNDERFLOW, ERROR: exception;

procedure PUSH (ITEM: in STRING) is
begin
    if TOP=SIZE then
        raise STACK_OVERFLOW;
    else
        TOP:= TOP+1;
        STACK(TOP):= ITEM;
    end if;
end PUSH;

procedure POP (ITEM: out STRING) is
begin
    if TOP=0 then
        raise STACK_UNDERFLOW;
    else
        ITEM:= STACK(TOP);
        TOP:= TOP-1;
    end if;
end POP;

procedure PRINT is
begin
    for I in 1..TOP loop
        put_line(STACK(I));
    end loop;
end PRINT;
```

```
procedure MENU is
      CHOICE: INTEGER;
begin
      put_line(" ");
      put_line("1--> Add item to stack");
      put_line(" ");
      put_line("2--> Remove item from stack");
      put_line(" ");
      put_line("3--> Print out all items in stack");
      put_line(" ");
      put_line("4--> Exit from program");
      put_line(" ");
      put("Enter appropriate choice: ");
      get(CHOICE);
      case CHOICE is
            when 1 =>
                  put("Enter item: ");
                  get(ITEM);
                  PUSH(ITEM);
                  put_line(" ");
            when 2 =>
                  POP(ITEM);
                  put("Item removed: ");
                  put(ITEM);
                  put_line(" ");
            when 3 =>
                  put("Stack contents: ");
                  put_line(" ");
                  PRINT;
                  put_line(" ");
            when 4 =>
                  YES:= TRUE;
            when others =>
                  raise ERROR;
      end case;
exception
      when STACK_UNDERFLOW =>
            put_line("Stack underflow!");
      when STACK_OVERFLOW   =>
            put_line("Stack overflow!");
      when ERROR            =>
            put_line("Input error!");
end MENU;
```

```
begin   --Main program
      YES:= FALSE;
      loop
            MENU;
            exit when YES;
      end loop;
end STACK_EXAMPLE;
```

10.9 SUMMARY

• Exceptions are events that cause suspension of normal program execution. The ability to handle exceptions is essential for the reliability of real-time systems.

• Exceptions may be declared, raised, and handled by the programmer. Raising an exception refers to bringing the exception to attention. An exception handler is a portion of program text that specifies the response to the exception. Execution of the exception handler is called ''handling'' the exception.

• The predefined exceptions are CONSTRAINT_ERROR, NUMERIC_ERROR, SELECT_ERROR, STORAGE_ERROR, and TASKING_ERROR.

• Exceptions are propagated dynamically from the program unit that raised the exception to the unit that called the unit until a handler is found or until the top level or main program is reached. If a handler is not found, the program is terminated.

Exercises for Chapter 10

1. We wish to define addition, subtraction, and multiplication for variables of ''subtype SMALL is range 0..9;''. Use overloading to write functions that define these operations with exceptions so that overflow returns 9 and underflow returns 0.

2. Rework Examples 1, 2, and 3 of Section 7.6 in terms of unconstrained arrays. Use the array attributes available (see Section 5.3) to test for legality of the operations based on the input array dimensions and define exception handlers if the operation is not legal.

3. For the type MONTH defined by

   ```
   type MONTH is (JAN, FEB, MAR, APR, MAY, JUN, JUL, AUG, SEP, OCT, NOV,
                  DEC);
   ```

   write a function NEXT_MONTH that returns next month from input of this month. Use the predefined exception CONSTRAINT_ERROR to return JAN when DEC is the input. Also use the attributes for enumeration types in your function.

4. In Program 7.8-2, replace the procedure ERROR with the exception ER-ROR and its corresponding exception handler. Modify the program to raise ERROR.

5. Assume that the function SQRT is available and raises NUMERIC_ER-ROR when the input parameter is negative. Define a function SQRT_ABS that uses SQRT to return the square root of the input parameter if the parameter is greater than or equal to zero and returns the square root of the negative of the input parameter if the input parameter is less than zero.

6. Use Program 4.5-1 to define a function, EXP, that returns $\exp(x)$ for the input parameter x. Define an exception handler so that your function returns FLOAT'LAST if the input parameter is too large.

Chapter 11

TASKS

Tasks are program units that may be executed in parallel or concurrently with other tasks. Parallel tasks may be implemented on multicomputers, on multiprocessors, or on a single processor. On a single processor the concurrent execution is modeled with interleaved sequential execution, since only one task can really be active. In this chapter we describe the tasking facilities that are available in Ada.

Concurrent execution facilities in a programming language are important for several reasons. First, many physical systems are more naturally modeled by concurrent processes. For example, consider the services of a bank, or the functions of the various departments in an organization or governmental body, or the steps in the construction of an object or an airline reservation system. All these clearly involve concurrent activities or tasks. Tasking is also an important aspect in the operation and control of embedded computer systems. Second, concurrent execution may speed up the processing time required in some applications. For example, in solving a large system of equations, if the problem can be subdivided and a corresponding algorithm determined so that several processors can be working on portions of the problem or algorithm concurrently, the problem may be solvable in less time than if only one processor had been used.

The syntactical structure of a task is similar to that of a package (see Chapter 13) in that it has two basic parts: a specification part and a body. The fundamental difference is that a package can be considered to be a passive program unit, whereas a task can be considered to be an active program unit.

The means of communication and synchronization between tasks is achieved using the concept of a rendezvous between a task issuing an entry call

185

and a task accepting the call by an accept statement. An entry call is similar to a procedure call except that the calling and called tasks are distinct and synchronized. The select statement enables a task to respond to several different possible entry calls. Other facilities include a conditional entry call, a timed entry call, a delay statement, and a selective wait statement. In this chapter we describe these features of Ada and illustrate their use with examples.

11.1 TASK SPECIFICATION AND TASK BODY

A task declaration, like a package declaration (see Chapter 13), consists of two distinct pieces of text. These are the task specification part, which describes the task's external appearance, and the task body, which describes the task's internal behavior. These two parts may be juxtaposed in the program text and may be compiled separately. We now consider the details of these two parts and show how they differ from the corresponding parts of a package program unit.

The specification part of a task consists of a header giving the name of the task and a declarative part that describes the appearance of the task to the outside world. The declarative part can contain only entry declarations. The inclusion of entry declarations distinguishes the specification part of a task from that of a package.

We now give two examples of the specification part of a task.

```
type LINE is array (1..80) of CHARACTER;

task LINE_TO_CHARACTER is
      entry PUT_LINE (L : in LINE);
      entry GET_CHARACTER (C : out CHARACTER);
end LINE_TO_CHARACTER;

type MESSAGE is array (1..80) of CHARACTER;

task MAILBOX is
      entry SEND (INMAIL : in MESSAGE);
      entry RECEIVE (OUTMAIL : out MESSAGE);
end MAILBOX;
```

The "entry" specifications, which are syntactically like procedure specifications, are explained in more detail in Section 11.3.

The task body contains hidden local declarations that are elaborated when the task is initiated and a sequence of statements that define the execution of the task. The elaboration of the body establishes the body as defining the execution of the task. If the specification part of a task contains "entry" specifications, the body of the task must contain corresponding "accept" statements. Note that if no "entry" specifications are given in the specification part of a task and if no "accept" specifications appear in the task body, the task appears no different from a package; however, the task is an active module whereas the package is passive.

In Program 11.1-1, we give two examples of possible task bodies for the preceding task specifications.

PROGRAM 11.1-1

```
with TEXT_IO; use TEXT_IO;
procedure TASK_SPECIFICATION_AND_BODY is

    type LINE is array (1..80) of CHARACTER;

    task LINE_TO_CHARACTER is
        entry PUT_LINE (L : in LINE);
        entry GET_CHARACTER (C : out CHARACTER);
    end LINE_TO_CHARACTER;

    type MESSAGE is array(1..80) of CHARACTER;

    task MAILBOX is
        entry SEND (INMAIL : in MESSAGE);
        entry RECEIVE (OUTMAIL : out MESSAGE);
    end MAILBOX;

    task body LINE_TO_CHARACTER is
        BUFFER: LINE;
    begin
        loop
                accept PUT_LINE (L: in LINE) do
                    BUFFER:= L;
                end PUT_LINE;
                for I in 1..80 loop
                    accept GET_CHARACTER (C: out CHARACTER) do
                        C:= BUFFER(I);
                    end GET_CHARACTER;
                end loop;
        end loop;
    end LINE_TO_CHARACTER;

    task body MAILBOX is
        BOX: MESSAGE;
    begin
        loop
                accept SEND (INMAIL: in MESSAGE) do
                    BOX:= INMAIL;
                end;
```

```
                    accept RECEIVE (OUTMAIL: out MESSAGE) do
                            OUTMAIL:= BOX;
                    end;
                end loop;
            end MAILBOX;

begin   --Parent task
                --Statements that use the two tasks LINE_TO_CHARACTER and
                --MAILBOX in a meaningful way go here
            put_line("End of program");
end TASK_SPECIFICATION_AND_BODY;
```

The operation of these tasks is explained in the sections that follow.

11.2 TASK INITIATION AND EXECUTION

In the preceding section we showed how to specify a task. Before describing the detailed statements associated with tasks, it is important to understand the underlying concept of a task, its activation, and its parent.

Every task in Ada is written in the declarative part of some enclosing program unit, which is called its parent. The parent task may be a subprogram, a declare block, a package, or another task. The execution of the parent task determines the start and finish of the execution of the task. If several tasks are specified in the declarative part of the parent, they will be executed concurrently with one another and with the parent task. Each is executed in its own sequential order, independent of the order of the others, unless there are explicit statements to relate them. Task communication is discussed in more detail in Section 11.3. Each task may come to the end of its statements and thus finish its execution, or it may be brought to an end by the influence of the other tasks. The parent task is considered to have completed its execution when it has come to the end of its statements and when all the tasks declared in it have finished their execution.

The structure of a multitask program usually consists of a parent with the tasks that perform the required actions declared in the declarative part of the parent. The body of the parent is responsible for overall control. In particular, the parent should ensure that the tasks are running properly and terminate them when necessary. The Ada language does not specify the order in which tasks declared within the declarative part are activated.

We illustrate with the following simple example.

PROGRAM 11.2-1

```
with TEXT_IO; use TEXT_IO;
procedure PARENT_TASK is
      TEMPERATURE: FLOAT:=10.0;
      DONE: BOOLEAN:=FALSE;

task WARNING is
end WARNING;

task body WARNING is
begin
      loop
            if TEMPERATURE <= 32.0 then
                  put_line(" Temperature is too low!");
                  put_line(" ");
            end if;
            exit when DONE;
      end loop;
end WARNING;

begin
      put( TEMPERATURE);
      TEMPERATURE:= 40.0;
      put( TEMPERATURE);
      TEMPERATURE:= 30.0;
      put( TEMPERATURE);
      TEMPERATURE:= 50.0;
      put( TEMPERATURE);
      DONE:= TRUE;
end PARENT_TASK;
```

In this example, the task WARNING begins execution with its parent. The body of the task tests the value of TEMPERATURE and prints a warning message if it is below 32. This is done concurrently with the parent and any other tasks with the same parent task. The Boolean variable DONE is used to terminate the task. DONE is set to TRUE at the end of the parent task, which permits the task WARNING to exit the loop and thereby terminate.

We now consider the execution of each of the tasks defined in Section 11.1, emphasizing the synchronization that must exist between the called task and the calling program or calling task when an "accept" statement is executed. The process of synchronization between an entry call and an accept statement is referred to as a rendezvous. We begin by considering the LINE_TO_CHARACTER task.

Execution of the parent task causes the task body for the task LINE_TO_CHARACTER to be executed concurrently with the parent task. Upon the initiation of the LINE_TO_CHARACTER task, a buffer for lines is created, followed by the execution of an infinite loop that alternatively accepts a PUT_LINE entry call from another task and accepts 80 consecutive GET_CHARACTER calls from one or more other tasks.

When execution reaches the statement "accept PUT_LINE . . .", the LINE_TO_CHARACTER task must perform a rendezvous with a PUT_LINE entry call from another task before execution of this task can continue. During the rendezvous, the execution of the parent task is suspended while the sequence of statements between "do" and "end" in the called task is executed. When this sequence of statements has been executed, the rendezvous is complete and the parent task may continue its execution concurrently with the LINE_TO_CHARACTER task.

In this example, the single statement "BUFFER:= L;" would be executed during the rendezvous. The execution of this statement causes the line of text L from the parent task to be transmitted to the buffer of the called task LINE_TO_CHARACTER. The statements that are executed during a rendezvous are usually concerned with the transmission of data between the parent task and the called task.

When the MAILBOX task is activated, the local variable BOX is created and the task then goes into an infinite loop that alternately accepts SEND and RECEIVE entries from other tasks.

11.3 TASK SYNCHRONIZATION AND COMMUNICATION

The entry/accept specifications are the primary mechanisms for communication and synchronization among tasks.

The syntax for entry specifications is very similar to the syntax for procedure specifications. For example, the entry specification may have parameters with the same binding modes (i.e., in, out, in out) as procedure parameters and may be called from other tasks by "entry" calls that are indistinguishable from procedure calls. However, there is a fundamental difference. A procedure call immediately invokes the called procedure, whereas an entry call cannot be executed until it has been synchronized with an accept statement in the body of the task. The syntax for an entry call is similar to that for a procedure call. It is simply the entry name followed by any actual parameters in parentheses.

The actions that are to be performed when an entry is called are specified in the corresponding accept statement. The general syntax for an "accept" statement is:

```
accept ENTRY_NAME (FORMAL PARAMETERS) do
      sequence of statements;
end ENTRY_NAME;
```

The formal parameters given in the entry and accept must match. An accept statement for an entry may appear only in the task body of the task that contains the entry. This means that a task can execute accept statements only for its own entries. The sequence of statements between the "do" and "end" following an "accept" statement is called the critical section. The critical section is optional. The execution of the calling or parent task is suspended during the execution of the critical section. This permits critical computations associated with an accept statement to be performed without interference from the parent task.

In the LINE_TO_CHARACTER task of Section 11.2, the critical section of "accept PUT_LINE . . ." is the single statement "BUFFER:= L;". This statement transfers the line L to the buffer. By permitting the parent task to continue execution while this statement is being executed, it might become possible for the parent task to modify the line L while it is being transmitted to the buffer.

To execute an accept statement, there must be synchronization between the task in which the accept statement occurs and a task containing an entry call for the entry name associated with the accept statement. There are two possibilities. First, if during the execution of the task an accept statement is reached before it has been called by an entry call, the execution of the task is suspended until an entry call is received. Second, if the parent task issues an entry call before the corresponding accept statement has been reached in the called task, the execution of the parent task is suspended until the accept statement is executed. When the entry call finds the corresponding accept ready, a rendezvous occurs. The corresponding critical section is executed while the execution of the parent task is suspended. As soon as the critical section has been completed, both the parent task and the called task continue their own concurrent executions.

Since more than one task can issue an entry call for the same task entry, it is possible for entry calls to occur faster than they can be handled by the corresponding accept statements. In such a case, the entry calls are stored in a queue that is associated with the entry name and handled in first-come, first-served order. Thus each execution of a corresponding accept statement removes one entry call from the queue. A task may have more than one accept statement for an entry name in its task body, but there will be only a single queue of waiting entry calls for each entry name. A task may be in only one queue at a time. In general, every entry of every task has an associated queue for entry calls that have not yet been serviced.

Let us now consider these concepts in conjunction with the two tasks, LINE_TO_CHARACTER and MAILBOX, that we have already defined.

We consider the LINE_TO_CHARACTER task first. Suppose that the parent task issues the calling statement

```
LINE_TO_CHARACTER.PUT_LINE (MY_LINE);
```

where MY_LINE is of type LINE and is defined in the parent task. There are two possibilities for a rendezvous, depending on whether the parent task issues the preceding call before or after the corresponding accept statement has been reached by the called task. Whichever task gets there first waits for the other. When the rendezvous is achieved, MY_LINE of the parent task is passed to the buffer of the called task, LINE_TO_CHARACTER. The task LINE_TO _CHARACTER alternately fills the buffer (by accepting a call of PUT_LINE) and empties it (by accepting 80 successive calls of GET_CHARACTER). Calls of the entries can be processed only when the corresponding accept statement is reached. Thus many different tasks could be held up if they were attempting to call PUT_LINE, since they can be accepted only after a group of 80 calls of GET_CHARACTER. The buffer may be emptied by several different tasks calling GET_CHARACTER. It is also possible for several tasks to be held up on calls of GET_CHARACTER until a task issues a call of PUT_LINE.

As mentioned previously, the MAILBOX task goes into an infinite loop that alternately accepts SEND and RECEIVE entries from other tasks. If entry calls for the entry SEND occur faster than the entries can be accepted, they are placed in a queue.

An entry may be renamed as a procedure using the key word "renames" to avoid excessive use of the dot notation. For example,

procedure WRITE(L: **in** LINE) **renames** LINE_TO_CHARACTER.PUT_LINE;

permits us to issue an entry call as

WRITE(MY_LINE);

instead of

LINE_TO_CHARACTER.PUT_LINE(MY_LINE);

where MY_LINE is of type LINE.

11.4 THE SELECT STATEMENT

The accept statement enables a task to wait for the occurrence of some event that is indicated by the calling of the corresponding entry. In many concurrent processes it may be impossible to predict the order in which events will occur. Since each event is characterized by an entry call, we would like to permit the task to choose its next action from among several entry calls. The select statement permits us to do this.

The syntax for the select statement is:

```
select
    when CONDITION_1    =>
        select-alternative;
        sequence of statements;
    or when CONDITION_2 =>
        select-alternative;
        sequence of statements;
    else
        sequence of statements;
end select;
```

The select statement begins with the keyword "select" and ends with "end select". CONDITION_1 and CONDITION_2 are called guards. There may be any number of guards; the statement above has two. A "select-alternative" may be an accept statement, described earlier, a delay statement, or a **terminate,** which causes the task to terminate. The delay statement has the structure.

```
delay EXPRESSION_SPECIFYING_DELAY_TIME;
```

The delay statement is discussed in more detail in the next section. If the select statement contains a delay statement, it cannot have an "else" alternative or a **terminate.** If it has a **terminate** alternative, it cannot have an alternative that begins with "delay" or an "else" clause. Finally, there can be at most one **terminate** alternative.

The select statement is evaluated by first evaluating the guards. If the guard is true then it is said to be open. An absent guard is taken to be true. If all guards are false, the exception SELECT_ERROR is raised. Only open guards are considered in the subsequent selection. If an open alternative begins with an accept statement and a corresponding entry call has been received, a rendezvous will occur. Several entry calls associated with a task may occur before a select statement is executed. In this case several different rendezvous may be possible. There may also be several alternatives beginning with an unconditional accept. When these cases occur, one possible rendezvous is chosen at random. If an open alternative begins with a "delay" statement, it will be chosen if no accept alternative has been accepted after the specified delay. Delay expressions are evaluated immediately after the corresponding guard has been evaluated. A **terminate** alternative will cause the task to terminate immediately. Finally, if no alternative can be immediately selected and there is an "else" alternative, the latter is executed. If there is no "else" alternative, the task waits for an open alternative.

A special form of the select statement is known as a conditional entry call. This permits a task that calls an entry to have an alternative action if the called task is not prepared to accept the call immediately. An example of a conditional entry call is:

select
      REQUEST; ––Entry call
      ––Sequence of statements related to REQUEST
else
      ––Alternative action if REQUEST is not immediately accepted
end select;

In the preceding example, REQUEST is an entry call. If a rendezvous is not immediately possible, the alternative action following "else" is performed.

To illustrate the use of the select statement, we consider the classic reader–writer problem. The reader–writer problem is the problem of reading and writing in a protected data base. The basic issue is to prevent writers from changing information while readers are trying to read it. We assume that any number of readers are permitted to read if there is no writer, but every writer must have exclusive access before beginning to write. In Program 11.4-1, we allow only a single read or write operation at a time.

PROGRAM 11.4-1

```
with TEXT_IO; use TEXT_IO;
procedure READER_WRITER_TASK is
      type ELEM is array (1..80) of CHARACTER;
            ––Type ELEM should be declared to satisfy the requirements of the
            ––problem

      task READER_WRITER is
            entry READ (V: out ELEM);
            entry WRITE (E: in ELEM);
      end;

      task body READER_WRITER is
            VARIABLE: ELEM;
      begin
            accept WRITE (E: in ELEM) do
                  VARIABLE:= E;
            end;
```

```
        loop
              select
                          accept READ (V: out ELEM) do
                                V:= VARIABLE;
                          end;
                or
                          accept WRITE (E: in ELEM) do
                                VARIABLE:= E;
                          end;
                    end select;
              end loop;
        end READER_WRITER;

begin   --Parent task
              --Statements that use the READER_WRITER task in a meaningful way
              --go here. This program will not terminate because the task contains
              --an infinite loop, thereby preventing the task from ever terminating
        put_line("End of program");
end READER_WRITER_TASK;
```

The task specification names this task as READER_WRITER with two entries, READ and WRITE. The task body declares a local protected variable, VARIABLE, with a sequence of statements that starts with an accept statement for the entry WRITE. This guarantees that the first call accepted is for WRITE so that it is impossible to read the variable before it is assigned a value. If another task calls READ before any task had called WRITE, the calls to READ will be queued until a call to WRITE has been accepted. The task then enters an infinite loop with a single select statement that accepts a READ entry that reads in the protected variable or accepts a WRITE entry that writes out the protected variable. The selection of READ or WRITE entries is repeated indefinitely because it is contained within an infinite loop.

We now describe the operation of the select statement depending on whether entry calls of READ or WRITE or both or neither have been made. If neither READ or WRITE entry calls have been made, the task is suspended until one of these calls is made, whereas on the corresponding accept statement is executed. If entry calls of READ are queued and there are no queued entry calls of WRITE, the first call of READ is accepted. If entry calls of WRITE are queued and there are no queued calls of READ, the first call of WRITE is accepted. If entry calls of both READ and WRITE are queued, a random choice is made.

Recall that the MAILBOX task performed SEND and RECEIVE operations in strictly alternating order. The receive operation was considered to have removed the message from the mailbox. In this READER_WRITER task, we can perform analogous operations but the read operation does not remove the value, and so we may perform repeated read operations. Analogously, we can also perform repeated write operations. The restriction imposed is that we allow only one reader or one writer to access the variable at any given instant.

To illustrate the use of guards in a select statement, we present the following program segment, which may be of little or no practical use.

```
select
        when WRITE'COUNT=0 =>
                accept START_READ;
                READERS:= READERS + 1;
        or
                accept STOP_READ;
                READERS:= READERS - 1;
        or
                when READERS:= 0 =>
                accept WRITE(E: in ELEM) do
                        VARIABLE:= E;
                end;
                loop
                        select
                                accept START_READ;
                                READERS:= READERS + 1;
                        else
                                exit;
                        end select;
                end loop;
end select;
```

The attribute WRITE'COUNT is the number of tasks currently in the queue for the entry WRITE. The use of the count attribute in guards should be done carefully, since the guard gives the value when the guard is evaluated. Its value could change because of other tasks entering the queue. This program segment contains accept statements for STOP_READ and START_READ and an integer READERS that counts the number of readers. It also shows a select statement embedded in a select statement.

Program 11.4-2 illustrates the use of the tasking features that have been described to simulate a four-function calculator.

PROGRAM 11.4-2

```
with TEXT_IO; use TEXT_IO;
procedure CALCULATOR is
        KEY    :   CHARACTER:='?';
        NUM    :   FLOAT;
        DIVIDE_BY_ZERO  :   exception;
```

```
task CALCULATE is
      entry ADD (X: in FLOAT);      --Add to running total
      entry SUB (X: in FLOAT);      --Subtract from running total
      entry MUL (X: in FLOAT);      --Multiply running total
      entry DIV  (X: in FLOAT);     --Divide running total
      entry EQU (X: out FLOAT);     --Return the running total
      entry CLEAR;                  --Reset running total to zero
end CALCULATE;

task body CALCULATE is
      TOTAL : FLOAT:=0.0;
begin
      loop
            select
                  accept ADD (X: in FLOAT) do
                        TOTAL:= TOTAL + X;
                  end ADD;
            or
                  accept SUB (X: in FLOAT) do
                        TOTAL:= TOTAL − X;
                  end SUB;
            or
                  accept MUL (X: in FLOAT) do
                        TOTAL:= TOTAL * X;
                  end MUL;
            or
                  accept DIV (X: in FLOAT) do
                        TOTAL:= TOTAL / X;
                  end DIV;
            or
                  accept EQU (X: out FLOAT) do
                        X:= TOTAL;
                  end EQU;
            or
                  accept CLEAR do
                        TOTAL:= 0.0;
                  end CLEAR;
            or
                  terminate;
            end select;
      end loop;
end CALCULATE;
```

```
procedure EXPLAIN is
begin
      put_line(" ");
      put_line(" This is a simple desk calculator. It can add (+),");
      put_line( subtract (−), multiply (*), and divide (/). Type the");
      put_line(" function key followed by the amount.");
      put_line(" ");
      put_line(" You can print the total with the equals key (=). The");
      put_line(" exclamation point (!) clears the total. Type @ to quit.");
end EXPLAIN;

procedure CALC is
begin
      while KEY /= '@' loop
            case KEY is
                  when '+' | '−' | '*' | '/' =>
                        get (NUM);
                        put_line(" ");
                  when others => null;
            end case;
            case KEY is
                  when '+' => CALCULATE.ADD(NUM);
                  when '−' => CALCULATE.SUB(NUM);
                  when '*' => CALCULATE.MUL(NUM);
                  when '/' => if NUM = 0.0 then
                                    raise DIVIDE_BY_ZERO;
                              else
                                    CALCULATE.DIV(NUM);
                              end if;
                  when '=' => CALCULATE.EQU(NUM);
                        put(NUM);
                        put_line(" ");
                  when '!' => CALCULATE.CLEAR;
                        put_line(" ");
                  when '?' => EXPLAIN;            −−KEY is initialized to '?'
                  when '@' => null;
                  when others =>
                        put_line(" Choices are +, −, *, /, !, @. Type ? for ");
                        put("help.");
            end case;
            put(":");
            get(KEY);
      end loop;
end CALC;
```

```
begin
      put_line(" Ada Four-Function Calculator");
      CALC;
exception
      when DIVIDE_BY_ZERO =>
              put_line(" Divide-by-zero error.");
              put(" Enter new divisor: ");
              CALC;
end CALCULATOR;
```

11.5 THE DELAY STATEMENT

The delay statement is used to suspend the execution of a task for a time of specified duration. The syntax for the delay statement is:

```
delay EXPRESSION_SPECIFYING_DELAY_TIME;
```

where the value of EXPRESSION_SPECIFYING_DELAY_TIME is of the predefined type DURATION, which is a positive or negative number of seconds. The maximum value is implementation dependent but should be at least the number of seconds in a day (i.e., 86400). Larger delays would have to be programmed with a loop. The type definition for the fixed point type DURATION is:

```
type DURATION is delta {implementation_defined}
                range  {implementation_defined};
```

The predefined specifications for Ada specify a library package CALENDAR, which defines type TIME as follows:

```
type TIME is
      record
              YEAR:    INTEGER range 1901..2099;
              MONTH:   INTEGER range 1..12;
              DAY:     INTEGER range 1..31;
              SECOND: DURATION;
      end record;
```

the operations "+" and "−" for type TIME as follows:

```
function "+" (A: TIME;        B: DURATION) return TIME;
function "+" (A: DURATION;  B: TIME        ) return TIME;
function "−" (A: TIME;        B: DURATION) return TIME;
function "−" (A: TIME;        B: TIME        ) return DURATION;
```

and the function CLOCK, which returns the TIME when it is called (i.e., **function** CLOCK **return** TIME;). A simple delay statement is

delay 15.0;

which specifies that the task is to suspend execution for at least 15 seconds. A delay of zero or a negative argument has no effect.

Program 11.5-1 is an example of a simple timer.

PROGRAM 11.5-1

```
with TEXT_IO; use TEXT_IO;
procedure TIMER is
     task ONE_MINUTE_TIMER is
          entry START;
          entry STOP;
     end ONE_MINUTE_TIMER;

     task body ONE_MINUTE_TIMER is
     begin
          loop
               select
                    accept START;
                    delay 60.0;
               or
                    accept STOP;
               or
                    terminate;
               end select;
          end loop;
     end ONE_MINUTE_TIMER;
```

begin

    put("Start of one minute timer.");

    ONE_MINUTE_TIMER.START;   --This starts the delay

        --Sequence of statements that take less than one minute to execute

    ONE_MINUTE_TIMER.STOP;

        --The statements that follow cannot begin execution until one minute

        --has elapsed

    put_line(" ");

    put("End of one minute timer.");

end TIMER:

Note that in this example the parent task and the ONE_MINUTE_TIMER task are executing concurrently. However, the parent task is held up by the entry call "ONE_MINUTE_TIMER.STOP;" until the ONE_MINUTE_TIMER task is synchronized for the rendezvous, which will occur after one minute has elapsed. If the sequence of statements that follows the start of the one minute timer takes longer than one minute to execute, the ONE_MINUTE_TIMER task is held up until the parent task issues the entry call "ONE_MINUTE_TIMER.STOP;". This results in an immediate rendezvous permitting the parent task to continue its execution.

    The delay statement can be used in conjunction with the select statement to create a timed entry call. A timed entry call issues a call if and only if a rendezvous is possible within the specified delay time. The specified delay is given in an "or" clause. If the rendezvous occurs within the time period, the entry call and any statements associated with it are executed, otherwise, the sequence of statements following the delay statement is executed. A simple example illustrating this is the following.

select

    REQUEST;

or

    delay 30.0;

    put(" Sorry, but request cannot be satisfied!");

end select;

In the preceding example, REQUEST is an entry call that is made as an ordinary statement. This task must now wait until the called task is prepared to accept that entry. The structure of this select statement limits to 30 seconds the time that it is prepared to wait. If the called task does not accept the entry within 30 seconds, the message will be printed and execution will continue with those statements that follow the "end select;".

In the preceding example, if the statement "REQUEST;" is replaced by the statement "accept REQUEST;" we can check that the entry REQUEST is called within the prescribed delay time. If the delay expires, the message is printed, the entry REQUEST is no longer acceptable, and execution continues with the statements that follow the "end select;".

Suppose that we further modify the preceding example to:

```
select
      accept REQUEST;
else
      delay 30.0;
      put(" Sorry, but request cannot be satisfied!");
end select;
```

In this case, the delay is quite different from the two preceding examples. If an entry call of REQUEST cannot be accepted at once, the "else" part is immediately executed. That is, we immediately delay for 30 seconds and then print the message.

11.6 TASK TERMINATION

The normal termination of a task occurs when the end of the task body has been reached and all locally declared tasks have terminated their execution. In general, any subprogram, module, or block containing local task declarations cannot be exited until all local tasks have terminated their execution.

The abort statement can be used to terminate a task. Its syntax is:

```
abort TASK_1, TASK_2, . . . ,TASK_N;
```

where TASK_1, TASK_2, . . . ,TASK_N are the names of the tasks to be aborted. An abort statement causes the unconditional asynchronous termination of all the tasks mentioned in the abort statement and the abnormal termination of all tasks for which it is the direct or indirect parent task. On completion of the abort statement the named tasks are no longer active. If a named task is waiting in an entry queue, it is removed from the queue. If an aborted task is engaged in a rendezvous, the other task will receive an exception error. If the aborted task is in a delay state, the delay is canceled. An abort statement should be used only in extreme situations that require unconditional termination. If the called task is aborted, the calling task receives the TASKING_ERROR exception. In less extreme cases the exception FAILURE could be raised and an exception handler created that permitted the task to execute some cleanup actions before termination. The exception FAILURE is an attribute of every task. The statement to raise FAILURE for task T is "raise T'FAILURE;". A task may abort any task including itself and its parent.

Another mechanism for terminating a task is to use the terminate alternative in a select statement. This is used to indicate that the task may be normally terminated at this point. There may not be more than one terminate statement in a select statement. Also there may not be a terminate statement and a delay statement in the same select statement. As an example consider the following.

```
loop
    select
            accept SEND (INMAIL: in MESSAGE) do
                BOX:= INMAIL;
            end SEND;
    or
            accept RECEIVE (OUTMAIL: out MESSAGE) do
                OUTMAIL:= BOX;
                end RECEIVE;
    or
            terminate;
        end select;
end loop;
```

This is a modification of our previous MAILBOX task. Now the MAILBOX task may properly terminate between executing either of the two accept statements, but it may not terminate within an accept statement. The terminate option is chosen if the unit on which the task depends has reached its end and all sibling and dependent tasks are terminated or are able to select a terminate option. In such a case, this entire set of tasks is dormant, since these tasks are the only ones that could call their entries. Hence the entire set of tasks is terminated.

11.7   TASK TYPES

A task specification may also define task types. A task type is useful when a number of tasks have similar properties, as might happen in the modeling of systems with multiple copies of equipment or resources all operating concurrently and all having similar specifications. Objects may then be declared to be of this type, as with any type and object declarations. Objects of task types can be components of arrays and records or they can be access types (see Chapter 12). The value of a task type object denotes a task whose value is defined by the elaboration of the object or by its creation with an allocator. After the value has been defined, the entries may be called. Task type objects are similar to limited private types in that assignment and testing for equality are not available. If one desires to assign task identifiers, access types may be used. Access types may be assigned even if the access value designates a task. There are no constraints associated with task type objects.

The syntax for specifying a task type is the same as for an individual task except that we begin with "task type . ." instead of "task. .". As an example to illustrate the specification of task types and the declaration of objects of these task types, suppose that we have up to 10 sensors and that we wish to drive each one by a distinct task, say SENSOR_DRIVER. A template for similar tasks might have the following task type declaration.

```
task type SENSOR_DRIVER is
      entry ON;
      entry OFF;
end SENSOR_DRIVER;

task body SENSOR_DRIVER is
      --Statements that define operation of SENSOR_DRIVER
end SENSOR_DRIVER;
```

The task body would be the same for all the sensors, since we are assuming that they are identical. The task body follows the same rules as before.

To create an actual task, we use the normal form of object declaration. For example,

```
X: SENSOR_DRIVER;
```

declares X to be a task of type SENSOR_DRIVER. Task objects can be used in structured types. For example,

```
XA: array (1 . . 10) of SENSOR_DRIVER;
```

declares XA to be an array of 10 tasks with each component a task of type SENSOR_DRIVER. A record containing tasks could be declared as follows.

```
type TASK_RECORD is
      record
              X: SENSOR_DRIVER;
              Z: FLOAT;
      end record;

XR: TASK_RECORD;
```

The entries of the preceding tasks would be called using the task object name. For example,

X.ON;
XA(I).ON;
XR.X.ON;

As a second example suppose that we have 10 line printers that we wish to drive using the task PRINTER_DRIVER. A possible specification is:

type LINE **is array** (1..132) **of** CHARACTER;

task type PRINTER_DRIVER **is**
      entry PRINT (L: **in** LINE);
end PRINTER_DRIVER;

task body PRINTER_DRIVER **is**
      --Statements that define operation of PRINTER_DRIVER
end PRINTER_DRIVER;

PRINTER: **array** (1..10) **of** PRINTER_DRIVER;

An entry call must give the index value and the relevant parameters. For example,

PRINTER(NUMBER).PRINT(MY_LINE);

represents an entry call to printer, NUMBER, where NUMBER is between 1 and 10 and passes the parameter MY_LINE of type LINE.

The following are additional examples to illustrate the specification of task types and the declaration of objects of these task types.

task type RESOURCE **is**
      entry SEIZE;
      entry RELEASE;
end RESOURCE;

task type KEYBOARD_DRIVER **is**
      entry READ (C: out CHARACTER);
      entry WRITE (C: in CHARACTER);
end KEYBOARD_DRIVER;

type KEYBOARD **is access** KEYBOARD_DRIVER;
      --See Chapter 12
COMPUTER: RESOURCE;
CRT, TELETYPE: KEYBOARD_DRIVER;
TYPING_POOL: **array** (1..10) **of** KEYBOARD_DRIVER;
TERMINAL: KEYBOARD:= **new** KEYBOARD_DRIVER;

We can refer to these task objects using the usual dot notation as follows.

```
COMPUTER.SEIZE;
CRT.READ(CHAR);              --CHAR is of type CHARACTER
TYPING_POOL(7).WRITE(CHAR);
TERMINAL.READ(CHAR);
```

Note that task objects are not variables; rather, they behave as constants even though they cannot be declared as constants. The parameters to a subprogram may be of task types. They are passed by reference and never copied, which means that the formal and actual parameters always refer to the same task. The activation of objects of task type occurs when the elaboration of the declarations is complete. The execution of the parent task is not allowed to proceed until the elaboration has been completed. The declared tasks and the parent task then proceed to execute in parallel. If an exception is raised during the elaboration, it is propagated to the parent task and behaves as if it had been raised immediately following the "begin" of the parent task.

11.8 SUMMARY

- Tasks are program units that may be executed concurrently. They are useful in programs that interact in real time with physical processes in the real world and in the modeling of parallel activities.
- A task consists of a specification part and a body. The specification part can contain only "entry" statements. The body of the task contains corresponding "accept" statements.
- Task initiation is automatic. Local tasks become active when the parent task reaches the "begin" following the task declarations. They are executed concurrently with one another and with the parent task.
- Task synchronization and communication is accomplished via the "entry" and "accept" statements. A rendevous occurs when the execution of an "accept" statement in one task is synchronized with an "entry" call from another task for the entry name associated with the accept statement.
- The select statement permits a task to select from one of several possible rendezvous. The delay statement may be used in conjunction with the select statement to create a timed entry call. The select statement also permits conditional entry calls and selective waits.
- Normal task termination occurs when the task reaches the end of its task body and all locally declared tasks have terminated their execution. Tasks may also be terminated by using a terminate alternative in a select statement or by using the abort statement.
- Task types are useful in applications with similar but distinct tasks.

Exercises for Chapter 11

1. Consider a family preparing dinner. Suppose that the father cooks the steak outside, the mother prepares the salad, and the child sets the table. Define a procedure DINNER that contains three local tasks for parallel preparation of dinner and illustrates the declaration, activation, and termination of tasks.

2. A binary semaphore task provides synchronization with no data transfer. It can be used to ensure mutually exclusive access to a critical resource such as a shared variable. If P and V are entries to the semaphore task, it can be used for mutual exclusion as follows.

   P; ––Entry call preceding mutually exclusive access sequence of statements
       ––for which mutually exclusive access must be guaranteed
   V; ––Entry call terminating mutually exclusive access

   Write the task specification and task body for the binary semaphore task.

3. Suppose that we wish a variable to be accessible to many tasks but we wish to prevent more than one task from accessing it at the same time. Also suppose that we wish to provide facilities to read the variable and to write a new value to it. Develop a task that provides the entries READ and WRITE for accomplishing this. *Hint.*   Use the select statement.

4. Write the body of a task whose specification is:

   task BUILD_RATIONAL **is**
        entry PUT_NUM(P: INTEGER);
        entry PUT_DEN(Q: INTEGER);
        entry GET_RATIONAL(X: **out** RATIONAL);
   end BUILD_RATIONAL;

   and alternately puts together a rational number from calls of PUT_NUM and PUT_DEN and then delivers the result on a call of GET_RATIONAL.

5. Rewrite the body of the task BUILD_RATIONAL of Exercise 4 so that the calls of PUT_NUM and PUT_DEN are accepted in any order.

Chapter 12

DYNAMIC ALLOCATION AND RECURSION

Many of the data structures already introduced require that memory be set aside when a program is compiled. At times it is desirable to be able to dynamically allocate memory for data structures during actual program execution.

Pascal and PL/1 provide the programmer with dynamic allocation of memory through the use of pointer variables. Ada follows the practice of providing the programmer the mechanism for dynamic allocation.

Dynamic allocation is often used to create data structures such as linked lists, trees, and graphs. Many list-processing algorithms may incorporate pointers and dynamic allocation. A fundamental reality associated with the use of dynamic allocation is that the amount of memory that will be used in the creation of the data structure is not known until the program is executed. The amount of memory required is the amount of memory used!

To illustrate the typical over allocation of computer memory, we consider the following Ada program segment.

```
type RARRAY is array(1..1000) of FLOAT;
     A    : RARRAY;
     SIZE : INTEGER;
     TEMP: FLOAT;
```

209

```
begin
        put_line(" AVERAGE VALUE COMPUTATION");
        put_line(" ------------------------");
        put("Enter the size of the list of numbers to be averaged: ");
        get(SIZE);
        put_line(" ");
        if SIZE <= 1000 then
                for I in 1..SIZE loop
                        put("Enter A(");
                        put(I);
                        put("): ");
                        get(TEMP);
                        A(I):= TEMP;
                end loop;
        end if;
```

In the program segment above, memory space that can accommodate 1000 floating point numbers is set aside as soon as the declaration for RARRAY is elaborated. Only a fraction of this space may actually be required in the execution of the program. For example, if SIZE=200, only 20% of the memory that has been allocated will be utilized.

In this chapter we introduce Ada's access types (pointer variables) and dynamic allocation of memory. To display the utility of access types, access types are presented along with some useful data structures. You will then be able to see access types used in an appropriate setting.

We also introduce recursion in this chapter. Many important applications of access types utilize recursion, and we present several examples.

12.1 SIMPLE ACCESS TYPES; POINTERS

The construct for declaring an access type is:

```
type USER_DEFINED_NAME is access DATA_TYPE;
```

We illustrate the declaration of access types and objects with the following example.

```
type POINTER is access INTEGER;
type AINTEGER is array(1..3) of INTEGER;
type PARRAY is access AINTEGER;
A,B,C: POINTER;
D     : PARRAY;
```

A, B, and C are names for memory locations that point to an integer. D is the name of a memory reference that points to an array of three integers. Access objects are separately created by an allocation assignment consisting of the reserved word "new" followed by the type of the object and then possibly the initial value of the object. The syntax for a dynamic allocation assignment is illustrated by the following example.

```
A:= new POINTER(4);
B:= new POINTER(12);
C:= new POINTER(12);
D:= new PARRAY(1,2,5);
```

Access types may be thought of as templates. In a program, when an access variable is dynamically assigned (e.g., D:= **new** PARRAY(1,2,5);), a memory reference is associated with the symbol D that points to the starting location of the template PARRAY. The actual amount of memory dynamically allocated, during program execution, is dependent on the template PARRRAY. The integers 1, 2, and 5 are assigned to the copy of the template pointed to by D.

The operations that are allowed for access types are assignment and testing for equality.

We obtain the contents of an access variable by using the reserved word "all" as follows.

```
IDENTIFIER.all
```

We now illustrate, by example, various kinds of access variable assignment and output.

```
A:= B;
C.all:= B.all;
A:= null;
for I in 1..3 loop
      D(I):= I;    --We do not need to write "D(I).all:=I"
end loop;
put(C.all);
```

In the first line, the location of pointer variable A is set equal to the location of pointer variable B. Both A and B become names for the same memory reference. It follows that the value stored in A is the same as the value stored in B, since A and B refer to the same memory reference.

In the second line, the value stored in location C is assigned the value stored in location B. The name C still refers to a memory location different from the name B.

In the third line, A is set to a common reference location called ''null''. In the last line, the value pointed to by C is sent to the terminal for output. Program 12.1-1 illustrates these concepts.

PROGRAM 12.1-1

```
with TEXT_IO; use TEXT_IO;
procedure DYNAMIC_ALLOCATION is
        type POINTER is access INTEGER;
        A,B: POINTER;
begin
        A:=new POINTER(5);      --We allocate a new storage location A
                                --We assign the value 5 to the new location
        B:=A;                   --We set the location of B to that of A
        put("A=");
        put(A.all);
        put(" B=");
        put(B.all);             --The value of B must equal the value of A
        put_line(" ");
        B.all:=6;               --The value of A must equal that of B since A=B
        put("A=");
        put(A.all);
        put(" B=");
        put(B.all);
        put_line(" ");
        A:=new POINTER(10);     --We create a new location for A
                                --We set the value of A in the new location at 10
        put("A=");
        put(A.all);
        put(" B=");
        put(B.all);             --The values of A and B are different
        put_line(" ");
        B.all:=A.all;           --The value in B is set to the new value of A
        put("A=");              --The locations of A and B are different
        put(A.all);
        put(" B=");
        put(B.all);             --A will equal B
        put_line(" ");
        A.all:=12;              --The value in the new location of A is set to 12
        put("A=");
        put(A.all);
        put(" B=");
        put(B.all);             --B is in a different location from A so its value is
                                --different
end DYNAMIC_ALLOCATION;
```

Access types can also refer to unconstrained arrays. For example,

type MATRIX **is array** (INTEGER **range** <>, INTEGER **range** <>) **of** INTEGER;
type MY_MATRIX **is access** MATRIX;

We can dynamically allocate new matrices as in the following.

M: **new** MATRIX(1..25, −10..10);

The matrix M could be initialized to zeros as follows.

M: **new** MATRIX(1..25 => (−10..10 => 0));

The statement

M: **new** MATRIX;

is illegal because the array object must have bounds specified.

True dynamic dimensioning of arrays (the ability to have a user specify the size of an array at run time) is possible in Ada by exploiting the foregoing concept. We illustrate this with a program segment that uses the type declarations above.

```
NUMBER_ROWS, NUMBER_COLUMNS: INTEGER;
put("Enter the number of rows in the matrix: ");
get(NUMBER_ROWS); put_line(" ");
put("Enter the number of columns in the matrix: ");
get(NUMBER_COLUMNS);
        --Now we dynamically create a matrix with the entered dimensions
M:= new MATRIX(1..NUMBER_ROWS, 1..NUMBER_COLUMNS);
        --We illustrate a typical assignment to the matrix M
M(3,5):= −45;
        --We illustrate a typical random access from the matrix M
put(M(3,5));   --The number −45 will be printed
```

The memory space used for all dynamically dimensioned arrays is deallocated when execution of the logical unit containing the array declarations terminates. Thus if the programmer wishes to save the contents of a dynamically dimensioned array and be able to access the information throughout the program, the array declaration should be global. That is, it should have a scope that covers all logical units in the Ada program.

12.2 RECORD ACCESS TYPES AND RECURSION

Most often, access types that are declared to be records are used in applications programming. Since a record data structure may require considerable memory storage, it is very desirable to be able to dynamically allocate storage for records. We illustrate an access record's declaration as follows.

```
type TREE;
type NODE is access TREE;
type TREE is
    record
            INFORMATION: INTEGER;
            LEFT       : NODE;
            RIGHT      : NODE;
        end record;
ROOT, PREVIOUS, CURRENT: NOTE;
```

Please note that we must establish that TREE is a data type (in the statement "type TREE") before we fully define that data type. Type "NODE" is defined as a pointer to the data type "TREE" and then type "TREE" is defined as a record, with one field containing information associated with the node and two fields defined to be of type "NODE". This circular or recursive definition is quite unsettling when first encountered. Declarations are elaborated in sequential order, so it is first necessary to give an incomplete declaration of TREE, then declare NODE, and finally complete the declaration of TREE. Pascal uses a similar recursive definition for its pointer types.

Let us examine the meaning of the access record more closely. We have created a template "NODE" that may be used to dynamically create a tree data structure. Nodes may be created dynamically by invoking the reserved word "new" (as in "so what else is . . . ?") followed by the access type "TREE". Each node is assumed to contain information in the form of an integer. In addition, each node contains two pointers, "LEFT" and "RIGHT". These access variables point to the locations (in memory) of two more nodes. If we consider the pointer "LEFT" as the pointer to a left descendant of the node, and the pointer "RIGHT" as the pointer to a right descendant of the node, we will have implemented a binary tree data structure. In such a data structure, each node points to two additional nodes, including the possibility of pointing to **null**. All binary trees must have a "root" node. Thus we must have an access variable that points to the root of the binary tree. We may call this variable "ROOT" if we wish. Initially there are no record objects allocated, only the pointers ROOT, PREVIOUS, and CURRENT, which by default take the value **null.** Likewise, when we dynamically create a new TREE, the LEFT and RIGHT fields of the record are assigned initial default values of **null.**

To access any field of the record "NODE" we use the same dot notation that is used for any record type. For example, to access the INFORMATION for ROOT, we would call ROOT.INFORMATION.

In Program 12.2-1, we illustrate the tree data structure in the context of a full program. Suppose that we wish to take a file of numbers (input sequentially from a terminal) and sort this file from smallest to largest. A simple solution to this problem might be to form an array of these numbers and then to use one of the sorting algorithms presented in Chapter 7 (e.g., exchange sort or bubble sort).

A more efficient approach for solving this problem involves the construction of a binary tree data structure from the numbers as they are entered. We have already constructed a binary tree similar to the type that we need to build now. In Section 8.1.7 we presented a binary tree structure to solve the problem of locating duplicates in a list of integers. In Program 12.2-1 we utilize dynamic allocation via access types to construct our binary tree.

In building our binary tree, the first number to be entered becomes the root. The second number entered is compared to the root: if it is smaller, it becomes the left offspring of the root; if it is equal or larger, it becomes the right offspring of the root. The third number entered also is compared to the root: if it is smaller than the root, it is compared to the left offspring of the root (if one exists); if it is equal to or larger than the root, it is compared to the right offspring of the root (if one exists). As soon as a leaf of the tree is reached (no offspring exists with which to compare the third entry), the third entry is inserted at that place in the tree. As each new number is entered from the terminal, it is first compared to the root of the tree. If it is smaller than the root, we move down the left branch of the tree; if it is equal to or larger than the root, we move down the right branch. This process of comparison and movement down the tree continues until a "null" node is hit (at a leaf node of the tree). Then a node for the number that has just been entered is created at the appropriate place in the tree.

When all the numbers have been entered and the binary tree has been constructed, the sorted list of numbers can be printed out by performing an "inorder" traversal of the binary tree. This recursive procedure is as follows.

```
procedure TRAVERSE(P: NODE) is
begin
        if P /= null then
        TRAVERSE(P.LEFT)      --We recursively call TRAVERSE sending in the
                              --parameter P.LEFT
        put(P.INFO);          --We output the information contained in the node P
        put_line(" ");
        TRAVERSE(P.RIGHT)     --We recursively call TRAVERSE sending in the
                              --parameter P.RIGHT
        end if;
end TRAVERSE;
```

To explain how this "in-order" traversal of the binary tree works we walk through a numerical example. We recommend that the reader also consult any reference textbook on the subject of data structures (e.g., Reference 4) and review the material on in-order traversal of binary trees.

Suppose that the file of numbers to be entered is 4, 2, 6, 8, 1, and 3. The tree structure that is produced from these numbers is shown in Figure 12.1.

Suppose that the access variable ROOT points to the root of the tree depicted in Figure 12.1. Then we would call TRAVERSE(ROOT). To explain

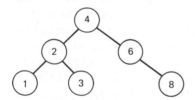

Figure 12.1 Tree example.

the "in-order" traversal algorithm given above, we use the notation ml4 to refer to the memory location of the node whose information content is 4 or mlI for the memory location of the node whose information content is I. The recursion works as follows.

```
TRAVERSE(ml4)    --From the call TRAVERSE(ROOT)
TRAVERSE(ml2)    --From the call TRAVERSE(ml4.LEFT)
TRAVERSE(ml1)    --From the call TRAVERSE(ml2.LEFT)
TRAVERSE(null)   --From the call TRAVERSE(ml1.LEFT)
--We complete the call TRAVERSE(null), since we reach the end statement of that
--TRAVERSE call. We return to the unfinished execution of TRAVERSE(ml1). We
--have completed the statement TRAVERSE(P.LEFT) in TRAVERSE(ml1). Now we
--execute the next statement, which is PRINT(P.INFO).
"1" gets printed    --Second statement in TRAVERSE(ml1)
--Now we go to the final statement in TRAVERSE(ml1)
```

TRAVERSE(**null**)   −−From the call TRAVERSE(ml1.RIGHT)
−−Since we reach the end statement of TRAVERSE(null), we complete the business
−−of TRAVERSE(ml1). We return to the unfinished execution of TRAVERSE(ml2). In
−−that call we completed TRAVERSE(ml2.LEFT).
"2" gets printed   −−Second statement in TRAVERSE(ml2)
−−Now we go to the final statement in TRAVERSE(ml2)
TRAVERSE(ml3)   −−From the call TRAVERSE(ml2.RIGHT)
TRAVERSE(**null**)   −−From the call TRAVERSE(ml3.LEFT)
"3" gets printed   −−Second statement of TRAVERSE(ml3)
TRAVERSE(**null**)   −−From the call TRAVERSE(ml3.RIGHT)
−−Now the TRAVERSE(ml2) is completed. We return to the unfinished execution of
−−TRAVERSE(ml4). The first statement, TRAVERSE(ml4.LEFT), has been completed.
"4" gets printed   −−Second statement in TRAVERSE(ml4)
TRAVERSE(ml6)   −−From the call TRAVERSE(ml4.RIGHT)
TRAVERSE(**null**)   −−From the call TRAVERSE(ml6.LEFT)
"6" gets printed   −−Second statement in TRAVERSE(ml6)
TRAVERSE(ml8)   −−From the call TRAVERSE(ml6.RIGHT)
TRAVERSE(**null**)   −−From the call TRAVERSE(ml8.LEFT)
"8" gets printed   −−Second statement in TRAVERSE(ml8)
TRAVERSE(**null**)   −−From the call TRAVERSE(ml8.RIGHT)
−−With TRAVERSE(ml8) completed and TRAVERSE(ml6) completed, it follows that
−−TRAVERSE(ml4) is completed. All the unfinished business has been completed,
−−so the algorithm terminates.

As evident in the foregoing walk-through of the "in-order" recursive algorithm, a "stack" of information is created in which the TRAVERSE is
executed in last-call-made, first-call-executed order. Fortunately, when this
algorithm is encoded as an Ada subprogram, all the complex bookkeeping that
was performed by hand in the walk-through is done automatically by the computer. Did you notice that the numbers printed out were sorted from smallest to
largest?

Program 12.2-1 shows an entire Ada program that implements the concepts
presented above for sorting a file of numbers.

PROGRAM 12.2-1

```
with TEXT_IO; use TEXT_IO;
procedure BINARY_TREE_SORT is
        type TREE;
        type NODE is access TREE;
        type TREE is
            record
                    INFO:  INTEGER;
                    LEFT:  NODE;
                    RIGHT: NODE;
            end record;
```

```
    ROOT, CURRENT, PREVIOUS: NODE;
    N: INTEGER;

procedure TRAVERSE(P: NODE) is
begin
    if P /= null then
            TRAVERSE(P.LEFT);
            put(P.INFO);
            put_line(" ");
            TRAVERSE(P.RIGHT);
    end if;
end TRAVERSE;

function MAKETREE(X: INTEGER) return NODE is
    R: NODE;
begin
    R:= new TREE;
    R.INFO:= X;
    R.LEFT:= null;
    R.RIGHT:= null;
    return R;
end MAKETREE;

procedure SETLEFT(X: INTEGER; W: in out NODE) is
    Q: NODE;
begin
    if W.LEFT /= null then
            put_line("Illegal setleft operation.");
    else
            --We dynamically create a new node Q
            Q:= MAKETREE(X);
            W.LEFT:= Q;
    end if;
end SETLEFT;

procedure SETRIGHT(X: INTEGER; W: in out NODE) is
    Q: NODE;
begin
    if W.RIGHT /= null then
            put_line("Illegal setright operation.");
    else
            --We dynamically create a new node Q
            Q:= MAKETREE(X);
            W.RIGHT:= Q;
    end if;
end SETRIGHT;
```

```
begin   ——Main program
     put("Enter the first number from your file: ");
     get(N);
     put_line("  ");
     ——We dynamically create the root of the tree
     ROOT:= MAKETREE(N);
     put_line("Enter the file of numbers (end with the number −9999)");
     get(N);
     put_line("  ");
     while N /= −9999 loop
          CURRENT:= ROOT;
          while CURRENT /= null loop
               PREVIOUS:= CURRENT;
               if N < PREVIOUS.INFO then
                    CURRENT:= PREVIOUS.LEFT;     ——Move to left
               else
                    CURRENT:= PREVIOUS.RIGHT;   ——Move to right
               end if;
          end loop;
          if N < PREVIOUS.INFO then
               SETLEFT(N,PREVIOUS);                    ——Add node to left
          else
               SETRIGHT(N,PREVIOUS);                  ——Add node to right
          end if;
          get(N);
          put_line("  ");
     end loop;
     put_line("  ");
     put_line("The sorted list");
     put_line("—————————");
     ——We do an "in-order" traversal of the tree
     TRAVERSE(ROOT);
end BINARY_TREE_SORT;
```

12.3   LINKED LISTS USING DYNAMIC ALLOCATION

In this section we present another application of dynamic allocation using a record structure.

We now rework Program 8.1-3, a list maintenance scheme using the data structure of linked lists; we use dynamic allocation to accomplish the same goals of being able to add, delete, and access records from a data base that is maintained in order. In Program 8.1-3, since an array of records was used as the vehicle for implementing the linked-list data structure, computer memory to store this data base was allocated before even a single entry in the data base was entered. In Program 12.3-1, memory for records in the data base is created "on demand." To simplify the problem, the list that we maintain in program 12.3-1 is a list of integers.

PROGRAM 12.3-1

```
with TEXT_IO; use TEXT_IO;
procedure LINKED_LISTS_USING_DYNAMIC_ALLOCATION is
      type LINKED_LIST;
      type NODE is access LINKED_LIST;
      type LINKED_LIST is
            record
                  INFO: INTEGER;   --There may be many information fields
                  NEXT: NODE;
            end record;
      AVAIL, LIST: NODE;
      INFORMATION: INTEGER;
                  E: BOOLEAN;   --We use this to exit from the program

procedure PRINTOUT is
      P: NODE;
begin
      put_line(" ");   put_line(" ");   put_line(" ");
      if LIST = null then
            put_line("No records available.");
      else
            P:= LIST;
            while P /= null loop
                  put(P.INFO);
                  put_line(" ");
                  P:= P.NEXT;
            end loop;
      end if;
end PRINTOUT;

procedure GETNODE(T: out NODE) is
begin
      if AVAIL /= null then
            T:= AVAIL;
            AVAIL:= AVAIL.NEXT;
      else
            --We dynamically obtain a new node
            T:= new LINKED_LIST;
      end if;
end GETNODE;
```

```
procedure FREENODE(P: in out NODE) is
      ——Garbage collection is done
begin
      P.NEXT:= AVAIL;
      AVAIL:= P;
end FREENODE;

procedure DELETE is
      PREVIOUS, CURRENT: NODE;
                  FOUND: BOOLEAN;
begin
      put_line(" ");
      put("Enter information to key on: ");
      get(INFORMATION);
      ——We search for the node just before the node containing the key
      FOUND:= FALSE;
      PREVIOUS:= null;
      CURRENT:= LIST;
      while (CURRENT /— null) and (not FOUND) loop
            if CURRENT.INFO = INFORMATION then
                  FOUND:= TRUE;
            else
                  PREVIOUS:= CURRENT;
                  CURRENT:= CURRENT.NEXT;
            end if;
      end loop;
      if CURRENT = null then
            put_line(" ");
            put_line("No matchup exists.");
            put_line(" ");
      else
            if CURRENT = LIST then
                  LIST:= CURRENT.NEXT;
            else
                  PREVIOUS.NEXT:= CURRENT.NEXT;
            end if;
            FREENODE(CURRENT);
            put_line(" ");
            put("We have purged ");
            put(INFORMATION);
            put(" from the list.");
            put_line(" ");
      end if;
end DELETE;
```

```
procedure INSAFTER(PREVIOUS: in out NODE; INFORMATION: INTEGER) is
      Q: NODE;
begin
      if PREVIOUS = null then
            put_line("Void insertion.");
      else
            GETNODE(Q);
            Q.INFO:= INFORMATION;
            Q.NEXT:= PREVIOUS.NEXT;
            PREVIOUS.NEXT:= Q;
      end if;
end INSAFTER;

procedure ADD is

procedure PLACE(LIST: in out NODE; INFORMATION: INTEGER) is
      CURRENT, PREVIOUS: NODE;
                        FOUND: BOOLEAN;
begin  --PLACE
      FOUND:= FALSE;
      CURRENT:= LIST;
      PREVIOUS:= null;
      while (CURRENT /= null) and (not FOUND) loop
            if INFORMATION <= CURRENT.INFO then
                  FOUND:= TRUE;
            else
                  PREVIOUS:= CURRENT;
                  CURRENT:= CURRENT.NEXT;
            end if;
      end loop;
      if PREVIOUS = null then
            --Record is the first in the list
            --We create a new node
            GETNODE(PREVIOUS);
            PREVIOUS.INFO:= INFORMATION;
            --We link the new element to the old first element
            PREVIOUS.NEXT:= LIST;
            --We make PREVIOUS the first element
            LIST:= PREVIOUS;
      else
            --The new element must be inserted just after the node PREVIOUS
            INSAFTER(PREVIOUS,INFORMATION);
      end if;
end PLACE;
```

```
begin  --ADD
      put_line(" ");
      put("Enter information to add to list: ");
      get(INFORMATION);
      PLACE(LIST,INFORMATION);
end ADD;

procedure MENU is
      CHOICE: INTEGER;
begin
      put_line(" ");
      put_line("1--> Add new record");
      put_line(" ");
      put_line("2--> Delete record");
      put_line(" ");
      put_line("3--> Printout records");
      put_line(" ");
      put_line("4--> Exit from program");
      put_line(" ");
      put("Enter appropriate choice: ");
      get(CHOICE);
      case CHOICE is
            when 1 => ADD;
            when 2 => DELETE;
            when 3 => PRINTOUT;
            when others => E:= TRUE;
      end case;
end MENU;

begin  --Main program
      E:= FALSE;
      --When AVAIL = null, we must allocate new space when creating a node
      AVAIL:= null;
      --When LIST = null, the list is empty
      LIST:= null;
      loop
            MENU;
            exit when E;
      end loop;
end LINKED_LISTS_USING_DYNAMIC_ALLOCATION;
```

12.4 HASH SORTING USING DYNAMIC ALLOCATION

In this section we present a final application of access records. In Program 12.4-1 we perform hash sorting on a set of integers, 1 to 100. We do not know in advance how many integers will be sorted. As each succeeding integer is entered from the terminal, it is placed into one of 10 lists (bins). Each of the 10 lists is maintained in order. When all the numbers have been entered, each of the lists is printed out sequentially. Since all the numbers in list one are less than all the numbers of list two, and so forth, the output list is sorted.

PROGRAM 12.4-1

```
--This program allows a user to enter N integers, each from 1 to 100
--The numbers are pushed into bins according to the following rule:
--      1-10   => bin 1
--     11-20   => bin 2
--      . . .
--     91-100  => bin 10.
--The contents of each bin are maintained in ascending order. Then the contents
--of bins 1 to 10 are printed out in order
with TEXT_IO; use TEXT_IO;
procedure DYNAMIC_HASH_SORT is
      type LINKED_LIST;
      type NODE is access LINKED_LIST;
      type LINKED_LIST is
            record
                  INFO: INTEGER;
                  NEXT: NODE;
            end record;
      BIN: array(1..10) of NODE;
      N, BINNUMBER: INTEGER;

procedure OUTPUT_LIST is
      P: NODE;
begin
      for I in 1..10 loop
            --P points to the beginning of a list
            P:= BIN(I);
            while P /= null loop
                  put(P.INFO);
                  put_line(" ");
                  P:= P.NEXT;
            end loop;
      end loop;
end OUTPUT_LIST;
```

```
procedure PLACE(BN: INTEGER; X: INTEGER) is
        P, Q: NODE;
      FOUND: BOOLEAN;

procedure PUSH_HEAD(BN,X: INTEGER) is
      P: NODE;
begin
      --We dynamically create a new node
      P:= new LINKED_LIST;
      P.INFO:= X;
      P.NEXT:= BIN(BN);
      --BIN(BN) is a pointer to the beginning of a list
      BIN(BN) := P;
end PUSH_HEAD;

procedure INSAFTER(Q: NODE; X: INTEGER) is
      P: NODE;
begin
      if Q = null then
            put_line("Void insertion.");
      else
            --We dynamically create a new node
            P:= new LINKED_LIST;
            P.INFO:= X;
            P.NEXT:= Q.NEXT;
            Q.NEXT:= P;
      end if;
end INSAFTER;

begin   --PLACE
      FOUND:= FALSE;
      Q:= null;
      --Q will trail P as we trace through linked list
      P:= BIN(BN);
      --P points to the beginning of a list
      while (P /= null) and (not FOUND) loop
            if X <= P.INFO then
                  --We have found the insertion point
                  FOUND:= TRUE;
            else
                  Q:= P;
                  P:= P.NEXT;
            end if;
      end loop;
```

```
      if Q = null then
             ——X must be inserted at the beginning of bin BN
             PUSH_HEAD(BN,X);
      else
             INSAFTER(Q,X);
      end if;
end PLACE;

begin   ——Main program
      for I in 1..10 loop
             ——We set the pointer to each of the lists to "null"
             BIN(I) := null;
      end loop;
      put_line("Enter your list of integers");
      put_line("Exit with an integer out of the range from 1 to 100");
      get(N);
      put_line(" ");
      while (N>=1) and (N<=100) loop
             BINNUMBER:= (N—1)/10+1;   ——When N=10, BINNUMBER=1
             PLACE(BINNUMBER,N);
             get(N);
             put_line(" ");
      end loop;
      OUTPUT_LIST;
end DYNAMIC_HASH_SORT;
```

12.5 MORE ON RECURSION

In Section 12.1 we introduced recursion in connection with the in-order traversal of a binary tree. There we saw the complex bookkeeping that the compiler was able to perform automatically. What price, if any, is paid for recursion?

Since recursion requires the generation of an internal stack, many recursive calls by a subprogram may raise the STORAGE_ERROR exception, indicating the exhaustion of computer memory. Recursion is often memory intensive.

An algorithm that employs recursion often runs more slowly than the same algorithm written without recursion. This follows because recursive operations on some machines are relatively slow.

The major advantage offered by recursion is the economy of code that is often possible for performing complex operations (e.g., traversing a tree). The simplicity of thinking and economy of program code provided by recursion is a benefit enjoyed by the programmer. If the price that must be paid for this benefit is too high, iteration or some alternative to recursion should be sought.

In the next several sections we present some applications of recursion.

12.6 GREATEST COMMON DIVISOR USING RECURSION

Program 12.6-1 gives another illustration of recursion. We use the Euclid algorithm to solve the problem of finding the greatest common divisor of two integers. The algorithm may be stated as follows: the greatest common divisor of A and B is equal to A if B is zero and is equal to the greatest common divisor of B and the remainder of A divided by B, if B is nonzero.

PROGRAM 12.6-1

```
with TEXT_IO; use TEXT_IO;
procedure GREATEST_COMMON_DIVISOR is
      A,B: INTEGER;

function GCD(A,B: INTEGER) return INTEGER is
begin
      if B=0 then
            return A;
      else
            return GCD(B,A mod B);
      end if;
end GCD;

begin   --Main program
      put_line("Greatest common divisor of A and B");
      put_line(" ");
      put("Enter A: ");
      get(A);
      put_line(" ");
      put("Enter B: ");
      get(B);
      put_line(" ");
      put("Greatest common divisor of ");
      put(A);
      put(" and ");
      put(B);
      put(" is ");
      put(GCD(A,B));
end GREATEST_COMMON_DIVISOR;
```

12.7 BINARY SEARCH OF SORTED ARRAY USING RECURSION

A well-known technique for searching an array of sorted objects for some key is the method of binary searching. Using this method, a key is compared to the middle of the list. Then, depending on whether the key is less than or greater than the element in the middle of the list, the search commences in either the first half or the second half of the list. The remaining half-list is divided again to produce a quarter-list (assuming that a matchup has not been found). This narrowing of the search into smaller and smaller sublists continues until either a matchup has been found or the entire list has been searched. In Program 12.7-1 we implement the binary search algorithm using recursion.

PROGRAM 12.7-1

```
with TEXT_IO; use TEXT_IO;
procedure BINARY_SEARCH is
        type RARRAY is array(1..1000) of INTEGER;

function BINSRCH(A: RARRAY; LOW,HIGH: INTEGER;
                    X: INTEGER) return INTEGER is
        MID,T: INTEGER;
begin
        if LOW > HIGH then
                T:=0;
        else
                MID:= (LOW+HIGH)/2;
                if X = A(MID) then
                        T:= MID;
                else
                        if X < A(MID) then
                                T:= BINSRCH(A,LOW,MID−1,X);
                        else
                                T:= BINSRCH(A,MID+1,HIGH,X);
                        end if;
                end if;
        end if;
        return T;   −−If not found, zero is returned
end BINSRCH;

        N,T,KEY: INTEGER;
                A: RARRAY;
begin   −−Main program
        put("Enter the size of the array to be created: ");
        get(N);
        for I in 1..N loop
                put("Enter A(");
                put(I);
                put("): ");
                get(T);
                A(I) := T;
        end loop;
```

```
    put_line(" ");
    put("Enter the integer to key on: ");
    get(KEY);
    T:= BINSRCH(A,1,N,KEY);
    put("The element ");
    put(KEY);
    put(" is located in position ");
    put(T);
end BINARY_SEARCH;
```

12.8 PERMUTATION OF OBJECTS USING RECURSION

Suppose we desire all the permutations of *N* integers. In Program 12.8-1, using recursion, we are able to achieve this goal. See whether you can "walk" through this program and understand its operation.

PROGRAM 12.8-1

```
with TEXT_IO; use TEXT_IO;
procedure PERMUTATIONS is
    type IARRAY is array(1..10) of INTEGER;
    A: IARRAY;
    N: INTEGER;

procedure PERMUTE(L: INTEGER; A: in out IARRAY) is
    T: INTEGER;
begin
    if L > 1 then
        PERMUTE(L-1,A);
        for I in reverse 1..L-1 loop
            T:= A(L);
            A(L):= A(I);
            A(I):= T;
            PERMUTE(L-1,A);
            T:= A(L);
            A(L):= A(I);
            A(I):= T;
        end loop;
    else
        for J in 1..N loop
            T:= A(J);
            put(T);
        end loop;
```

```
            put_line(" ");
        end if;
end PERMUTE;

begin  --Main program
        put("Enter the size of the number to be permuted: ");
        get(N);  --N must be 1..10
        for I in 1..N loop
            A(I):= I;
        end loop;
        PERMUTE(N,A);
end PERMUTATIONS;
```

12.9 ADAPTIVE INTEGRATION USING RECURSION

For our final illustration and application of recursion in this chapter we examine a technique for adaptive numerical integration. After a function F(X) has been written into the program by a user, the user is asked to input the lower and upper limits of integration. The interval is cut in half. The lower half is integrated, followed by the upper half. If the difference between the sum of the two halves and the integral over the total interval is less than some predetermined level, the integration ceases. If not, each half of the integral is obtained by continuing the recursion and cutting each respective portion into two more halves. Study Program 12.9-1 and see whether the method makes sense to you. You may also wish to consult a standard reference book on numerical methods (e.g., Reference 5) and review the two-point Gaussian method for numerical integration.

PROGRAM 12.9-1

```
with TEXT_IO; use TEXT_IO;
procedure ADAPTIVE_INTEGRATION is
        LOWER, UPPER, ANSWER: FLOAT;

--The user must supply his or her own integrand

function F(X: FLOAT) return FLOAT is
begin
        return X;
end F;
```

```
procedure INTEGRAL(A,B: FLOAT; ANS: out FLOAT) is
      X1: constant FLOAT:=0.5773502692;
      ANST, ANSR, ANSL, ANS1, ANS2, EPS: FLOAT;

procedure INT(A,B: FLOAT; AN: out FLOAT) is
      --We use a two-point Gauss
      C,D,S: FLOAT;
begin
      C:= (B-A)/2.0;
      D:= (B+A)/2.0;
      S:= F(-C*X1+D)+F(C*X1+D);
      AN:= C*S;
end INT;

begin   --INTEGRAL
      if A < B then
            EPS:= 2.0E-5;   --The user may wish to change this relative error
                            --bound
            ANS:= 0.0;
            INT(A,B,ANST);
            INT(A,(A+B)/2.0,ANSL);
            INT((A+B)/2.0,B,ANSR);
            if abs(ANST-ANSL-ANSR) > EPS*ABS(ANST) then
                  INTEGRAL(A,(A+B)/2.0,ANS1);
                  ANS:= ANS+ANS1;
                  INTEGRAL((A+B)/2.0,B,ANS2);
                  ANS:= ANS+ANS2;
            else
                  ANS:= ANS+ANST;
            end if;
      end if;
end INTEGRAL;

begin   --Main program
      put("Enter lower limit: ");
      get(LOWER);
      put_line(" ");
      put("Enter upper limit: ");
      get(UPPER);
      put_line(" ");
      INTEGRAL(LOWER,UPPER,ANSWER);
      put("The integral=");
      put(ANSWER);
end ADAPTIVE_INTEGRATION;
```

12.10 SUMMARY

• Access types are similar to reference or pointer types of other programming languages. Access types permit dynamic allocation of memory during program execution.

• The use of access types permits true dynamic dimensioning of arrays to be accomplished at run time.

• Access types are useful in applications involving linked-list, tree, and graph data structures.

• Access variables are deallocated when the unit containing them is terminated.

• All subprograms can be called recursively. Many important applications of access types utilize recursion.

Exercises for Chapter 12

1. With pencil in hand, walk through Program 12.7-1 and search for the key 3 in the array 1, 6, 7, 9, 3, 2.

2. With pencil in hand (perhaps the same one as for Exercise 1), walk through Program 12.8-1 for size 3. Write out all the recursive calls and the output produced by each call.

3. With pencil in hand (you may have to sharpen it by this time), walk through the first several recursive calls in Program 12.9-1. Do you follow the scheme for this recursive integration?

4. Modify the linked-list program to allow a string of 30 characters to be used for an alphabetical ordering instead of integer ordering.

5. A post-order traversal of a tree is given by the following subprogram.

```
procedure POST_ORDER(A: NODE) is
begin
        if A /= null then
                POST_ORDER(A.LEFT);
              - POST_ORDER(A.RIGHT);
                put(A.INFO);
                put_line(" ");
        end if;
end POST_ORDER;
```

where NODE is defined as in Program 12.2-1. Walk through this algorithm for the accompanying tree and write out the output.

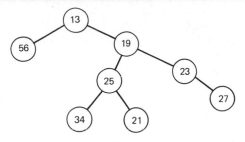

6. Write a function COUNT that returns the number of nodes in a binary tree.

Chapter 13

LET'S PACKAGE WHAT WE'VE DONE

Large computational resources such as software libraries are made up of smaller software building blocks. In Chapter 7 we discussed subprograms in the form of procedures and functions. Subprograms coupled with user-defined data structures including record types may be woven together to form larger software modules. These software modules can be used to form the basic fabric of a software library. Each module represents a component in such a library.

One of the major strengths of Ada is the existence of a language construct that supports the creation of software modules, called packages. Generally the package unit contains functionally related data structures and subprograms that can be used in other programs as a computational resource, or used as a module in a software library.

Ada allows the programmer to separate the specification of a package from its implementation (body). Thus computational resources (modules in the form of packages) can be made available to an Ada programmer without revealing the implementation details of these modules. Often the programmer does not wish to be burdened with such details. Similarly, the authors of the package may not wish to reveal the contents of their package. The specification part of a package includes sufficient detail to allow a programmer using the package to create an interface to his or her program.

A user's guide may be constructed for a package by inserting comments and explanations in the specification part of the package. Frequently, the programmer using the package will have access only to the package specification.

235

Thus, if the practice just outlined is employed, the programmer will have a handy user's guide with the package specification source.

Since the specification part of a package may be compiled separately from the implementation part (in Chapter 16 we discuss compilation units), the implementation details may be changed (e.g., an algorithm improved or changed) by the authors of the package without requiring a revision of the programs that utilize the package.

The package construct may greatly contribute to effective software maintenance and software engineering. We discuss these ideas in Chapter 16.

In this chapter we present the constructs associated with Ada packages. We illustrate these constructs and the significance of packages by grouping some earlier subprograms together into packages as well as creating new packages.

13.1 PACKAGES OF DATA TYPES AND DATA OBJECTS

Perhaps the simplest kind of package consists of only a specification part. This specification part may include constants, types, and variable declarations that are logically related (the language imposes no constraint concerning the logical relationship between the various data types and identifiers—only good programming practice dictates this). These types and identifiers may then be made available to other programs that utilize the package. We illustrate this with the following Ada package.

```
package PERSONAL_DATA is
     type PERSON is
          record
                    HEIGHT, WEIGHT: INTEGER;
                    ADDRESS        : array(1..25) of CHARACTER;
                    PHONE          : array(1..12) of CHARACTER;
                    STATE          : array(1..2) of CHARACTER;
                    ZIP            : array(1..10) of CHARACTER;
                    SCORE1, SCORE2, SCORE3, SCORE4: INTEGER;
                    COMMENTARY     : array(1..80) of CHARACTER;
          end record;
     P                                 : array(1..500) of PERSON;
end PERSONAL_DATA;
```

We illustrate how such a package may typically be used.

```
with PERSONAL_DATA; use PERSONAL_DATA;
procedure ILLUSTRATION_OF_PACKAGE_USE is
        T,J: INTEGER;
         C: CHARACTER;
begin
       for I in 1..500 loop
              put("Enter score 3 for person ");   put(I);   put(": ");
              get(T);
              P(I).SCORE3:= T;
              put_line(" ");
              put("Enter commentary for person ");   put(I);
              put(" (end with '/')");
              put_line(" ");
              get(C);
              J:= 1;
              while (C /= '/') and (J <= 80) loop
                     P(I).COMMENTARY(J):= C;
                     J:= J+1;
                     get(C);
              end loop;
       end loop;
end ILLUSTRATION_OF_PACKAGE_USE;
```

We have assumed that the package PERSONAL_DATA has been compiled separately from the program that utilizes it. The statement "with PER-
SONAL_DATA" causes the compiler to fetch this precompiled file and link it
to the user's program. The statement "use PERSONAL_DATA" makes available all the data types and identifiers defined in the specification part of the
package within the scope of the logical unit that employs the "use" command.
It is as if these data types and objects were declared to be part of the user's
program and are being accessed within the logical unit that employs the "use"
command. If a package is defined within a program, its resources may be made
available to another logical unit that employs the "use" command.

As the package PERSONAL_DATA illustrates, the specification part of a
package containing data type and object declarations is constructed as follows.

```
package USER_DEFINED_IDENTIFIER is
       --Data type and object declarations
end USER_DEFINED_IDENTIFIER;
```

Access to a package may be accomplished within a program without the
"use" command. The same type of dot notation that is available for accessing
fields of a record may be used to access an identifier of a package. For example,

suppose the package PERSONAL_DATA were defined within a user's program. Then PERSONAL_DATA.P(13).SCORE1 would be a legal reference to the variable P defined within the package.

How do packages differ from records? We just mentioned a similarity between accessing the fields of a record and accessing the objects of a package. There are profound differences between the use of the two constructs record and package. A record is a data template, which may be used in declaring data objects. A program cannot assign values to a data template; it can only assign values to objects (variables) declared to be of the type given by the record. On the other hand, a package may consist of more than data templates. It may include data objects and, as we see in the next section, subprograms.

13.2   PACKAGES THAT CONTAIN SUBPROGRAMS

As previously indicated, a set of functionally related subprograms may be grouped together to form a software module or a package. Such a package has two parts: the package specification and the package body.

The package specification, which (as we discuss in detail in Chapter 16) can be compiled separately, may contain data type and data object declarations, subprogram (procedure and function) headings, private data types (discussed in Section 13.3), and nested package specifications.

The package body, which also can be compiled separately, may contain declarations of local variables and auxiliary subprograms needed to implement subprograms defined in the specification part, initialization specifications, and implementation of the subprograms defined in the specification part of the package.

We defer discussion concerning the order of compilation of package subunits (specification and body) or any other matters relating to the compilation hierarchy to Chapter 16.

In Program 13.2-1 we illustrate the package structure by defining a package, VECTORS, for converting a vector from rectangular to polar form. We define the package separate from the program and assume that the package (both specification and body) was compiled before the program.

PROGRAM 13.2-1

```
with MATH_LIB; use MATH_LIB;
package VECTORS is   --Package specification
    type RECTANGULAR is
        record
            HORZ, VERT: FLOAT;
        end record;
```

```
    type POLAR is
        record
                MODULUS, ANGLE: FLOAT;
        end record;
    function RECT_POLAR_CONVERSION(A: RECTANGULAR) return POLAR;
    function POLAR_RECT_CONVERSION(A: POLAR) return RECTANGULAR;
end VECTORS;

package body VECTORS is   --Package implementation
    PI: constant FLOAT:= 3.141593;
            --This local constant is not accessible to the program that utilizes
            --package VECTORS but is accessible to the package body
function RECT_POLAR_CONVERSION(A: RECTANGULAR) return POLAR is
                B: POLAR;
        QUADRANT: INTEGER;
                R: FLOAT;
begin
    B.MODULUS:= SQRT(A.HORZ*A.HORZ + A.VERT*A.VERT);
    --We determine what quadrant the angle is in
    if (A.HORZ>0.0) and (A.VERT>0.0) then
        QUADRANT:=1;
    elsif (A.HORZ<0.0) and (A.VERT>0.0) then
        QUADRANT:=2;
    elsif (A.HORZ<0.0) and (A.VERT<0.0) then
        QUADRANT:=3;
    elsif (A.HORZ>0.0) and (A.VERT<0.0) then
        QUADRANT:=4;
    elsif (A.HORZ=0.0) then
        if A.VERT>0.0 then
                QUADRANT:=5;
        elsif A.VERT<0.0 then
                QUADRANT:=6;
        elsif A.VERT=0.0 then
                QUADRANT:=9;
        end if;
    elsif (A.VERT=0.0) then
        if A.HORZ>0.0 then
                QUADRANT:=7;
        elsif A.HORZ<0.0 then
                QUADRANT:=8;
        elsif A.HORZ=0.0 then
                QUADRANT:=9;
        end if;
    end if;
```

```
     if A.HORZ /= 0.0 then
          R:= abs(ARCTAN(A.VERT/A.HORZ));
     end if;
     case QUADRANT is
          when 1 => B.ANGLE:= R;
          when 2 => B.ANGLE:= PI/2.0-R;
          when 3 => B.ANGLE:= PI/2.0+R;
          when 4 => B.ANGLE:= -R;
          when 5 => B.ANGLE:= PI/2.0;        --Vector on positive vertical axis
          when 6 => B.ANGLE:= -PI/2.0;       --Vector on negative vert. axis
          when 7 => B.ANGLE:= 0.0;           --Vector on positive horz. axis
          when 8 => B.ANGLE:= -PI;           --Vector on negative horz. axis
          when 9 => B.ANGLE:= 0.0;           --Vector has no magnitude
     end case;
     return B;
end RECT_VERT_CONVERSION;

function POLAR_RECT_CONVERSION(A: POLAR) return RECTANGULAR is
     B: RECTANGULAR;
begin
     B.HORZ:=  A.MODULUS * COS(A.ANGLE);
     B.VERT:=  A.MODULUS * SIN(A.ANGLE);
     return B;
end POLAR_RECT_CONVERSION;

end VECTORS;
```

Program 13.2-2 uses the package VECTORS.

PROGRAM 13.2-2

```
with VECTORS, TEXT_IO; use VECTORS, TEXT_IO;
     --Makes the package VECTORS available to this program
procedure VECTOR_MANIPULATIONS is
     E: RECTANGULAR;   --This data structure defined within package VECTORS
     F: POLAR;              --This data structure defined within package VECTORS
     T: FLOAT;
begin
     put("Enter the horizontal component of a vector:  ");
     get(T);
     E.HORZ:= T;
     put_line("  ");
     put("Enter the vertical component of a vector:  ");
     get(T);
     E.VERT:= T;
     F:= RECT_POLAR_CONVERSION(E);
```

```
        put_line(" ");
        T:= F.MODULUS;
        put("The modulus of the vector is ");
        put(T);
        put_line(" ");
        T:= F.ANGLE;
        put("The angle (in radians) of the vector is ");
        put(T);
end VECTOR_MANIPULATIONS;
```

In Program 13.2-1 the package VECTORS specifies two data structures (i.e., records RECTANGULAR and POLAR) as well as two subprograms (i.e., functions RECT_POLAR_CONVERSION and POLAR_RECT_CONVERSION). Only the data structures and formal subprogram parameters necessary to interface the package with the outside world (i.e., the user's program) are given in the package specification. The local variable PI and the implementation details of subprograms RECT_POLAR_CONVERSION and POLAR _RECT_CONVERSION are hidden from the package user. These implementation details may be changed without affecting VECTOR_MANIPULATIONS, provided the package specification has not been altered. As illustrated in Program 13.2-1, the headings for the two subprograms must appear again in the package body. In general the body of a package is defined as follows.

```
package body USER_DEFINED_NAME is
        --Local data types and objects not accessible to package user
        --Local subprograms not accessible to package user
        --Subprograms accessible to user and declared in the
        --Specification part of the package
end USER_DEFINED_NAME;
```

Variables that are declared either in a package specification or in body retain their value between subprogram calls in the package.

13.3 PRIVATE DATA TYPES

Not only may a package hide the implementation details of subprograms from the user, it may deny access to data structures defined in the package. To accomplish this requires the use of private data types.

Private data types are implemented by splitting the package specification into two parts, visible and private (hidden). Several private types may be declared in the same package specification. Private data types are declared as follows.

type USER_DEFINED_NAME_1 **is private**;
type USER_DEFINED_NAME_2 **is private**;
  --Other types are defined
private
  --This is the private part of the package specification and must occur last
type USER_DEFINED_NAME_1 **is**
  --Description of data type
type USER_DEFINED_NAME_2 **is**
  --Description of data type

For private data types, the operations of assignment and testing for both equality and inequality are available (as they are for any data type except limited private, which is defined later) in the program that uses the package.

We illustrate the use of private data types in Program 13.3-1 by reworking Program 13.2-1. The data structures RECTANGULAR and POLAR, which were part of the visible portion of the package VECTORS, are hidden in Program 13.3-1. The user can declare a variable to be of type RECTANGULAR or of type POLAR but cannot access or input either the horizontal or the vertical components of the vector. This follows because the detailed specification of the private data structure is off limits to the user. To allow the user the ability to either create a vector or access components of a vector we add several subprograms to the procedure VECTOR_MANIPULATIONS contained in Program 13.2-1.

PROGRAM 13.3-1

with MATH_LIB; **use** MATH_LIB;
package VECTORS **is** --Package specification
  type RECTANGULAR **is private**;
  type POLAR **is private**;
  function RECT_POLAR_CONVERSION(A: RECTANGULAR) **return** POLAR;
  function POLAR_RECT_CONVERSION(A: POLAR) **return** RECTANGULAR;
  function HORZ_VECT(A: RECTANGULAR) **return** FLOAT;
  function VERT_VECT(A: RECTANGULAR) **return** FLOAT;
  function MODULUS_VECT(A: POLAR) **return** FLOAT;
  function ANGLE_VECT(A: POLAR) **return** FLOAT;
  procedure CREATE_RECT(A,B: **in** FLOAT; C: **out** RECTANGULAR);
  procedure CREATE_POLAR(A,B: **in** FLOAT; C: **out** POLAR);
private
  type RECTANGULAR **is**
    record
      HORZ, VERT: FLOAT;
    end record;

```
      type POLAR is
         record
                  MODULUS, ANGLE: FLOAT;
         end record;
end VECTORS;

package body VECTORS is   --Package implementation
      PI: constant FLOAT:= 3.141593;
            --This local constant is not accessible to the program that utilizes
            --package VECTORS but is accessible to the package body
function HORZ_VECT(A: RECTANGULAR) return FLOAT is
begin
      return A.HORZ;
end HORZ_VECT;

function VERT_VECT(A: RECTANGULAR) return FLOAT is
begin
      return A.VERT;
end VERT_VECT;

function MODULUS_VECT(A: POLAR) return FLOAT is
begin
      return A.MODULUS;
end MODULUS_VECT;

function ANGLE_VECT(A: POLAR) return FLOAT is
begin
      return A.ANGLE;
end ANGLE_VECT;

procedure CREATE_RECT(A,B: in FLOAT; C: out RECTANGULAR) is
begin
      C.HORZ:= A;
      C.VERT:= B;
end CREATE_RECT;

procedure CREATE_POLAR(A,B: in FLOAT; C: out POLAR) is
begin
      C.MODULUS:= A;
      C.ANGLE:= B;
end CREATE_POLAR;
```

```
function RECT_POLAR_CONVERSION(A: RECTANGULAR) return POLAR is
          B: POLAR;
     QUADRANT: INTEGER;
          R: FLOAT;
begin
     B.MODULUS:= SQRT(A.HORZ*A.HORZ + A.VERT*A.VERT);
     --We determine what quadrant the angle is in
     if (A.HORZ>0.0) and (A.VERT>0.0) then
          QUADRANT:=1;
     elsif (A.HORZ<0.0) and (A.VERT>0.0) then
          QUADRANT:=2;
     elsif (A.HORZ<0.0) and (A.VERT<0.0) then
          QUADRANT:=3;
     elsif (A.HORZ>0.0) and (A.VERT<0.0) then
          QUADRANT:=4;
     elsif (A.HORZ=0.0) then
          if A.VERT>0.0 then
               QUADRANT:=5;
          elsif A.VERT<0.0 then
               QUADRANT:=6;
          elsif A.VERT=0.0 then
               QUADRANT:=9;
          end if;
     elsif (A.VERT=0.0) then
          if A.HORZ>0.0 then
               QUADRANT:=7;
          elsif A.HORZ<0.0 then
               QUADRANT:=8;
          elsif A.HORZ=0.0 then
               QUADRANT:=9;
          end if;
     end if;
     if A.HORZ /= 0.0 then
          R:= A.VERT/A.HORZ;
     end if;
     case QUADRANT is
          when 1 => B.ANGLE:= ARCTAN(R);
          when 2 => B.ANGLE:= PI/2.0 - abs(ARCTAN(R));
          when 3 => B.ANGLE:= PI/2.0 + abs(ARCTAN(R));
          when 4 => B.ANGLE:= -abs(ARCTAN(R));
          when 5 => B.ANGLE:= PI/2.0;
          when 6 => B.ANGLE:= -PI/2.0;
          when 7 => B.ANGLE:= 0.0;
          when 8 => B.ANGLE:= -PI;
          when 9 => B.ANGLE:= 0.0;
     end case;
```

     return B;
end RECT_VERT_CONVERSION;

function POLAR_RECT_CONVERSION(A: POLAR) **return** RECTANGULAR **is**
     B: RECTANGULAR;
begin
     B.HORZ:= A.MODULUS * COS(A.ANGLE);
     B.VERT:= A.MODULUS * SIN(A.ANGLE);
     return B;
end VERT_RECT_CONVERSION;

end VECTORS;

Program 13.3-2 uses package VECTORS, defined above.

PROGRAM 13.3-2

with VECTORS, TEXT_IO; **use** VECTORS, TEXT_IO;
procedure VECTOR_MANIPULATIONS_MODIFIED **is**
       E: RECTANGULAR;
       F: POLAR;
    T1,T2,T: FLOAT;

begin
     put("Enter the horizontal component of a vector: ");
     get(T1);
     put_line(" ");
     put("Enter the vertical component of a vector: ");
     get(T2);
     CREATE_RECT(T1,T2,E);
     F:= RECT_POLAR_CONVERSION(E);
     put_line(" ");
     T:= MODULUS_VECT(F);
     put("The modulus of the vector is ");
     put(T);
     put_line(" ");
     T:= ANGLE_VECT(F);
     put("The angle (in radians) of the vector is ");
     put(T);
end VECTOR_MANIPULATIONS_MODIFIED;

    If types RECTANGULAR and POLAR had been declared to be local to
the package body, the user would not know of their existence and would not be
able to provide an interface to the subprograms. Also the subprograms that

define a formal parameter in terms of RECTANGULAR or POLAR would have to be redefined without the use of these record types.

Have you seen the differences between Programs 13.2-1 and 13.3-1? In Program 13.3-1, components cannot be directly assigned to a vector. The subprogram CREATE_RECT or CREATE_POLAR must be used for the purpose named. Also the horizontal, vertical, modulus, or angle components of vectors cannot be accessed directly. The subprograms HORZ_VECT, VERT_VECT, MODULUS_VECT, or ANGLE_VECT must be used. If these four subprograms were not provided in the package VECTORS, the user would not be able to access these vector components.

By denying the user access to the details of data types RECTANGULAR and POLAR, the implementation details of subprograms such as HORZ_ VERT or MODULUS_VECT could be changed without requiring changes or recompilation in any host program that uses the package.

13.4 LIMITED PRIVATE DATA TYPES

If a data type is declared to be "limited private", the available operations in the program that uses the package are further restricted. The restrictions on limited private data types are the following.

1. Functions cannot return a variable declared to be of limited private type.
2. Constants of a limited private type cannot be defined.
3. Formal parameters of limited private type in a subprogram cannot have default values.
4. Variable declarations cannot include initialization.
5. There are no operations predefined on limited private types. That is, the usual equality testing and assignment are not defined.

The syntax for limited private declarations is as follows.

```
type USER_DEFINED_NAME is limited private;
      --Other type definitions
private
      type USER_DEFINED_NAME is
          --Description of type
```

We illustrate the use of the limited private data types in Program 13.4-1.

PROGRAM 13.4-1

```
with TEXT_IO; use TEXT_IO;
procedure ILLUSTRATE_LIMITED_PRIVATE_DATA_TYPES is

package ILLUSTRATION is
      type SECURE is limited private;
      procedure SECURITY(A: out SECURE);
      private
      type SECURE is
            record
                  INFO: INTEGER;
            end record;
end ILLUSTRATION;

package body ILLUSTRATION is

procedure SECURITY(A: out SECURE) is
begin
      A.INFO:= 5;
end SECURITY;

end ILLUSTRATION;

use ILLUSTRATION;
      C,D: SECURE;
begin   --Main program
      SECURITY(C);
      SECURITY(D);
      --if C=D then          This operation is illegal, since C and D are declared
      --put("Hurray!");      to be of a limited private type and equality testing is
      --else                 not defined
      --put("Boo!");
      --end if;
end ILLUSTRATE_LIMITED_PRIVATE_DATA_TYPES;
```

We could, if we wish, define a special equality operator for the SECURE data type. In fact, limited private types might be most often defined in cases when one wishes to redefine the meaning of equality testing for objects of a given type. In such a case, one would create an overloaded "=" function that defines the special type of equality desired. The "=" operator cannot be overloaded for any type other than limited private type.

13.5   ILLUSTRATIVE ADA PROGRAMS

In this section we present practical illustrations of the power and utility of packages. Some of the programs are reworked versions of earlier programs and some are new.

13.5.1 Linear Systems Package: A Partial Rework of Program 7.8-2

Program 13.5-1 gives the package LINEAR_SYSTEMS. This package is followed by two programs that use it. We assume that the package is separately compiled.

PROGRAM 13.5-1

```
with TEXT_IO; use TEXT_IO;
package LINEAR_SYSTEMS is
        MAXSIZE: constant INTEGER:=50;
        subtype INDEX is INTEGER range 1..MAXSIZE;
        type RMATRIX is array (INDEX, INDEX) of FLOAT;
        type RARRAY is array (INDEX) of FLOAT;
        type IARRAY is array (INDEX) of INTEGER;
        procedure LU_FACTOR(N: in INTEGER; A: in out RMATRIX);
        procedure SOLVE(N: in INTEGER; A: in RMATRIX; C: in RARRAY;
                    X: out RARRAY);
        procedure MATRIX_INVERSE(N: INTEGER: A: in out RMATRIX;
                        B: out RMATRIX);
end LINEAR_SYSTEMS;

package body LINEAR_SYSTEMS is
        SUB: IARRAY;
        SINGULAR: exception;   ——This exception is hidden from the user

        procedure LU_FACTOR(N: in INTEGER: A: in out RMATRIX) is
                    INDX,J: INTEGER;
            PIVOT,MAX,AB,T: FLOAT;
        begin   ——LU_FACTOR
            if N > MAXSIZE then
                    put_line(" ");
                    put("Can solve up to only ");
                    put(MAXSIZE);
                    put_line(" simultaneous equations.");
                    put_line(" ");
            else
                    for I in 1..N loop
                            SUB(I):=I;   ——We initialize subscript array
                    end loop;
```

```
    for K in 1..N−1 loop
        MAX:=0.0;
        for I in K..N loop
            T:= A(SUB(I),K);
            AB:= abs(T);
            if AB > MAX then
                MAX:=AB;
                INDX:=I;
            end if;
        end loop;
        if MAX <= 1.0E−7 then
            raise SINGULAR;
        end if;
        J:= SUB(K);
        SUB(K):= SUB(INDX);
        SUB(INDX):= J;
        PIVOT:= A(SUB(K),K);
        for I in K+1..N loop
            A(SUB(I),K):= −A(SUB(I),K)/PIVOT;
            for J in K+1..N loop
                A(SUB(I),J):= A(SUB(I),J) +
                A(SUB(I),K)*A(SUB(K),J);
            end loop;
    end loop;
end loop;
for I in 1..N loop
        if A(SUB(I),I) = 0.0 then
            raise SINGULAR;
        end if;
    end loop;
end if;
exception when SINGUALR=>
    put_line(" ");   put_line(" ");
    put_line("The matrix of coefficients is singular");
    put_line(" ");
    put_line("Cannot continue processing");
    put_line(" ");
end LU_FACTOR;
```

```
    procedure SOLVE(N: in INTEGER; A: in RMATRIX; C: in RARRAY;
                    X: out RARRAY) is
begin
    if N=1 then
            X(1):= C(1)/A(1,1);
    else
            X(1):= C(SUB(1));
            for K in 2..N loop
                X(K):= C(SUB(K));
                for I in 1..K−1 loop
                    X(K):= X(K) + A(SUB(K),I)*X(I);
                end loop;
            end loop;
            X(N):= X(N)/A(SUB(N),N);
            for K in reverse 1..N−1 loop
                for I in K+1..N loop
                    X(K):= X(K) − A(SUB(K),I)*X(I);
                end loop;
                X(K):= X(K)/A(SUB(K),K);
            end loop;
    end if;
end SOLVE;

    procedure MATRIX_INVERSE(N: INTEGER; A: in out RMATRIX;
                            B: out RMATRIX) is
        X,E: RARRAY;
        SUB: IARRAY;
begin   −−MATRIX_INVERSE
        LU_FACTOR(N,A);   −−The matrix A will be changed by this
                          −−procedure
        for I in 1..N loop
            for J in 1..N loop
                E(J):= 0.0;
            end loop;
            E(I):= 1.0;
            SOLVE(N,A,E,X);
            for J in 1..N loop
                B(J,I):= X(J);
            end loop;
        end loop;
end MATRIX_INVERSE;

end LINEAR_SYSTEMS;
```

We use package **LINEAR_SYSTEMS** in Program 13.5-2 to solve a system of linear equations.

PROGRAM 13.5-2

```ada
with LINEAR_SYSTEMS, TEXT_IO; use LINEAR_SYSTEMS, TEXT_IO;
procedure SIMULTANEOUS_EQUATIONS is
        SIZE: INTEGER;
          A: RMATRIX;
        X,B: RARRAY;
          T: FLOAT;

procedure MESSAGE is
begin
        put_line("We solve N simultaneous equations of the form");
        put_line(" ");
        put_line("                  A*X=B");
        put_line(" ");
        put_line("where A is an n × n matrix of coefficients and B");
        put_line("is a column vector of coefficients.");
        put_line(" ");
end MESSAGE;

procedure INPUT is
begin
        put("Enter the number of equations to be solved: ");
        get(SIZE);
        if SIZE > MAXSIZE then
                put_line(" ");
                put("Cannot solve more than ");
                put(MAXSIZE);
                put_line(" equations.");
                put_line(" ");
                INPUT;
        end if;
        put_line(" ");
        for I in 1..SIZE loop
                for J in 1..SIZE loop
                        put("Enter A(");
                        put(I);
                        put(",");
                        put(J);
                        put("): ");
                        get(T);
                        A(I,J):= T;
                end loop;
        end loop;
```

```
        put_line(" ");
        for K in 1..SIZE loop
                put("Enter B(");   put(K);   put("): ");
                get(T);
                B(K):= T;
        end loop;
end INPUT;

procedure OUTPUT is
        T: FLOAT;
begin
        put_line(" ");
        put_line("The solution");
        put_line("--------");
        for I in 1..SIZE loop
                T:= X(I);
                put(T);
                put_line(" ");
        end loop;
end OUTPUT;

begin   --SIMULTANEOUS_EQUATIONS
        MESSAGE;
        INPUT;
        --The matrix A will be changed by LU_FACTOR
        LU_FACTOR(SIZE,A);
        SOLVE(SIZE,A,B,X);
        OUTPUT;
end SIMULTANEOUS_EQUATIONS;
```

We use package LINEAR_SYSTEMS in Program 13.5-3 to calculate the inverse of a matrix.

PROGRAM 13.5-3

```
with LINEAR_SYSTEMS, TEXT_IO; use LINEAR_SYSTEMS, TEXT_IO;
procedure MATRIX_INVERSION is
        SIZE: INTEGER;
        G,INV: RMATRIX;
            T: FLOAT;

procedure MESSAGE is
```

```
begin
      put_line("                    Matrix Inversion"),
      put_line("                    —————————");
      put_line(" ");
end MESSAGE;

procedure INPUT(SIZE: out INTEGER; A: out RMATRIX) is
      T: FLOAT;
begin
      put("Enter the number of rows or columns in the matrix: ");
      get(SIZE);
      if SIZE > MAXSIZE then
            put_line(" ");
            put("Cannot invert more than a ");
            put(MAXSIZE);
            put(" × ");
            put(MAXSIZE);
            put(" matrix.");
            put_line(" ");
            INPUT(SIZE,A);
            ——A subprogram may recursively call itself; see Chapter 12
      else
            put_line(" ");
            for I in 1..SIZE loop
                  for J in 1..SIZE loop
                        put("Enter A(");
                        put(I);
                        put(",");
                        put(J);
                        put("): ");
                        get(T);
                        A(I,J):= T;
                  end loop;
            end loop;
            put_line(" ");
      end if;
end INPUT;

procedure OUTPUT is
      T: FLOAT;
```

```
begin
     put_line(" ");
     put_line("The solution");
     put_line("--------");
     for I in 1..SIZE loop
          for J in 1..SIZE loop
                    T:= INV(I,J);
                    put("INV(");
                    put(I);
                    put(",");
                    put(J);
                    put(")=");
                    put(T);
                    put_line(" ");
          end loop;
     end loop;
end OUTPUT;

begin   --MATRIX_INVERSION
     MESSAGE;
     INPUT(SIZE,G);
     MATRIX_INVERSE(SIZE,G,INV);
     OUTPUT;
end MATRIX_INVERSION;
```

The LINEAR_SYSTEMS package is size dependent. That is, the LINEAR_SYSTEMS package will not allow one to solve a system of equations larger than 50 or to invert a matrix larger than 50 × 50. In Program 13.5-4 we rework Program 13.5-1 and remove size dependency by using unconstrained arrays and matrix attributes.

PROGRAM 13.5-4   LINEAR SYSTEMS PACKAGE WITHOUT SIZE DEPENDENCY

```
with TEXT_IO; use TEXT_IO;
package LINEAR_SYSTEMS is
     type RMATRIX is array (INTEGER range <>, INTEGER range <>) of
                         FLOAT;
     type RARRAY is array (INTEGER range <>) of FLOAT;
     type IARRAY is array (INTEGER range <>) of INTEGER;
     procedure LU_FACTOR(A: in out RMATRIX);
     procedure SOLVE(A: in RMATRIX; C: in RARRAY; X: out RARRAY);
     procedure MATRIX_INVERSE(A: in out RMATRIX; B: out RMATRIX);
end LINEAR_SYSTEMS;
```

```ada
package body LINEAR_SYSTEMS is
    SUB: IARRAY;

    procedure LU_FACTOR(A: in out RMATRIX) is
                INDX,J: INTEGER;
        PIVOT,MAX,AB,T: FLOAT;

    procedure ERROR is   --This procedure is hidden from user
    begin
        put_line(" ");
        put_line(" ");
        put_line("The matrix of coefficients is singular");
        put_line(" ");
        put_line("Cannot continue processing");
        put_line(" ");
    end ERROR;

    begin   --LU_FACTOR
        for I in 1..A'LAST(1) loop
            SUB(I):= I;   --We initialize subscript array
        end loop;
        for K in 1..A'LAST(1)-1 loop
            MAX:= 0.0;
            for I in K..A'LAST(1) loop
                T:= A(SUB(I),K);
                AB:= abs(T);
                if AB > MAX then
                    MAX:= AB;
                    INDX:= I;
                end if;
            end loop;
            if MAX <= 1.0E-7 then
                ERROR;
            end if;
            J:= SUB(K);
            SUB(K):= SUB(INDX);
            SUB(INDX):= J;
            PIVOT:= A(SUB(K),K);
            for I in K+1..A'LAST(1) loop
                A(SUB(I),K):= -A(SUB(I),K)/PIVOT;
                for J in K+1..A'LAST(1) loop
                    A(SUB(I),J):= A(SUB(I),J) +
                    A(SUB(I),K)*A(SUB(K),J);
                end loop;
            end loop;
        end loop;
```

```
        for I in 1..A'LAST(1) loop
                if A(SUB(I),I) = 0.0 then
                        ERROR;
                end if;
        end loop;
end LU_FACTOR;

procedure SOLVE(A: in RMATRIX; C: in RARRAY; X: out RARRAY) is
        K: INTEGER;
begin
        if A'LAST(1) = 1 then
                X(1):= C(1)/A(1,1);
        else
                X(1):= C(SUB(1));
                for K in 2..A'LAST(1) loop
                        X(K):= C(SUB(K));
                        for I in 1..K−1 loop
                                X(K):= X(K) + A(SUB(K),I)*X(I);
                        end loop;
                end loop;
                X(A'LAST(1)):= X(A'LAST(1))/A(SUB(A'LAST(1)),A'LAST(1));
                K:= A'LAST(1);
                loop
                        K:= K−1;
                        for I in K+1..A'LAST(1) loop
                                X(K):= X(K) − A(SUB(K),I)*X(I);
                        end loop;
                        X(K):= X(K)/A(SUB(K),K);
                        exit when K=1;
                end loop;
        end if;
end SOLVE;

procedure MATRIX_INVERSE(A: in out RMATRIX; B: out RMATRIX) is
        X,E: RARRAY;
        SUB: IARRAY;

        −−This procedure is invisible to the user

        procedure RESOLVE(A: RMATRIX; C: in out RARRAY; X: out
                          RARRAY) is
        begin
                if A'LAST(1) = 1 then
                        X(1):= C(1)/A(1,1);
                end if;
```

```
        X(1):= C(SUB(1));
        for K in 2..A'LAST(1) loop
            X(K):= C(SUB(K));
            for I in 1..K-1 loop
                X(K):= X(K) + A(SUB(K),I)*X(I);
            end loop;
        end loop;
        X(A'LAST(1)):= X(A'LAST(1)) / A(SUB(A'LAST(1)),A'LAST(1));
        for K in reverse 1..A'LAST(1)-1 loop
            for I in K+1..A'LAST(1) loop
                X(K):= X(K) - A(SUB(K),I)*X(I);
            end loop;
            X(K):= X(K)/A(SUB(K),K);
        end loop;
    end RESOLVE;

begin   --MATRIX_INVERSE
    LU_FACTOR(A);   --The matrix A will be changed by LU_FACTOR
    for I in 1..A'LAST(1) loop
        for J in 1..A'LAST(1) loop
            E(J):= 0.0;
        end loop;
        E(I):= 1.0;
        RESOLVE(A,E,X);
        for J in 1..A'LAST(1) loop
            B(J,I):= X(J);
        end loop;
    end loop;
end MATRIX_INVERSE;

end LINEAR_SYSTEMS;
```

We use the package LINEAR_SYSTEMS defined above to solve linear systems of equations. This is done in Program 13.5-5.

PROGRAM 13.5-5

```
with LINEAR_SYSTEMS, TEXT_IO; use LINEAR_SYSTEMS, TEXT_IO;
procedure SIMULTANEOUS_EQUATIONS is
        --The array RMATRIX is dimensioned by the user
        A: RMATRIX(1..75,1..75);
        X,B: RARRAY(1..75);
        S: IARRAY(1..75);   --We do not use this array but effectively dimension
                            --the unconstrained array IARRAY

        T: FLOAT;

procedure MESSAGE is
```

```
begin
      put_line("We solve N simultaneous equations of the form");
      put_line(" ");
      put_line("              A*X=B");
      put_line(" ");
      put_line("where A is an n × n matrix of coefficients and B");
      put_line("is a column vector of coefficients.");
      put_line(" ");
end MESSAGE;

procedure INPUT is
begin
      for I in 1..75 loop
            for J in 1..75 loop
                  put("Enter A(");
                  put(I);
                  put(",");
                  put(J);
                  put(") : ");
                  get(T);
                  A(I,J) := T;
            end loop;
      end loop;
      put_line(" ");
      for K in 1..75 loop
            put("Enter B(");
            put(K);
            put(") : ");
            get(T);
            B(K) :=T;
      end loop;
end INPUT;

procedure OUTPUT is
      T: FLOAT;
begin
      put_line(" ");
      put_line("The solution");
      put_line("--------");
      for I in 1..75 loop
            T:= X(I);
            put(T);
            put_line(" ");
      end loop;
end OUTPUT;
```

```
begin  --SIMULTANEOUS_EQUATIONS
      MESSAGE;
      INPUT;
      LU_FACTOR(A);  --The matrix A will be changed by LU_FACTOR
      SOLVE(A,B,X);
      OUTPUT;
end SIMULTANEOUS_EQUATIONS;
```

13.5.2 Package of Special Input/Output

A standard package for input and output is defined as part of the Ada environment. In Program 13.5-6 we develop a short package of special Pascal-like output routines. This package may then be used with any Ada program. It is frequently desirable, when writing code for output, to write a message in the form of a string in front of the variable whose value we wish to print. For example, we may wish to write out "The answer=" in front of the printed value of the variable. In the package SPECIAL_OUTPUT, any string of up to 70 characters may precede the variable whose value we wish to print. This capability is provided for floating point, integer, character, and Boolean variables.

PROGRAM 13.5-6

```
with TEXT_IO; use TEXT_IO;
procedure SPECIAL_OUTPUT is

package SPECIAL_IO is
      subtype ST is STRING(1..70);
      procedure SKIP_LINE(I: INTEGER);
      procedure WRITELN(S: ST; I: INTEGER);
      procedure WRITELN(S: ST; I: FLOAT);
      procedure WRITELN(S: ST; I: CHARACTER);
      procedure WRITELN(S: ST; I: BOOLEAN);
end SPECIAL_IO;

package body SPECIAL_IO is

procedure SKIP_LINE(I: INTEGER) is
begin
      for J in 1..I loop
            put_line(" ");
      end loop;
end SKIP_LINE;
```

```
procedure WRITELN(S: ST; I: INTEGER) is
begin
      put(S);
      put(I);
      put_line(" ");
end WRITELN;

procedure WRITELN(S: ST; I: FLOAT) is
begin
      put(S);
      put(I);
      put_line(" ");
end WRITELN;

procedure WRITELN(S: ST; I: CHARACTER) is
begin
      put(S);
      put(I);
      put_line(" ");
end WRITELN;

procedure WRITELN(S: ST; I: BOOLEAN) is
begin
      put(S);
      if I then
            put("true");
      else
            put("false");
      end if;
      put_line(" ");
end WRITELN;

end SPECIAL_IO;

use SPECIAL_IO;
      A: INTEGER;
      B: FLOAT;
      C: CHARACTER;
      D: BOOLEAN;
begin   --Main program
      A:= 1;
      B:= 1.0;
      C:= 'A';
      D:= TRUE;
      WRITELN("The answer=",A);
      WRITELN("The answer is ",B);
      WRITELN("The next character=",C);
```

```
        SKIP_LINE(5);
        WRITELN("The answer is ",D);
end SPECIAL_OUTPUT;
```

13.6 SUMMARY

- Packages are the highest level of abstraction in Ada. A package specification may consist of data declarations as well as subprograms. Variables inside a package exist between subprogram calls in the package. The body of a package may be compiled separately from its specification.

- The package specification should serve as a user's guide. Examples illustrating the use of all the subprograms defined in the package should be provided. The purpose of each subprogram, references to the algorithms used in a subprogram, and general background information should be supplied in narrative form with the package specification. All this supporting information must be in the form of comments along with the formal package specification.

- The package construct invites programmers to build software libraries. The data structures and subprograms that make up a package become software resources that can be shared by many users. We predict the growth of a large Ada "package" industry. We anticipate packages to be developed in the areas of graphics, input and output, scientific and engineering computation, word processing, business, data base management, education, and games, to name a few. Because of the total portability of Ada, system designers and software developers should, in the near future, have easy access to the highest quality software in these as well as other fields.

- The scope of the software contained in a package may be broadened to include the scope of the logical unit or units that "use" the package.

- By declaring some data types to be "private" in the specification part of a package, the user is denied access to the internal details of the data structure. The operations of testing for equality (or inequality) as well as assignment are supported for "private" data types.

- By declaring data types to be "limited private" in the specification part of a package, the user, in addition to being denied access to the internal details of the data structure, may not test for equality (or inequality) or make assignment statements using data objects declared to be of "limited private" type.

Exercises for Chapter 13

1. Write a matrix algebra package. Overload the operators "+", "−", and "*".

2. Write a package LONG_INTEGERS that allows long integers to be subtracted and multiplied.

3. Write a package that allows double precision (16 digits) addition, subtraction, multiplication, and division to be performed. *Hint.* Use some of the concepts developed in package LONG_INTEGERS.

4. Using some of the subprograms introduced in Chapter 7, write a package for sorting.

5. Write a complex number package.

6. Write a package for generating pseudo-random numbers uniformly distributed between zero and one.

7. Write a string manipulation package beginning with the subprograms defined in Program 7.8-1.

Chapter 14

TUNNEL VISION: SCOPING AND VISIBILITY

One of Ada's strengths is that its structure supports the development of large software projects. Often, teams of programmers must be able to easily interface their respective contributions to a large software project. To accomplish this, it is essential that each programmer establish a programming structure for the logical units under his or her responsibility, so that the individual's units will mesh with the overall effort.

We have already presented most of the ingredients of the Ada language that support the development of large software projects. In this chapter we take stock of these features of Ada and focus on them. We examine the logical structure of Ada programs. We discuss the relationships among the basic entities in a program.

Our concern here is with the scope and visibility of constants, variables, types, subprogram entities, and package entities. The special rules that apply to tasks and exception handling are taken up in Chapters 10 and 11, respectively.

The position or positions in a program at which a declared entity may be used depend on the visibility rule for that entity. We summarize and illustrate the visibility rules for various Ada entities.

Our interest in this chapter lies in the logical structure of Ada programs. In Chapter 16 we will be concerned with the physical structure of an Ada program; that is, compilation units.

Ada supports the following logical units: blocks (introduced in this chapter), subprograms (including the main program), packages, and tasks. For each of these logical units there may be both a specification and a body. Embedded within any logical unit may be other logical units. We examine how these logical units may be interfaced (tasks are excluded here; see Chapter 11) and thus how teams of programmers may contribute to an overall software effort.

14.1 BLOCKS

The major purpose of the Ada construct called a "block" is to hide one or more declarations external to the block.

A "block" is a section of program code located in the executable part of some logical unit (subprogram, main program, package, or task) that begins with the reserved word "declare" followed by some declarations, then the reserved word "begin", and some statements; it concludes with the reserved word "end". The "declare" statement introduces one or more declarations whose scope includes everything between the point of declaration and the "end" statement of the block. These declarations are not visible outside the boundaries of the block. The size of a block is not limited except by the memory constraints of the computer used to develop the program. Often, blocks are a relatively small structure in a program.

The syntax for constructing a block is as follows.

```
USER_DEFINED_BLOCK_NAME: declare   ——The user-defined name is optional
——Declarations
begin
      ——Executable statement(s)
end USER_DEFINED_BLOCK_NAME;
```

We illustrate with the following example.

```
HELLO: declare
        A,B,C: INTEGER;
begin
      put("Enter A: ");
      get(A);
      put_line(" ");
      put("Enter B: ");
      get(B);
      C:=A−B;
      put("C=");
      put(C);
end HELLO;
```

The variables A, B, and C are essentially local to the body of code contained between the "begin" and "end" statement of the block HELLO. If A,

B, or C were defined in the logical unit containing the block HELLO, those logical unit variables would not be visible within the block HELLO, since they occupy different memory locations and represent different variables even though they have the same name.

We further illustrate these concepts in Program 14.1-1.

PROGRAM 14.1-1

```
with TEXT_IO; use TEXT_IO;
procedure ILLUSTRATION_OF_BLOCK is
        A,B,C,D: INTEGER;
begin   --Main program
        A:=1;
        B:=2;
        C:=3;
        D:=4;
        ISOLATE: declare
                    A,B,C: INTEGER;
              begin
                    A:=-1;
                    B:=-2;
                    C:=-3;
                    put(A);          --The value -1 will be printed
                    put_line(" ");
                    put(B);          --The value -2 will be printed
                    put_line(" ");
                    put(C);          --The value -3 will be printed
                    put_line(" ");
                    put(D);          --The value 4 will be printed
                    put_line(" ");
              end ISOLATE;
        put(A);                      --The value 1 will be printed
        put_line(" ");
        put(B);                      --The value 2 will be printed
        put_line(" ");
        put(C);                      --The value 3 will be printed
        put_line(" ");
end ILLUSTRATION_OF_BLOCK;
```

From Program 14.1-1, it is evident that the "block" structure allows you to create a body of program code in which some or all of the declarations are outside the block but whose scope covers the block (e.g., global variables A, B, and C in Program 14.1-1) may be made invisible within the block.

All the identifiers that are introduced in the declarative section of a block must be distinct from one another but may of course have the same names as identifiers external to the block. The only exceptions to this are overloaded enumeration literals and subprograms, which are discussed in Section 14.6.

We now consider the consequence of nesting blocks within each other. In particular, how can variables that are hidden by a block be accessed? Program 14.1-2 provides an answer to this question and illustrates nested blocks.

PROGRAM 14.1-2

```
with TEXT_IO; use TEXT_IO;
procedure NESTED_BLOCKS is

        procedure P1 is
                A,B,C: INTEGER;
        begin
                A:=1;
                B:=2;
                C:=3;
                BLOCK_1: declare
                        A,B,C: FLOAT;
                    begin
                        A:=-1.0;
                        B:=-2.0;
                        C:=-3.0;
                        put(A);                 --The value -1.000000 is printed
                        put_line(" ");
                        put(B);                 --The value -2.000000 is printed
                        put_line(" ");
                        put(C);                 --The value -3.000000 is printed
                        put_line(" ");
                        BLOCK_2:declare
                                A,B,C:    CHARACTER;
                            begin
                                A:='F';
                                B:='U';
                                C:='N';
                                put(A);                 --The value F is printed
                                put_line(" ");
                                put(B);                 --The value U is printed
                                put_line(" ");
                                put(C);                 --The value N is printed
                                put_line("  ");
                                put(BLOCK_1.A);    --The value -1.000000
                                                   --is printed
```

```
                                   put_line(" ");
                                   put(BLOCK_1.B);   --The value -2.000000
                                                     --is printed
                                   put_line(" ");
                                   put(BLOCK_1.C);   --The value -3.000000
                                                     --is printed
                                   put_line(" ");
                                 end BLOCK_2;
                      end BLOCK_1;
             put(A);                               --The value 1 is printed
             put_line(" ");
             put(B);                               --The value 2 is printed
             put_line(" ");
             put(C);                               --The value 3 is printed
             put_line(" ");
             --put(BLOCK_2.A);                      --These statements
             --put_line(" ");                       --would be illegal
             --put(BLOCK_2.B);                      --because the
             --put_line(" ");                       --declarations within a
             --put(BLOCK_2.C);                      --block are invisible
         end P1;                                   --outside the block

begin   --Main program
     P1;
end NESTED_BLOCKS;
```

As Program 14.1-2 illustrates, the variables declared in BLOCK_1 may be accessed from within nested BLOCK_2 by using a dot notation. On the other hand, none of the variables declared either in BLOCK_1 or in BLOCK_2 may be accessed outside BLOCK_1. This follows because the scope of block variables is limited strictly to the boundaries of the given block.

The same principles of scoping and visibility that we have discussed and illustrated for block variables apply to all block declarations, namely, procedures, packages, and tasks.

14.2 SCOPE OF LABELS

A statement in an Ada program may be labeled so that it can be called in a "goto" statement. The first occurrence of a label identifier (which may be at the head of a labeled statement or in a "goto" statement) acts as a declaration of the label identifier. The scope of a label is contained within a logical unit, the unit in which the label identifier occurs.

14.3 SCOPE OF LOOP PARAMETERS

As we have seen in numerous programs introduced in earlier chapters, the scope of a loop parameter, such as "I" in "for I in 1..10 loop", consists of the body of code up to the statement "end loop". Within the scope of the loop, "I" acts as if it were declared to be a constant of the type defined by the range of the loop. It would be illegal to attempt any assignment to "I" within the scope of the loop. If the logical unit containing the loop had declared the variable "I", this variable would be invisible within the loop because it is a different "I" from the "I" of the loop.

If before terminating the loop it is necessary to know the last value that the loop parameter had, then its value must be assigned to another variable before ending the loop.

If a block is contained within a loop in which the block declares variable "I", then within the block the variable "I" is treated as a local variable decoupled from the implicitly declared loop parameter "I". This is illustrated in Program 14.3-1.

PROGRAM 14.3-1

```
with TEXT_IO; use TEXT_IO;
procedure SCOPE_OF_LOOP_PARAMETERS is
begin
      for I in 1..5 loop
            put("Outer I=");
            put(I);
            put_line(" ");
            ISOLATE: declare
                        I: INTEGER;
                  begin
                        I:=6;
                        put("Inner I=");
                        put(I);
                        put_line(" ");
                  end ISOLATE;
      end loop;
end SCOPE_OF_LOOP_PARAMETERS;
```

The output of Program 14.3-1 is:

```
OUTER I=1
 INNER I=6
OUTER I=2
 INNER I=6
```

```
OUTER I=3
 INNER I=6
OUTER I=4
 INNER I=6
OUTER I=5
 INNER I=6
```

14.4 BLOCK STRUCTURE WITH SUBPROGRAMS

A procedure or function acts in a manner similar to that of a "block." Procedures and functions differ from blocks because they have formal parameters. They are similar to a blocks insofar as they have local declarations of constants, types, variables, packages, tasks, and other subprograms.

All the formal parameters of a subprogram must be distinct from one another and from any declarations local to the subprogram. Both the formal parameters and local declarations have a scope from their point of declaration to the "end" statement of the subprogram.

Subprograms may be defined within some enclosing logical unit (in many cases this unit is the main program). All the variables external to the subprogram but whose scope covers the subprogram are visible within the subprogram, unless specifically hidden by giving a formal parameter or a local declaration the same name as the name within the enclosing logical unit.

We illustrate the scoping and visibility of subprogram formal parameters and local declarations in Program 14.4-1.

PROGRAM 14.4-1

```
with TEXT_IO; use TEXT_IO;
procedure SCOPE_AND_VISIBILITY_OF_SUBPROGRAM_ENTITIES is
      A,B,C,D: INTEGER;

      procedure OUTPUT is
      begin
            put(A);
            put_line(" ");
            put(B);
            put_line(" ");
            put(C);
            put_line(" ");
      end OUTPUT;
```

```
procedure P1 is
      A,B,C: INTEGER;

      procedure P2 is
            A,B,C: INTEGER;

            procedure OUTPUT is
            begin
                  put(A);
                  put_line(" ");
                  put(B);
                  put_line(" ");
                  put(C);
                  put_line(" ");
                  put(D);
                  put_line(" ");
            end OUTPUT;

      begin   --P2
            A:=-1;
            B:=-2;
            C:=-3;
            P2.OUTPUT;
      end P2;

begin   --P1
      A:=1;
      B:=2;
      C:=3;
      P2;
      OUTPUT;
end P1;

begin   --Main program
      A:=10;
      B:=11;
      C:=12;
      D:=13;
      P1;
      OUTPUT;
end SCOPE_AND_VISIBILITY_OF_SUBPROGRAM_ENTITIES;
```

The output of Program 14.4-1 is:

```
-1
-2
-3
```

13
10
11
12
10
11
12

The same names are used for identifiers in the main program, in subprogram P1, and in subprogram P2. When P2.OUTPUT is called in procedure P2, the only visible variables are the local P2 variables A, B, C, and the global variable D, defined to be −1, −2, −3, and 13. When OUTPUT is called in procedure P1, the only procedure OUTPUT that is visible to P1 is the first procedure OUTPUT. The entities (in this case both variables and subprograms) declared within P2 are invisible to P1 because P2 is nested within P1. The first procedure OUTPUT can only "see" the global (main program) variables A, B, and C, which have been defined to have the values 10, 11, and 12.

The isolation of local constants, types, and variables in Ada subprograms provides a natural mechanism for interfacing the work of a team of programmers. Each member of the team may define his or her own subprogram declarations without concern about the names declared by other members. Data would flow in and out of the various procedures through "in-out" parameters. All the variables in such a subprogram would be local variables. Thus a natural unit to use as the basis for the distribution of programming responsibility would be the subprogram. Each programmer would be responsible for writing one or more subprograms.

14.5   SCOPE AND VISIBILITY OF PACKAGES

Earlier sections of this chapter have demonstrated that blocks and subprograms may be used to limit the visibility of identifiers. On the other hand, packages may be used to expand the visibility of the identifiers used within them. The scope of some of the declarations in a package may extend beyond the boundaries of the package. Those declarations in the specification (or public) part of a package may be shared by many logical units that "use" the package. The declarations in the body (private part) of the package are not visible beyond the boundaries of the package.

The "use PACKAGE_NAME" construct makes available to a logical unit all of the public software resources defined in the package. These may include constants, types, variables, tasks, and subprograms.

Occasionally, there is duplication of a name given in a package and a name given in a logical unit using the package. To resolve any possible ambiguity that may result from using such a name, component selection is done. The name of the package is used, followed by a dot, followed by the entity being used in the package. We illustrate this process in Program 14.5-1.

PROGRAM 14.5-1

```
with TEXT_IO; use TEXT_IO;
procedure COMPONENT_SELECTION is

        package PROGRAMMING_RESOURCE is
            A,B,C: INTEGER:= 0;
            procedure P1(A: in out INTEGER);
        end PROGRAMMING_RESOURCE;

        package body PROGRAMMING_RESOURCE is

            procedure P1(A: in out INTEGER) is
            begin
                put(A*A);
                put_line(" ");
            end P1;

        end PROGRAMMING_RESOURCE;

A,B: INTEGER;
use PROGRAMMING_RESOURCE;
begin   --Main program
        A:=1;
        B:=2;
        C:=3;
        put(A);           --Refers to the A of the main program
        put_line(" ");
        put(B);           --Refers to the B of the main program
        put_line(" ");
        put(C);           --Refers to the C of the package
        put_line(" ");
        P1(B);
        put(PROGRAMMING_RESOURCE.A);   --Refers to the A of the package
        put_line(" ");
        put(PROGRAMMING_RESOURCE.B);   --Refers to the B of the package
        put_line(" ");
        put(PROGRAMMING_RESOURCE.C);   --Refers to the C of the package
end COMPONENT_SELECTION;
```

The output of Program 14.5-1 is:

```
1
2
3
4
0
0
3--Since C of the package has been changed to 3
```

The package PROGRAMMING_RESOURCE shares the names A and B with the main program. A reference to variables "A" or "B" in the main program must be interpreted as the "A" or "B" in the innermost unit, namely, the main program.

We illustrate this concept further in Program 14.5-2.

PROGRAM 14.5-2

```
with TEXT_IO; use TEXT_IO;
procedure MORE_COMPONENT_SELECTION is

        package WINDOW is
            type WASH is
                record
                        WATER: INTEGER;
                        BLADE: FLOAT;
                end record;
            B: WASH;
        end WINDOW;

        type WASH is
            record
                    A,B: INTEGER;
            end record;
        B: WASH;

use WINDOW;
begin   --Main program
        B.A:= 3;                    --Refers to the main program B
        B.B:= 4;                    --Refers to the main program B
        --B.WATER:= 1;              This statement would be illegal
        --B.BLADE:= 1.0;            This statement would be illegal
        WINDOW.B.WATER:= 5;     --Refers to the package B
        WINDOW.B.BLADE:= 5.0;   --Refers to the package B
end MORE_COMPONENT_SELECTION;
```

14.6 RULES FOR NAMING IDENTIFIERS

In general, identifiers must be given unique names within the same logical unit. We have already seen examples of the use of the same name for an identifier in different logical units. Now we state the conditions under which identifiers must be given unique names.

1. Components of a record type.
2. Values of an enumeration type.
3. Formal parameters, local declarations, block and loop identifiers, and statement labels introduced in a subprogram or package.

14.6.1 Identifiers in Enumeration Types

For any given enumeration type, the possible values must be distinct. Different enumeration types need not have disjoint values. That is, an enumeration value may be overloaded on two or more enumeration types.

In Program 14.6-1 we illustrate how ambiguities are removed in the case of value overloading of enumeration types.

PROGRAM 14.6-1

```
with TEXT_IO; use TEXT_IO;
procedure ENUMERATION_VALUE_OVERLOADING is
      type ONE is (A,B,C,D);
      type TWO is (C,D);
      O1,O2,O3,O4: ONE;
      T1,T2:        TWO;
begin
      O1:= A;
      O2:= B;
      O3:= ONE'(C);
      O4:= ONE'(D);
      T1:= TWO'(C);
      T2:= TWO'(D);
end ENUMERATION_VALUE_OVERLOADING;
```

In Program 14.6-1, the statement "ONE'(C)" is called a qualified statement. This is necessary because C may belong to either type ONE or type TWO.

An array that has as its index an enumeration type does not require further qualification for its index values. That is, if one or more of the values in the index is overloaded with another enumeration type, a qualified expression in refering to the array is never necessary. For example, if the type

type THREE **is array** (ONE) **of** FLOAT;
D: THREE;

is added to the declarations in Program 14.6-1, the statement "D(C):=3.5" would be legal. It would not be necessary to write "D(ONE'(C)):=3.5".

14.6.2 Overloading of Subprograms

The identifiers used to name subprograms may be overloaded, provided the formal parameter specifications differ from each other. In the standard input/output procedures, "get" and "put" are overloaded to perform input and output on different data types.

We illustrate the overloading of subprograms in Program 14.6-2.

PROGRAM 14.6-2

```
with TEXT_IO; use TEXT_IO;
procedure OVERLOADING_SUBPROGRAM_NAMES is

      A,B: FLOAT;
      C,D: INTEGER;
      procedure SAME(A: INTEGER; B: out INTEGER) is
      begin
            B:= 2*A+5;
      end SAME;

      procedure SAME(X,Y: in out FLOAT) is
            T: FLOAT;
      begin
            T:= X;
            X:= Y;
            Y:= T;
      end SAME;

begin  --Main program
      C:= 5;
      SAME(C,D);
      put(D);          --The output will be 15
      put_line(" ");
      A:= 1.0;
      B:= 1000.0;
      SAME(A,B);
      put(A);          --The output will be 1.000000e3
      put_line(" ");
      put(B);          --The output will be 1.000000
end OVERLOADING_SUBPROGRAM_NAMES;
```

In Program 14.6-2, the compiler is able to distinguish the two subprograms by their respective formal parameter signatures. The first subprogram SAME requires two integers, whereas the second subprogram SAME requires two floating point numbers.

14.7 SUMMARY

• The scope of an identifier is the portion of text in which the identifier is potentially visible.

• Identifiers may be hidden within regions of their scope by using local variables within nested units whose names are the same as those of the identifiers that are to be hidden.

• Ada allows local variables to be declared in subprograms, declare blocks, packages, and tasks.

• Subprogram names may be overloaded within a logical unit. The compiler resolves subprogram calls by examining the type and mode of parameters in the call.

• Data types, constants, subprograms, and variables that are declared within a subprogram, task, or declare block may not be accessed outside the logical unit.

Exercises for Chapter 14

1. If a program declares

   type A **is** (C,D,E,F);
   type B **is** (F,G,H);

   how would you distinguish the value "F" in type A from "F" in type B? Give an example.

2. What would be the output of the following Ada program?

   procedure QUESTION_2 **is**

   A: INTEGER;
   B: FLOAT;
   package BLUE_RIBBON **is**
       A,B: INTEGER:=4;
   end BLUE_RIBBON;

   procedure SIMILAR(A: INTEGER) **is**
   begin

```
            put_line("Hello everybody.");
        end SIMILAR;

    procedure SIMILAR(A: FLOAT) is
    begin
            put_line("Goodbye everybody.");
        end SIMILAR;

    procedure FIRST is
            A,B: INTEGER;
    begin
            A:=1;
            B:=2;
        end FIRST;

    begin    --Main program
            SIMILAR(B);
            SIMILAR(A);
            A:=-100;
            B:=-0.0;
          FIRST;
            put(A);
            put_line(" ");
            put(B);
            put_line(" ");
            put(BLUE_RIBBON.B);
    end QUESTION_2;
```

3. Identify the errors in the following program. Attempt to correct each error
   that you identify.

```
procedure TRY_TO_FIND_ALL_THE_ERRORS is
        C: GROCERY;
        D: BASKET;
package HANDLE is
        type GROCERY is (BAG, PRICE, INFLATION);
        type BASKET is (WOOL, WEAVE, PRICE);
        A,B: FLOAT;
end HANDLE;

procedure SMART(C: out GROCERY) is
begin
        C:= INFLATION;
end SMART;

procedure SMART(C: out GROCERY) is
begin
```

```
        C:= BAG;
end SMART;

begin   --Main program
        C:= BAG;
        D:= PRICE;
        SMART(C);
end TRY_TO_FIND_ALL_THE_ERRORS;
```

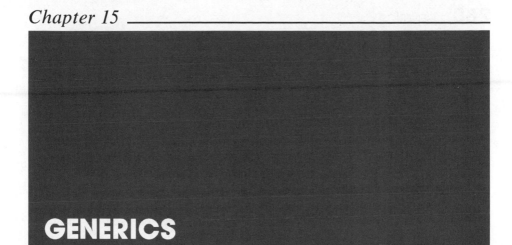

Chapter 15

GENERICS

In this chapter we describe the generic capabilities that are available in Ada. This facility of the language permits the development of general purpose subprograms and packages that perform computations on abstract data types.

The subprograms and packages that we have presented so far are restricted in that they require data objects and/or parameters to be of a specified type. For example, Program 7.7-1 gives a sorting algorithm for sorting an array of integers. If we were to change the problem to sorting an array of names, real numbers, or records, we would have to rewrite the procedure to take account of the new data type even though the underlying algorithm would remain the same. Generic program units permit the programmer to develop subprograms and packages that provide computational resources for abstract data types. So, for example, a generic sorting procedure implements a sorting algorithm independent of the type of objects that are to be sorted.

15.1 HAVE SOME GIN, ERIC?
WHAT IS A GENERIC?

Before formally defining generics as implemented in Ada, we informally present two illustrative examples.

The exchange of two objects is required in many calculations. In Program 7.7-1 we defined the following procedure to exchange two integers.

```
procedure EXCHANGE(X,Y: in out INTEGER) is
     TEMP: INTEGER;
begin
     TEMP:= X;
     X:= Y;
     Y:= TEMP;
end EXCHANGE;
```

If we wanted to exchange two objects that were not of type integer, we would have to rewrite this procedure for the new data type. The generic feature of Ada permits us to write this procedure so that it can be used for different data types. The generic version is:

```
generic
     type OBJECT is private;
     procedure EXCHANGE(X,Y: in out OBJECT);

procedure EXCHANGE(X,Y: in out OBJECT) is
     TEMP: OBJECT;
begin
     TEMP:= X;
     X:= Y;
     Y:= TEMP;
end EXCHANGE;
```

The first three lines are called a generic declaration. They specify that the procedure EXCHANGE is generic and that OBJECT is a generic parameter. For a generic subprogram, we must give the specification and the body separately. Since OBJECT is declared to be of private type, neither its structure nor its set of possible values is required to be known by the generic procedure. This generic program unit can be thought of as a template that defines operations on data items of an abstract type named OBJECT.

The generic subprogram EXCHANGE cannot be called directly. This is because the compiler has not yet established memory allocation for a variable of type OBJECT. The generic template EXCHANGE may be converted to an actual executable subprogram by a process called "instantiation" (we must create an "instance" of the subprogram). Look "instantiation" up in your dictionary! As two examples, we may define

```
procedure INTERCHANGE is new EXCHANGE(FLOAT);
```

or

procedure CHANGE **is new** EXCHANGE(OBJECT=>WEATHER_RECORD);

where WEATHER_RECORD is a data type previously defined. In both cases, we have instantiated generic procedure EXCHANGE and have created executable subprograms that may be used in the ordinary way.

Is generic instantiation a mechanism for text substitution? The answer is no! The scope of variables that cover the generic unit and are external to the generic unit are exported to the location at which the generic unit is instantiated. If text substitution were implied by generic instantiation, this would not be the case.

Our second example is designed to illustrate a generic package. In Program 10.8-1, we introduced operations on an important and simple data structure, the stack. We now present a generic package for stack manipulation. In this package we assume that all items in a stack are of the same type but that different stacks may have different types. We may instantiate the generic package to create new stacks for different type items. For each stack, we define procedures to push new items on the stack and to pop existing items off the stack.

We define two exceptions, STACK_OVERFLOW and STACK_UN-DERFLOW, which will propagate back to the user of the generic package so that the desired manipulation can be performed when the exceptions occur. We make the exception declarations global to the generic package so that all instantiations may use the same exceptions. If this were not done—if, for example, the exceptions were defined within the generic package—then each instantiation would produce a distinct exception. Since exceptions cannot be overloaded, we would be forced to use the dot notation to distinguish them. Indeed, this subtle matter of locating the exception declarations illustrates that nonlocal identifiers to a generic unit act according to where the generic unit is placed, not according to where the instantiation is placed!

PROGRAM 15.1-1

```
STACK_OVERFLOW, STACK_UNDERFLOW: exception;
generic
      SIZE: POSITIVE;
      type ELEMENT is private;

package STACK is
      procedure PUSH(ITEM: in ELEMENT);
      procedure POP(ITEM: in out ELEMENT);
end STACK;
```

```
package body STACK is
     SPACE: array (1..SIZE) of ELEMENT;
     TOP: INTEGER range 0..SIZE:= 0;

procedure PUSH (ITEM: in ELEMENT) is
begin
     if TOP = SIZE then
          raise STACK_OVERFLOW;
     end if;
     TOP:= TOP+1;
     SPACE(TOP):= ITEM;
end PUSH;

procedure POP (ITEM: in out ELEMENT) is
begin
     if TOP = 0 then
          raise STACK_UNDERFLOW;
     end if;
     ITEM:= SPACE(TOP);
     TOP:= TOP-1;
end POP;

end STACK;
```

It is not legal to use the binding mode "out" for any parameter in a generic subprogram. Thus procedure POP, above, uses an "in out" parameter.

This generic stack package can be instantiated to create a stack of integers with a maximum stack size of 25 as follows.

```
package INTEGER_STACK is new STACK(SIZE=> 25, ELEMENT=> INTEGER);
```

To create a stack of Boolean elements with a maximum size of 50, the following instantiation could be used.

```
package BOOLEAN_STACK is new STACK(50, BOOLEAN);
```

Finally, to create a stack of floating point numbers with a maximum size of 15, we could use the following instantiation.

```
package FLOAT_STACK is new STACK(15, FLOAT);
```

We now present a program for performing stack operations on an integer stack and a floating point number stack that uses the generic package STACK.

PROGRAM 15.1-2

```
with STACK, TEXT_IO; use STACK, TEXT_IO;
procedure GENERIC_STACKS is
      YES:            BOOLEAN;
      INTEGER_ITEM: INTEGER;
      FLOAT_ITEM:    FLOAT;
      ERROR:         exception;

package INTEGER_STACK is new STACK(SIZE => 25, ELEMENT => INTEGER);

package FLOAT_STACK is new STACK(50, ELEMENT => FLOAT);

use INTEGER_STACK,FLOAT_STACK;
procedure MENU is
      STACK_CHOICE, OPERATION_CHOICE: INTEGER;
begin
      put_line(" ");
      put("Which stack? ");
      put_line(" ");
      put_line(" ");
      put_line("1--> Integer stack");
      put_line(" ");
      put_line("2--> Boolean stack");
      put_line(" ");
      put("Enter appropriate choice: ");
      get(STACK_CHOICE);
      put_line(" ");
      put_line(" ");
      put("Which stack operation? ");
      put_line(" ");
      put_line(" ");
      put_line("1--> Add item to stack");
      put_line(" ");
      put_line("2--> Remove item from stack");
      put_line(" ");
      put_line("3--> Exit from program");
      put_line(" ");
      put("Enter appropriate choice: ");
      get(OPERATION_CHOICE);
      case OPERATION_CHOICE is
            when 1 =>
                  put("Enter item: ");
                  case STACK_CHOICE is
                        when 1 =>
                              get(INTEGER_ITEM);
```

```
                              PUSH(INTEGER_ITEM);      --The compiler
                              put_line(" ");           --determines the correct
                                                       --PUSH to use by the
                                                       --parameter
                                                       --INTEGER_ITEM
                    when 2 =>
                            get(FLOAT_ITEM);
                            PUSH(FLOAT_ITEM);
                            put_line(" ");
                    end case;
            when 2 =>
                    put("Item removed: ");
                    case STACK_CHOICE is
                            when 1 =>
                                    POP(INTEGER_ITEM);
                                    put(INTEGER_ITEM);
                                    put_line(" ");
                            when 2 =>
                                    POP(FLOAT_ITEM);
                                    put(FLOAT_ITEM);
                                    put_line(" ");
                    end case;
            when 3 =>
                    YES:= TRUE;
            when others =>
                    raise ERROR;
    end case;
    exception
            when STACK_UNDERFLOW => put_line("Stack underflow!");
            when STACK_OVERFLOW  => put_line("Stack overflow!");
            when ERROR           => put_line("Input error!");
end MENU;

begin   --Main program
    YES:= FALSE;
    loop
            MENU;
            exit when YES;
    end loop;
end GENERIC_STACKS;
```

15.2 GENERIC DECLARATIONS

15.2.1 Generic Type Parameters

Generic types may be one of the following; the meanings are given next to the types.

private ——Any data type with equality testing and assignment
——defined.

limited private ——Any data type with equality testing and assignment
——not defined.

(<>) ——A discrete type; enumeration, character or integer.

range <> ——An integer. Predefined integer operations assumed.

digits <> ——Floating point type. Predefined operations assumed.

delta <> ——Fixed point type. Predefined operations assumed.

As an example, consider the following.

```
generic
      type X is (<>);                              ——X is a discrete type
      function SUCCESSOR(OBJECT: X) return X;      ——Generic subprograms must
                                                   ——be specified separately

function SUCCESSOR(OBJECT: X) return X is
begin
      if X=X'LAST then
              return X'FIRST;
      else
              return X'SUCC(OBJECT);
      end if;
end SUCCESSOR;
```

Discrete types have the attributes FIRST, LAST, and SUCC. In the example above, since X is declared to be of generic type (<>), it follows that we may use the attributes indicated in the example.

If we have

type COLOR **is** (RED,BLUE,GREEN,ORANGE,BLACK,WHITE);

declared, we could define

function NEXT_COLOR **is new** SUCCESSOR(COLOR **range** BLUE..BLACK);

Then NEXT_COLOR(BLACK) would be BLUE.

We complete this section by explaining the meaning and restrictions imposed by the use of the various generic type parameters.

type T **is** (<>);
>   ——This restricts the type T to have actual parameter values of discrete type.
>   ——All attributes and operations for discrete types may be used in the generic
>   ——unit.

type T **is range** <>;
>   ——This names T as an integer type that is a smaller class than discrete type.
>   ——This permits stronger assumptions to be made in the generic unit
>   ——concerning the properties possessed by the generic parameters. For
>   ——example, we may assume that "*", "+", and other operations defined for
>   ——integer types are available in the generic unit.

type T **is private**;
>   ——This names T as the class of all types for which assignment and equality
>   ——are defined. This is a larger class than either of the preceding two but
>   ——now we can make no assumptions about the properties of the parameters
>   ——in the generic unit. We cannot assume the availability of addition,
>   ——multiplication, the successor attribute, and so on.

type T **is limited private**;
>   ——This names T as the class of all types with no operations available except
>   ——those defined by subprograms declared in the program unit.

type T **is delta** <>;
>   ——This names T as a fixed point type. All operations for fixed point type can
>   ——be assumed to be available for data objects of type T.

type T **is digits** <>;
>   ——This names T to be a floating point type with all floating point operations
>   ——and attributes available in the unit for data objects of type T.

15.2.2 Generic Subprogram Parameters

Subprograms can also serve as generic parameters. We must use the reserved word "with" as a prefix to the subprogram name if we wish to use the subprogram as a parameter. We list below the various generic subprogram parameter declaration types, with short explanations.

generic
>   **with** SUBPROGRAM_SPECIFICATION
>   >   ——The generic parameter is a subprogram. The full specification of the
>   >   ——subprogram must be given.

with SUBPROGRAM_SPECIFICATION **is** USER_DEFINED_NAME;
--The generic parameter is a subprogram with a default of USER
--DEFINED NAME. During instantiation (see Section 15.3) if the
--generic parameter is not specified, the default subprogram, USER
--DEFINED NAME, is used.
with SUBPROGRAM_SPECIFICATION **is** <>;
--The generic parameter is a subprogram that defaults to a
--subprogram with the same name during instantiation.

The subprogram supplied as the actual parameter (during instantiation) must have parameters and a result (if any) of the same type, binding mode(s), and constraints as the generic subprogram parameter. The parameter names and default values (if any) of the actual parameter do not matter.

As an example, suppose we wish to write a subprogram for finding the approximate maximum value of a function $F(x)$ between the real values A and B. Our strategy is to evaluate the function $F(x)$ over 10000 points, equally spaced between A and B, and then print out the maximum value. Unfortunately, we do not know the function $F(x)$ in advance. But we can define a generic subprogram parameter $F(x)$, and during instantiation, actually define the function whose maximum value we desire. Consider the following generic unit.

```
generic
      with function F(X: FLOAT) return FLOAT;
      function MAXIMUM_VALUE(LOWER_LIMIT,UPPER_LIMIT:FLOAT) return
          FLOAT;

function MAXIMUM_VALUE(LOWER_LIMIT,UPPER_LIMIT:FLOAT) return
      FLOAT is MAX,INCR,Z: FLOAT;
begin
      if LOWER_LIMIT>=UPPER_LIMIT
          then
                  put_line("Illegal parameters in MAXIMUM_VALUE");
                  return 0.0;
          else
                  INCR:=(UPPER_LIMIT-LOWER_LIMIT)/10000.0;
                  Z:=LOWER_LIMIT;
                  MAX:=F(Z);   --The generic parameter, F, is used
                  Z:=Z+INCR;
                  while Z<=UPPER_LIMIT loop
                      if F(Z)>MAX
                              then MAX:=F(Z);
                      end if;
```

```
                              Z:=Z+INCR;
                      end loop;
                      return MAX;
              end if;
end MAXIMUM_VALUE;
```

We now use this generic unit in the following program segment.

```
function CRAZY(W: FLOAT) return FLOAT is
begin
        return W*W/3.5+2.6*W*W*W;
end CRAZY;
```

```
function BANANA(U: FLOAT) return FLOAT is
begin
        return SIN(U)/(3.4+U*U)−4.0*U;
end BANANA;
```

```
function MAX_BANANA is new MAXIMUM_VALUE(BANANA);
function MAX_CRAZY is new MAXIMUM_VALUE(CRAZY);
−−We have created two instantiations of MAXIMUM_VALUE by transferring the
−−subprogram parameters BANANA and CRAZY, the names of two actual
−−subprograms, to the generic procedure MAXIMUM_VALUE
```

```
T: FLOAT;
put("The maximum value of CRAZY between 0 and 10 is :");
T:=MAX_CRAZY(0.0,10.0);
put(T);
put("The maximum value of BANANA between −2 and 5 is :");
T:=MAX_BANANA(−2.0,5.0);
put(T);
```

Next we present additional examples of how to employ generic subprogram parameters in an Ada program.

15.3 GENERIC INSTANTIATION

A generic unit is not a normal program unit because it cannot be called directly. Rather, it is a computational template that must be instantiated or created at compile time. This process involves compile time substitutions for the generic parameters (whether they be types or subprogram parameters). An instance of the generic subprogram can then be called in the usual way during the execution of the program. To instantiate a generic unit, a generic instantiation must appear in the declaration part of the procedure that requires use of the generic subprogram. Some examples of generic instantiation for the generic procedure defined in Section 15.1 are:

procedure SWAP_REAL **is new** EXCHANGE(FLOAT);
procedure SWAP_VECTOR **is new** EXCHANGE(VECTOR);
procedure SWAP_NAMES **is new** EXCHANGE(STRING);

where types VECTOR and STRING have been appropriately defined.

To use these instances of EXCHANGE, we would call them in the usual manner. For example,

SWAP_REAL(X,Y);
SWAP_NAMES(NAME1,NAME2);
SWAP_VECTOR(U,V);

Operations that are used within the body of a generic subprogram should be specified by other generic parameters. As an example, we consider the simple operation of squaring an arbitrary element that can be defined by the generic procedure.

generic
        type ELEM **is private**;
        with function "*"(X,Y: ELEM) **return** ELEM **is** <>;

function SQUARING(Z: ELEM) **return** ELEM **is**
begin
        return Z*Z;
end SQUARING;

Since we have not placed any restrictions on the type ELEM, it is not possible to perform the operation Z*Z unless the specification of subprogram "*" is provided explicitly as a generic parameter. It is quite possible that many instantiations of SQUARING will involve "*" for integers, floating point numbers, or other types for which "*" is predefined or defined, but it is also possible that an instantiation of SQUARING might involve types for which "*" is not implicitly defined.

Let us now consider several instantiations of this generic function. For example,

function SQUARE **is new** SQUARING(INTEGER, "*");

In this case the operation "*" is defined as

function "*"(X,Y: INTEGER) **return** INTEGER;

which is normal integer multiplication. We can therefore instantiate the generic procedure SQUARING using the default for "*" as follows.

function SQUARE **is new** SQUARING(INTEGER);

Another instantiation of SQUARING for type FLOAT is:

function SQUARE **is new** SQUARING(FLOAT);

Suppose we wish to instantiate this function for vectors. We assume that type VECTOR has been previously declared, say, for example, by

type VECTOR **is array** (1..1000) **of** FLOAT;

and that we then instantiate SQUARING using the following instantiation.

function SQUARE **is new** SQUARING(VECTOR, "*");

In this case the operation "*" for objects of type VECTOR needs to be specified. We may choose to define it as follows.

```
function "*" (A,B: VECTOR) return VECTOR is
     C: VECTOR;
begin
     for I in FIRST'VECTOR..LAST'VECTOR loop
          C(I):= A(I)*B(I);
     end loop;
     return C;
end "*";
```

If we did not wish to overload the operator "*" for vector multiplication, we could rename the function, say VEC_MULT, and then instantiate SQUARING by:

function SQUARE **is new** SQUARING(VECTOR, VEC_MULT);

In the preceding examples we have instantiated SQUARING several times with different parameters but have used the same function name, SQUARE. We have in essence overloaded the function name SQUARE in much the same way that we overloaded various operators in Section 7.6.

Generic parameters can also be specified by explicit association between the formal generic parameter name and the parameter value. For example,

function SQUARE **is new** SQUARING(ELEM => VECTOR, "*" => VEC_MULT);

and

function SQUARE_FLOAT **is new** SQUARING(ELEM => FLOAT);

are legal instantiations of SQUARING, illustrating explicit generic parameter association.

The next example shows a generic program structure that involves a type parameter in the generic clause, but the subprogram within the generic unit uses a comparison operator that may not be defined for the type. In this example, we define a function with two input parameters of an abstract type that returns the maximum of the two input parameters. The generic function may be defined as follows.

```
generic
      type T is private;
      with function "<"(U,V: T) return T is <>;
      function MAX(X,Y: T) return T;
function MAX(X,Y: T) return T is
begin
      if X < Y then
            return Y;
      else
            return X;
      end if;
end MAX;
```

Examples of instantiation of this function are:

```
function MAX_INTEGER is new MAX(INTEGER);
      ——Default "<" is used

function MAX_STRING is new MAX(STRING);
      ——"<" for type STRING is available in Ada
```

```
function MAX_VECTOR is new MAX(VECTOR);
     ——"<" for type VECTOR must be available
```

The program unit that is obtained after generic instantiation can be viewed as the function MAX with T replaced by the corresponding specified parameter. Thus, for example, MAX_VECTOR is the function MAX with T replaced by VECTOR. However, the comparison "<" in the definition of the function may not be defined for the type VECTOR unless it is specified by the programmer. The generic function defining MAX permits arguments of arbitrary type. The only operations that we can assume to be available for private types are assignment and comparison for equality.

15.4 EXAMPLES OF GENERIC SUBPROGRAMS

15.4.1 An Adaptive Generic Integration Subprogram

Our first nontrivial example involves adaptive integration, where the function to be integrated is a generic subprogram parameter. This example is a rework of Program 12.9-1. We have changed the original procedure INTEGRAL to a function subprogram and have defined the user function name as a generic parameter.

```
ERROR: exception;   ——Scope of exception covers the generic unit
generic
     with function F(X: FLOAT) return FLOAT is <>;
     ——Defaults to F if calling parameter is not specified
     function INTEGRAL(A,B: FLOAT) return FLOAT;

function INTEGRAL(A,B: FLOAT) return FLOAT is
     X1: constant FLOAT:= 0.5773502692;
     ANST, ANSR, ANSL, ANS1, ANS2, EPS: FLOAT;

procedure INT(A,B: FLOAT; AN: out FLOAT) is
     ——We use two-point Gauss
     C,D,S: FLOAT;
begin
     C:= (B−A)/2.0;
     D:= (B+A)/2.0;
     S:= F(−C*X1+D)+F(C*X1+D);
     AN:= C*S;
end INT;
```

```
begin  --INTEGRAL
     If A > B then
          raise ERROR;
     end if;
     EPS:= 2.0E-5;   --The user may wish to change this relative error bound
     ANS:= 0.0;
     INT(A,B,ANST);
     INT(A,(A+B)/2.0,ANSL);
     INT((A+B)/2.0,B,ANSR);
     if abs(ANST-ANSL-ANSR) > EPS*abs(ANST) then
          INTEGRAL(A,(A+B)/2.0,ANS1);
          ANS:= ANS+ANS1;
          INTEGRAL((A+B)/2.0,B,ANS2);
          ANS:= ANS+ANS2;
     else
          ANS:= ANS+ANST;
     end if;
     return ANS;
exception
     when ERROR =>
          put("The lower limit of integration must be less than the upper!");
end INTEGRAL;
```

The preceding function to integrate $F(X)$ from A to B could be part of a mathematical subroutine library. To use this generic function you would have to instantiate it for the specific function to be integrated. We give a specific example in Program 15.4-1.

PROGRAM 15.4-1

```
procedure GENERIC_FUNCTIONS is
     AREA: FLOAT;

function MY_F(X: FLOAT) return FLOAT is
begin
     if X <= 1.0 then
          return 1.0/X;
     if (X > 1.0) and (X <= 5.0) then
          return 1.0 + SQRT(X-1.0);
     if (X > 5.0) and (X <= 7.0) then
          return (X-5.0)**2;
end MY_F;
```

```
function F(X: FLOAT) returns FLOAT is
begin
        return 1.0/(1.0+X*X)
end F;

function INTEGRATE_SIN is new INTEGRAL(F => SIN);
        ——The explicit specification is not necessary here

function INTEGRATE_MY_F is new INTEGRAL(MY_F);
        ——Note that we cannot instantiate INTEGRAL with MY_F until MY_F has been
        ——defined and is accessible

function INTEGRATE is new INTEGRAL;
        ——Defaults to F for the input function to integrate

begin
        AREA:= INTEGRATE_SIN(0.0,1.0);
        put("Integral of sin from 0 to 1 is equal to ");
        put(AREA);
        put_line(" ");
        put_line(" ");
        AREA:= INTEGRATE_MY_F(0.1,7.0);
        put("Integral of function from 0 to 7 is equal to ");
        put(AREA);
        put_line(" ");
        put_line(" ");
        AREA:= INTEGRATE(0.0,2.0);
        put("Integral of F from 0 to 2 is equal to ");
        put(AREA);
end GENERIC_FUNCTIONS;
```

15.4.2 A Generic Sorting Algorithm

The following generic sorting procedure uses the exchange sort algorithm,
which was introduced in Programs 5.1-2 and 7.7-1. The generic feature of this
procedure is that it permits the sorting of elements of an abstract type.

PROGRAM 15.4-2

```
generic
        type OBJECT is private;
        type OBJECT_ARRAY is array (1..10000) of OBJECT;
        with ">"(U,V: OBJECT) return BOOLEAN is <>;
        procedure SORT(SIZE: INTEGER; A: OBJECT_ARRAY);
```

```
procedure SORT(SIZE: INTEGER; A: OBJECT_ARRAY) is
     POS,INDEX: INTEGER;

function MAX(A: OBJECT_ARRAY; UPPER: INTEGER) return INTEGER is
     MAX:       OBJECT;
     POSITION: INTEGER;
begin
     MAX:= A(1);
     POSITION:= 1;
     for I in 2..UPPER loop
          if A(I) > MAX then   ––This comparison needs to be defined for type
                               ––OBJECT
               MAX:= A(I);
               POSITION:= I;
          end if;
     end loop;
     return POSITION;
end MAX;

procedure EXCHANGE(X,Y: INTEGER) is
     TEMP: OBJECT;
begin
     TEMP:= A(X);
     A(Y):= A(Y);
     A(X):= TEMP;
end EXCHANGE;

begin
     INDEX:=SIZE+1;
     loop
          INDEX:= INDEX-1;
          POS:= MAX(A,INDEX);
          EXCHANGE(POS,INDEX);
          exIt when INDEX=2;
     end loop;
end SORT;
```

Program 15.4-3 gives an example of a procedure that uses the generic sorting algorithm to sort an array of words and an array of floating point numbers.

PROGRAM 15.4-3

```
procedure GENERIC_SORT is
      MAXSIZE: INTEGER:=100;
      type WORD is array (1..10) of CHARACTER;
      WORD_ARRAY is array (1..MAXSIZE) of WORD;
      FLOAT_ARRAY is array (1..MAXSIZE) of FLOAT;
      ERROR: exception;
function "<" (A,B: WORD) return BOOLEAN is
      T: BOOLEAN;
begin
      T:= FALSE;
      for I in 1..10 loop
            if A(I) < B(I) then
                  T:= TRUE;
                  exit;
            end if;
            if A(I) > B(I) then
                  exit
            end if;
      end loop;
      return T;   --In the event that A equals B, T will be FALSE
end "<";

WORD_SORT is new SORT(OBJECT => WORD, OBJECT_ARRAY =>
                  WORD_ARRAY);

FLOAT_SORT is new SORT(FLOAT, FLOAT_ARRAY);

begin   --Main program
      put(" Enter the number of words to be sorted:");
      get(SIZE);
      if SIZE>MAXSIZE then
            raise ERROR;
      end if;
      INPUT(SIZE,WORD_ARRAY);
            --We assume this routine to input words is available
      WORD_SORT(SIZE, WORD_ARRAY);
      OUTPUT(SIZE, WORD_ARRAY);
            --We assume this routine to output the sorted words is available
      put_line(" ");
      put(" Enter the number of floating point numbers to be sorted:");
      get(SIZE);
      if SIZE > MAXSIZE then
            raise ERROR;
      end if;
```

```
INPUT_FLOAT(SIZE,FLOAT_ARRAY);
        --We assume this routine to input floating point numbers is available
FLOAT_SORT(SIZE, FLOAT_ARRAY);
OUTPUT_FLOAT(SIZE, FLOAT_ARRAY);
        --We assume this routine to output the sorted floating point numbers
        --is available
exception
    when ERROR =>
            put_line(" ");
            put("The maximum number of items permitted is ");
            put(MAXSIZE);
            put_line(" ");
end GENERIC_SORT;
```

15.5 SUMMARY

- The generic does not simply create text replacement. Nonlocal parameters act according to the position of the generic unit, not the position of the instantiation of the generic unit.
- Generic parameters of modes ''in'' and ''in out'' are permitted in generic units.
- All expressions that are defined in a generic unit are evaluated as far as possible at the time of generic declaration.
- Generic subprograms may not be overloaded. The instantiations of generic subprograms may be overloaded.
- Generic units give the programmer the opportunity to implement algorithms on totally abstract data objects and subprograms.

Exercises for Chapter 15

1. Define generic procedures for INPUT and OUTPUT of arrays of abstract type. Then show how to instantiate them in Program 15.4-3.
2. Write a generic function EQUALITY to define the equality of two arrays of a limited private type.
3. Rewrite Program 15.4-2 so that the maximum size of the array is not specified in advance (e.g., 10000).
4. Write a generic complex number package. Declare

    type REAL **is digits** <>;

    Then instantiate the package by passing your own floating point type to the package.

5. Write the body of the generic package SETS, using the following package specification.

```
generic
      type ELEMENT is (<>);
package SETS is
      type SET is private;
      type GROUP is array(POSITIVE range <>) of ELEMENT;
      function CREATE_SET(Z: GROUP) return SET;
      function CREATE_SET(Z: ELEMENT) return SET;
      function UNION(X,Y: SET) return SET;
      function INTERSECTION(X,Y: SET) return SET;
      function DIFFERENCE(X,Y: SET) return SET;
      function "<" (Z: ELEMENT; Y: SET) return BOOLEAN;   --Inclusion
      function "<="(X,Y: SET) return BOOLEAN;             --Contains
      function ACCESS_SET(X: SET) return GROUP;
      function SIZE(Z: SET) return INTEGER;               --Number
                                                          --of elements
      NULL_SET,FULL_SET: constant SET;
      private
            type SET is array (ELEMENT) of BOOLEAN;
            NULL_SET: constant SET:=(SET'RANGE=>FALSE);
            FULL_SET: constant SET:=(SET'RANGE=>TRUE);
end SETS;
```

6. Define:

type DAYS_OF_WEEK **is** (MON,TUES,WED,THURS,FRI,SAT,SUN);

Using the package defined in Exercise 5, write a program that instantiates this package as follows.

package DAYS **is new** SETS(DAYS_OF_WEEK);

Your program should use every subprogram defined in the generic package.

Chapter 16

COMPILATION UNITS; SOFTWARE ENGINEERING

In Chapter 14 we discussed the structure of Ada programs in terms of logical program units. Now we treat the physical structure of Ada programs in terms of compilation units. A compilation unit is defined as a block of code that may be separately compiled.

Ada offers the programmer a variety of compilation unit options, which are discussed in detail below. Some compilation units are designed to serve as software resources that will be available to other programs. These are called library units. Other compilation units are designed to implement software facilities specified in parent units. These are called compilation subunits.

A compilation unit should contain a listing of the software facilities assumed to be available to it (if any), a specification of the software facilities provided by the unit, and perhaps the implementation details of the facilities provided. The latter feature may be omitted, since the implementation details can be provided in a separate compilation unit.

An Ada program may typically contain many separately compiled units linked together at compile time. Consistency checks are performed at compile time to ensure that the various compilation units are compatible. Compilation units may use the facilities of other units as well as introduce their own new facilities. Because of this, the order in which units are compiled is very important. We discuss this matter in detail in Section 16.3.

We now consider the construction of Ada programs from a collection of compilation units, the interfacing of these units, and the order in which they must be compiled.

16.1. COMPILATION UNITS

We have defined a compilation unit as a block of code that may be compiled separately. Every compilation unit (henceforth called *unit*) defines a context that determines the scope of its declarations. For example, library units may have declarations whose scope covers many nested compilation units. A subunit has another unit, its parent unit, which creates a context for the subunit. Tasks may only be subunits. Subprograms and packages may be library units or subunits. Subunits of the same parent must have distinct names. Library units must have distinct names.

A library unit may be either the declaration or body (or of course both) of a subprogram or a package. It may not be a task. A subunit may be the body of a subprogram, package, or task.

The context of a subunit is determined by its parent unit. This parent unit (which may be a subunit of some other parent unit) must provide a body stub at its outermost declarative level for each of its subunits. For example, consider the following.

```
procedure PARENT_UNIT is
     type COLOR is (RED, GREEN, BLUE);
     C: COLOR;

procedure P1(A,B: INTEGER) is separate;                    --Stub

function F1(D,E: FLOAT; C: COLOR) return BOOLEAN is separate;   --Stub

package C1 is
     type JAPANESE_CAR is (HONDA, SUBARU, DATSUN, TOYOTA);
     function F2(I: INTEGER) return INTEGER;
end C1;

package body C1 is separate;                               --Stub

begin   --PARENT_UNIT
     --Executable code that may use P1, F1, and C1
end PARENT_UNIT;
```

Here the subprogram PARENT_UNIT contains the complete specification of the subunits P1 and F1, in this case subprograms. All the formal parameters of P1 and F1 must be given in the body stub. The body of package C1 is specified as a subunit. The specification of the package C1 is not optional. If the body of C1 is to be a subunit (compiled separately), the specification of this package must be included in the declarative section of the parent unit.

The subunits P1, F1, and C1 may use variable C (declared in the parent unit to be COLOR) as if they had been defined as logical units contained within PARENT_UNIT. That is, the scope of variable C covers the subunits P1, F1, and C1. How can P1, F1, or the body of package C1 be separately compiled and use a reference to the variable C if the variable C is not declared in these subunits? Each of the subunits P1, F1, or C1 must begin with the declaration: "separate (PARENT_UNIT)". For example, the subunit F1 may be written as follows.

```
separate (PARENT_UNIT)   --Note no semicolon
function F1(D, E: FLOAT; C: COLOR) return BOOLEAN is
begin
      if (D >= E) and (C = RED) then
            return TRUE;
      else
            return FALSE;
      end if;
end F1;
```

The declaration "separate (PARENT_UNIT)" causes the compiler to make available to F1 all the declarations that would normally be available if F1 were defined in the parent unit at the position of the stub.

The default context available to all compilation units is the package STANDARD (given in Appendix B).

16.2 FACILITIES ACCESSIBLE TO A COMPILATION UNIT

By using the "with" prefix, all the public declarations in library units that are referenced by the "with" statement may be brought into scope for the unit being compiled. For example, suppose we wish to create a unit called NEW_UNIT. In this separate compilation unit we wish to use the software facilities of library units L1 and L2. We accomplish this as follows.

```
with L1,L2;
procedure NEW_UNIT is
     --Declarations and body of subprogram
end NEW_UNIT;
```

Suppose that L1 is a separately compiled package. If we wish to limit the exposure of L1's public declarations to some subprogram within NEW_UNIT, we may start that nested subprogram with the clause "use L1". Then this nested subprogram within NEW_UNIT may access any of the public declarations of unit L1.

We have seen earlier that subunits have access to all the facilities defined in the parent unit above the body specification for the subunit.

We illustrate the concepts above in Program 16.2-1. All separate compilation units are shown between pairs of lines.

PROGRAM 16.2-1

```
package L1 is
      type IARRAY is array (1..1000) of INTEGER;
      procedure MOVE(K: in out IARRAY; I: INTEGER);
end L1;

package body L1 is
      procedure MOVE(K: in out IARRAY; I: INTEGER) is
      begin
            for J in I..999 loop
                  K(J):= K(J+1);
            end loop;
      end MOVE;
end L1;
```

```
with L1; use L1;
procedure OUTER is
      G: IARRAY;
      --We are using a software resource defined in library unit L1
      POS: INTEGER;

procedure INPUT(H: out IARRAY) is separate;
--The body stub of a subunit

begin   --OUTER
      INPUT(G);
      --We input G and determine the position in G to delete
      MOVE(G,POS);
      --We delete the array element at POS and move the other elements down
end OUTER;
```

```
with TEXT_IO; use TEXT_IO;
separate (OUTER)
--This links this subunit to its parent unit
procedure INPUT(H:out IARRAY) is
```

begin
      ––We input the array H
      for I **in** 1 . . 1000 **loop**
            put("Enter element ");
            put(I);
            put(": ");
            get(H(I));
            put_line(" ");
      end loop;
      put("Enter the position of the element to delete: ");
      get(POS);
      ––The variable POS is accessible to this unit
      put_line(" ");
end INPUT;

In the subunit INPUT, the variable POS is accessible because it is declared above the body stub for INPUT in the parent unit OUTER. The data type IARRAY and the subprogram MOVE are two facilities contained in the library unit L1 that are being used by the unit OUTER.

Next we consider the order in which separate units should be compiled.

16.3 ORDER OF COMPILATION

The basic principle for determining the order of compilation is the following.

> *If one compilation unit uses the facilities of another compilation unit, the unit providing the facilities must be compiled before the unit using the facilities.*

The location of "with" clauses greatly influences the order of compilation. Any unit referred to in a "with" clause, must be compiled before the unit containing the "with" clause.

A parent unit must always be compiled before any of its subunits. Of course, before the parent unit can be "run," all its subunits must be compiled and available.

In Program 16.2-1, the required order of compilation would be: L1, OUTER, INPUT. L1 is required as a resource for OUTER thus must be compiled before OUTER. OUTER is required as a resource for INPUT and thus must be compiled before INPUT.

16.4 ORDER OF RECOMPILATION

During the cycle of software maintenance, algorithms contained in a program may be updated and improved, errors may be detected in portions of a program and corrected, or programming techniques may be modified to reflect new conditions. How does Ada support software maintenance?

A change in an Ada program (here we define an Ada program as the total collection of compilation units) may require parts or all of the individual compilation units to be recompiled. The following basic principle determines which, if any, units must be recompiled.

If a change is made in a compilation unit, any units in the program that would normally be compiled after the changed unit must be recompiled. Units that would normally be compiled before the changed unit do not have to be recompiled unless an interface to the changed unit has occurred.

One consequence of this principle is that one may improve an algorithm that is compiled as a subunit without having to recompile the parent unit. In fact, a person using the parent unit might not even be aware of the changes that have been made in the subunit. Only if the interface to the subunit (the body stub) is changed must the parent unit be recompiled.

As an example, in Program 16.2-1, if the subunit INPUT were changed in detail (without changing the stub in OUTER), the unit OUTER would not have to be recompiled. At run time the new, separately compiled subunit INPUT would be linked to the parent unit OUTER. On the other hand, if the package body L1 were changed, the units OUTER and INPUT would have to be recompiled, since OUTER depends on L1, and INPUT depends on OUTER.

16.5 COMMENTS ON SOFTWARE ENGINEERING

Top-down and bottom-up methodologies are commonly used in software design. Ada supports both these design strategies.

In bottom-up design, the programmer(s) constructs subprograms (parent units and associated subunits that implement the specifications contained in the parent units) that are later woven together into packages. The details of all subunits are completed before writing the code for the parent units that call the subunits. Each parent unit and its associated subunits are fully tested before building to the package level.

In top-down design, the general specifications for packages and their associated subprograms are created before any implementation details are provided. The program is then developed by a process of refinement. Parent units that specify (through a stub) other subunits are written before the subunits are implemented. That is, the software facilities assumed in the body stub are utilized in the parent unit before the subunit is written. Top-down design has been used successfully in the development of large programs, particularly programs that involve several programmers.

In practice both top-down and bottom-up design procedures are used in parallel. The top-down approach allows the design team clean problem definition, whereas the bottom-up approach forces the definition of important implementation details that may influence later program development.

16.6   A PROGRAMMING EXAMPLE

We conclude this chapter by reconsidering Program 13.5-1. All the separate compilation units are indicated by lines between the various units.

PROGRAM 16.6-1

```
package LINEAR_SYSTEMS is
      MAXSIZE: constant INTEGER:=50;
      subtype INDEX is INTEGER range 1..MAXSIZE;
      type RMATRIX is array (INDEX,INDEX) of FLOAT;
      type RARRAY is array (INDEX) of FLOAT;
      type IARRAY is array (INDEX) of INTEGER;
      procedure LU_FACTOR(N: in INTEGER; A: in out RMATRIX);
      procedure SOLVE(N: in INTEGER; A: in RMATRIX; C: in RARRAY;
                  X: out RARRAY);
      procedure MATRIX_INVERSE(N: INTEGER; A: in out RMATRIX;
                  B: out RMATRIX);
end LINEAR_SYSTEMS;
```

```
with TEXT_IO; use TEXT_IO;
package body LINEAR_SYSTEMS is
      SUB: IARRAY;
      SINGULAR: exception;   ––This exception is hidden from the user

      procedure LU_FACTOR(N: in INTEGER; A: in out RMATRIX) is
            INDX,J: INTEGER;
            PIVOT,MAX,AB,T: FLOAT;
      begin   ––LU_FACTOR
            if N > MAXSIZE then
                  put_line(" ");
                  put("Can solve up to only ");
                  put(MAXSIZE);
                  put_line(" simultaneous equations.");
                  put_line(" ");
```

```
        else
            for I in 1..N loop
                SUB(I):= I;   --We initialize subscript array
            end loop;
            for K in 1..N-1 loop
                MAX:= 0.0;
                for I in K..N loop
                    T:= A(SUB(I),K);
                    AB:= absS(T);
                    if AB > MAX then
                        MAX:= AB;
                        INDX:= I;
                    end if;
                end loop;
                if MAX <= 1.0E-7 then
                    raise SINGULAR;
                end if;
                J:= SUB(K);
                SUB(K) := SUB(INDX);
                SUB(INDX) := J;
                PIVOT:= A(SUB(K),K);
                for I in K+1..N loop
                    A(SUB(I),K) := -A(SUB(I),K)/PIVOT;
                    for J in K+1..N loop
                        A(SUB(I),J) := A(SUB(I),J) +
                        A(SUB(I),K)*A(SUB(K),J);
                    end loop;
                end loop;
            end loop;
            for I in 1..N loop
                if A(SUB(I),I) = 0.0 then
                    raise SINGULAR;
                end if;
            end loop;
        end if;
exception
    when SINGULAR =>
        put_line(" ");
        put_line(" ");
        put_line("The matrix of coefficients is singular");
        put_line(" ");
        put_line("Cannot continue processing");
        put_line(" ");
end LU_FACTOR;
```

```ada
procedure SOLVE(N: in INTEGER; A: in RMATRIX; C: in RARRAY;
                X: out RARRAY) is
begin
      if N=1 then
            X(1) := C(1)/A(1,1);
      else
            X(1) := C(SUB(1));
            for K in 2..N loop
                  X(K) := C(SUB(K));
                  for I in 1..K-1 loop
                        X(K) := X(K) + A(SUB(K),I)*X(I);
                  end loop;
            end loop;
            X(N) := X(N)/A(SUB(N),N);
            for K in reverse 1..N-1 loop
                  for I in K+1..N loop
                        X(K) := X(K) - A(SUB(K),I)*X(I);
                  end loop;
                  X(K) := X(K)/A(SUB(K),K);
            end loop;
      end if;
end SOLVE;

procedure MATRIX_INVERSE(N: INTEGER; A: in out RMATRIX;
                         B: out RMATRIX) is
      X,E: RARRAY;
      SUB: IARRAY;
      SUB: IARRAY;
begin   --MATRIX_INVERSE
      LU_FACTOR(N,A);   --The matrix A will be changed by LU_FACTOR
      for I in 1..N loop
            for J in 1..N loop
                  E(J) := 0.0;
            end loop;
            E(I) := 1.0;
            SOLVE(N,A,E,X);
            for J in 1..N loop
                  B(J,I) := X(J);
            end loop;
      end loop;
end MATRIX_INVERSE;

end LINEAR_SYSTEMS;
```

```
with LINEAR_SYSTEMS, TEXT_IO; use LINEAR_SYSTEMS, TEXT_IO;
procedure SIMULTANEOUS_EQUATIONS is
      SIZE: INTEGER;
      A:    RMATRIX;
      X,B:  RARRAY;
      T:    FLOAT;

procedure INPUT is separate;
procedure MESSAGE is separate;
procedure OUTPUT is separate;

begin  --SIMULTANEOUS_EQUATIONS
      MESSAGE;
      INPUT;
      LU_FACTOR(SIZE,A);   --The matrix A will be changed by LU_FACTOR
      SOLVE(SIZE,A,B,X);
      OUTPUT;
end SIMULTANEOUS_EQUATIONS;
```

```
separate (SIMULTANEOUS_EQUATIONS)
procedure MESSAGE is
begin
      put_line("We solve N simultaneous equations of the form");
      put_line(" ");
      put_line("                 A*X=B");
      put_line(" ");
      put_line("where A is an n × n matrix of coefficients and B");
      put_line("is a column vector of coefficients.");
      put_line(" ");
end MESSAGE;
```

```
separate (SIMULTANEOUS_EQUATIONS)
procedure INPUT is
begin
      put("Enter the number of equations to be solved: ");
      get(SIZE);
      if SIZE > MAXSIZE then
            put_line(" ");
            put("Cannot solve more than ");
            put(MAXSIZE);
            put_line(" equations.");
            put_line(" ");
            INPUT;
      end if;
```

```
        put_line(" ");
        for I in 1..SIZE loop
            for J in 1..SIZE loop
                    put("Enter A(");
                    put(I);
                    put(",");
                    put(J);
                    put(") : ");
                    get(T);
                    A(I,J) := T;
            end loop;
        end loop;
        put_line(" ");
        for K in 1..SIZE loop
                put("Enter B(");
                put(K);
                put(") : ");
                get(T);
                B(K) := T;
        end loop;
end INPUT;
```

```
separate (SIMULTANEOUS_EQUATIONS)
procedure OUTPUT is
        T: FLOAT;
begin
        put_line(" ");
        put_line("The solution");
        put_line("----------");
        for I in 1..SIZE loop
                T:= X(I);
                put(T);
                put_line(" ");
        end loop;
end OUTPUT;
```

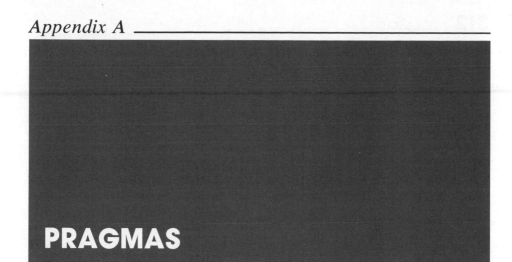

PRAGMAS

Pragmas are compiler instructions that are included in an Ada program. The format is:

pragma (PRAGMA NAME and [argument]);

A pragma may have an argument that is an identifier, a string or a number or numbers. The following are the predefined pragmas in Ada.

Controlled   The argument is an access type. It must appear in the same declaration section as the access type definition. It specifies that automatic storage reclamation should not be performed for objects of the access type except upon leaving the scope of the access type definition.

Elaborate   The single argument is the name of a secondary unit. This pragma specifies that the named secondary unit must be elaborated before the given compilation unit.

Inline   Subprogram names are the arguments. This pragma must appear in the same declarative part as the named subprograms. It specifies that the subprogram bodies should be expanded inline at each call.

Interface   Takes a language name and subprogram name as arguments. It must appear after the subprogram specification in the same declaration section or in the same package specification. It specifies that the body of the subprogram is written in the given language.

311

List Takes ON or OFF as an argument. This pragma may appear anywhere. It specifies that listing of the program unit is to be continued or suspended until a LIST pragma is given with the opposite argument.

Memory Size An integer is the argument. This pragma can appear only before a library unit. It establishes the required number of storage units in memory.

Optimize TIME or SPACE is the argument. This pragma can appear only in a declarative part, and it applies to the block or body enclosing the declarative part. It specifies whether time or space is the primary optimization criterion.

Pack A record or array type name is the argument. The pragma is located before the record or array type. It specifies that storage minimization should be the main criterion when selecting the representation of the given type.

Page This pragma has no argument. It specifies that the program text which follows the pragma should start on a new page of the compiler listing.

Priority Takes an expression as argument. It must appear in a task specification or the outermost declarative part of a main program. It specifies the priority of the task or the main program.

Storage Unit An integer is the argument. This pragma can appear only before a library unit. It establishes the number of bits per storage unit.

Suppress Takes a compiler check name and optionally also either an object name or a type name as arguments. It must appear in the declaration part of a unit (block or body). It specifies that the designated compiler check is to be suppressed in the unit. In the absence of the optional name, the pragma applies to all operations within the unit. Otherwise, its effect is restricted to operations on the named object or to operations on objects of the named type.

System-Name Takes a name as argument. This pragma is only allowed at the start of compilation. It establishes the name of the object machine.

PACKAGE TEXT IO

```
with IO_EXCEPTIONS;
package TEXT_IO is

        type FILE_TYPE is limited private;

        type FILE_MODE is (IN_FILE, OUT_FILE);

        type COUNT is range 0..implementation defined;

        subtype POSITIVE_COUNT is COUNT range 1..COUNT'LAST;

        subtype FIELD        is INTEGER range 0..implementation defined;
        subtype NUMBER_BASE is INTEGER range 2..16;

        UNBOUNDED : constant COUNT := 0;   --line and page length

        --File Management

        procedure CREATE(FILE : in out FILE_TYPE;
                    MODE : in FILE_MODE := OUT_FILE;
                    NAME : in STRING    := '''';
                    FORM : in STRING    := '''');

        procedure OPEN(FILE : in out FILE_TYPE;
                    MODE : in FILE_MODE;
                    NAME : in STRING;
                    FORM : in STRING := '''');
```

```
procedure CLOSE   (FILE : in out FILE_TYPE);
procedure DELETE  (FILE : in out FILE_TYPE);
procedure RESET   (FILE : in out FILE_TYPE; MODE : in FILE_MODE);
procedure RESET   (FILE : in out FILE_TYPE);

function  MODE    (FILE : in FILE_TYPE) return FILE_MODE;
function  NAME    (FILE : in FILE_TYPE) return STRING;
function  FORM    (FILE : in FILE_TYPE) return STRING;

function  IS_OPEN(FILE : in FILE_TYPE) return BOOLEAN;
```

--Control of default input and output files

```
procedure SET_INPUT   (FILE : in FILE_TYPE);
procedure SET_OUTPUT(FILE : in FILE_TYPE);


function STANDARD_INPUT   return FILE_TYPE;
function STANDARD_OUTPUT return FILE_TYPE;

function CURRENT_INPUT   return FILE_TYPE;
function CURRENT_OUTPUT return FILE_TYPE;
```

--Specification of line and page lengths

```
procedure SET_LINE_LENGTH(FILE : in FILE_TYPE; TO : in COUNT);
procedure SET_LINE_LENGTH(TO : in COUNT);

procedure SET_PAGE_LENGTH(FILE : in FILE_TYPE; TO : in COUNT);
procedure SET_PAGE_LENGTH(TO : in COUNT);

function LINE_LENGTH(FILE : in FILE_TYPE) return COUNT;
function LINE_LENGTH return COUNT;

function PAGE_LENGTH(FILE : in FILE_TYPE) return COUNT;
function PAGE_LENGTH return COUNT;
```

--Column, Line and Page Control

```
procedure NEW_LINE     (FILE : in FILE_TYPE; SPACING : in
                        POSITIVE_COUNT := 1);
procedure NEW_LINE     (SPACING : in POSITIVE_COUNT := 1);

procedure SKIP_LINE    (FILE : in FILE_TYPE; SPACING : in
                        POSITIVE_COUNT := 1);
procedure SKIP_LINE    (SPACING : in POSITIVE_COUNT := 1);

function  END_OF_LINE (FILE : in FILE_TYPE) return BOOLEAN;
function  END_OF_LINE  return BOOLEAN;
```

procedure NEW_PAGE   (FILE : **in** FILE_TYPE);
procedure NEW_PAGE;

procedure SKIP_PAGE   (FILE : **in** FILE_TYPE);
procedure SKIP_PAGE;

function   END_OF_PAGE(FILE : **in** FILE_TYPE) **return** BOOLEAN;
function   END_OF_PAGE **return** BOOLEAN;

function   END_OF_FILE (FILE : **in** FILE_TYPE) **return** BOOLEAN;
function   END_OF_FILE   **return** BOOLEAN;

procedure SET_COL(FILE : **in** FILE_TYPE; TO : **in** POSITIVE_COUNT);
procedure SET_COL(TO   : **in** POSITIVE_COUNT);

procedure SET_LINE(FILE : **in** FILE_TYPE; TO : **in** POSITIVE_COUNT);
procedure SET_LINE(TO   : **in** POSITIVE_COUNT);

function COL (FILE : **in** FILE_TYPE) **return** POSITIVE_COUNT;
function COL   **return** POSITIVE_COUNT;

function LINE (FILE : **in** FILE_TYPE) **return** POSITIVE_COUNT;
function LINE   **return** POSITIVE_COUNT;

function PAGE(FILE : **in** FILE_TYPE) **return** POSITIVE_COUNT;
function PAGE **return** POSITIVE_COUNT;

--Character Input-Output

procedure GET(FILE : **in** FILE_TYPE; ITEM : **out** CHARACTER);
procedure GET(ITEM : **out** CHARACTER);
procedure PUT(FILE : **in** FILE_TYPE; ITEM : **in** CHARACTER);
procedure PUT(ITEM : **in**   CHARACTER);

--String Input-Output

procedure GET(FILE : **in** FILE_TYPE; ITEM : **out** STRING);
procedure GET(ITEM : **out** STRING);
procedure PUT(FILE : **in** FILE_TYPE; ITEM : **in** STRING);
procedure PUT(ITEM : **in**   STRING);

procedure GET_LINE(FILE : **in** FILE_TYPE; ITEM : **out** STRING; LAST : **out**
            NATURAL);
procedure GET_LINE(ITEM : **out** STRING; LAST : **out** NATURAL);
procedure PUT_LINE(FILE : **in** FILE_TYPE; ITEM : **in** STRING);
procedure PUT_LINE(ITEM : **in** STRING);

--Generic package for Input-Output of Integer Types

generic
    type NUM **is range** <>;
package INTEGER_IO **is**

      DEFAULT_WIDTH : FIELD := NUM'WIDTH;
      DEFAULT_BASE : NUMBER_BASE := 10;

      procedure GET(FILE : **in** FILE_TYPE; ITEM : **out** NUM; WIDTH : **in**
                      FIELD := 0);
      procedure GET(ITEM : **out** NUM; WIDTH : **in** FIELD := 0);

      procedure PUT(FILE   : **in** FILE_TYPE;
                 ITEM   : **in** NUM;
                 WIDTH : **in** FIELD := DEFAULT_WIDTH;
                 BASE   : **in** NUMBER_BASE := DEFAULT_BASE);
      procedure PUT(ITEM   : **in** NUM;
                 WIDTH : **in** FIELD := DEFAULT_WIDTH;
                 BASE   : **in** NUMBER_BASE := DEFAULT_BASE);

      procedure GET(FROM : **in** STRING; ITEM : **out** NUM; LAST : **out**
                       POSITIVE);
      procedure PUT(TO   : **out** STRING;
                 ITEM   : **in** NUM;
                 BASE   : **in** NUMBER_BASE := DEFAULT_BASE);

  end INTEGER_IO;

--Generic packages for Input-output of Real Types

generic
    type NUM **is digits** <>;
package FLOAT_IO **is**

      DEFAULT_FORE : FIELD := 2;
      DEFAULT_AFT   : FIELD := NUM'DIGITS-1;
      DEFAULT_EXP   : FIELD := 3;

      procedure GET(FILE   : **in** FILE_TYPE; ITEM : **out** NUM; WIDTH : **in**
                      FIELD := 0);
      procedure GET(ITEM : **out** NUM; WIDTH : **in** FIELD := 0);

      procedure PUT(FILE   : **in** FILE_TYPE;
                 ITEM   : **in** NUM;
                 FORE   : **in** FIELD := DEFAULT_FORE;
                 AFT   : **in** FIELD := DEFAULT_AFT;
                 EXP   : **in** FIELD := DEFAULT_EXP);
      procedure PUT(ITEM   : **in** NUM;
                 FORE   : **in** FIELD := DEFAULT_FORE;

```
                      AFT         : in  FIELD := DEFAULT_AFT;
                      EXP         : in  FIELD := DEFAULT_EXP);

    procedure GET(FROM : in  STRING; ITEM : out NUM; LAST : out
                             POSITIVE);
    procedure PUT(TO      : out STRING;
                  ITEM    : in  NUM;
                  AFT     : in  FIELD := DEFAULT_AFT;
                  EXP     : in  FIELD := DEFAULT_EXP);
end FLOAT_IO;
generic
    type NUM is delta <>;
package FIXED_IO is

    DEFAULT_FORE : FIELD := NUM'FORE;
    DEFAULT_AFT  : FIELD := NUM'AFT;
    DEFAULT_EXP  : FIELD := 0;

    procedure GET(FILE   : in  FILE_TYPE; ITEM : out NUM; WIDTH : in
                             FIELD := 0);
    procedure GET(ITEM   : out NUM; WIDTH : in FIELD := 0);

    procedure PUT(FILE   : in  FILE_TYPE;
                  ITEM   : in  NUM;
                  FORE   : in  FIELD := DEFAULT_FORE;
                  AFT    : in  FIELD := DEFAULT_AFT;
                  EXP    : in  FIELD := DEFAULT_EXP);
    procedure PUT(ITEM   : in  NUM;
                  FORE   : in  FIELD := DEFAULT_FORE;
                  AFT    : in  FIELD := DEFAULT_AFT;
                  EXP    : in  FIELD := DEFAULT_EXP);

    procedure GET(FROM : in  STRING; ITEM : out NUM; LAST : out
                             POSITIVE);
    procedure PUT(TO      : out STRING;
                  ITEM    : in  NUM;
                  AFT     : in  FIELD := DEFAULT_AFT;
                  EXP     : in  FIELD := DEFAULT_EXP);

end FIXED_IO;

--Generic package for Input-Output of Enumeration Types

generic
    type ENUM is (<>);
package ENUMERATION_IO is

    DEFAULT_WIDTH : FIELD := 0;
    DEFAULT_IS_LC : BOOLEAN := FALSE;   --upper case
```

```
          procedure GET(FILE   : in   FILE_TYPE; ITEM : out ENUM);
          procedure GET(ITEM   : out ENUM);

          procedure PUT(FILE   : in FILE_TYPE;
                        ITEM    : in ENUM;
                        WIDTH   : in FIELD     := DEFAULT_WIDTH;
                        LC      : in BOOLEAN := DEFAULT_IS_LC);
          procedure PUT(ITEM   : in ENUM;
                        WIDTH   : in FIELD     := DEFAULT_WIDTH;
                        LC      : in BOOLEAN := DEFAULT_IS_LC);

          procedure GET(FROM : in              STRING; ITEM : out ENUM;
                                               LAST : out POSITIVE);
          procedure PUT(TO    : out            STRING;
                        ITEM    : in            ENUM;
                        LC      : in            BOOLEAN := DEFAULT_IS_LC);
     end ENUMERATION_IO;

     --Exceptions

     STATUS_ERROR : exception renames IO_EXCEPTIONS.STATUS_ERROR;
     MODE_ERROR   : exception renames IO_EXCEPTIONS.MODE_ERROR;
     NAME_ERROR   : exception renames IO_EXCEPTIONS.NAME_ERROR;
     USE_ERROR    : exception renames IO_EXCEPTIONS.USE_ERROR;
     DEVICE_ERROR : exception renames IO_EXCEPTIONS.DEVICE_ERROR;
     END_ERROR    : exception renames IO_EXCEPTIONS.END_ERROR;
     DATA_ERROR   : exception renames IO_EXCEPTIONS.DATA_ERROR;
     LAYOUT_ERROR : exception renames IO_EXCEPTIONS.LAYOUT_ERROR;

private
     --implementation dependent
end TEXT_IO;
```

PACKAGE STANDARD

```
--Refer to reference 2 for changes that have
--occurred in package STANDARD in 1982

package STANDARD is
      type BOOLEAN is (FALSE, TRUE);

      function "not" (X   : BOOLEAN) return BOOLEAN;
      function "and" (X,Y : BOOLEAN) return BOOLEAN;
      function "or"  (X,Y : BOOLEAN) return BOOLEAN;
      function "xor" (X,Y : BOOLEAN) return BOOLEAN;

      type SHORT_INTEGER is range {implementation defined};
      type INTEGER          is range {implementation defined};
      type LONG_INTEGER  is range {implementation defined};

      function "+" (X : INTEGER) return INTEGER;
      function "−" (X : INTEGER) return INTEGER;
      function abs (X : INTEGER) return INTEGER;

      function "+"     (X,Y : INTEGER) return INTEGER;
      function "−"     (X,Y : INTEGER) return INTEGER;
      function "*"     (X,Y : INTEGER) return INTEGER;
      function "/"     (X,Y : INTEGER) return INTEGER;
      function "rem" (X,Y : INTEGER) return INTEGER;
      function "mod" (X,Y : INTEGER) return INTEGER;
      function "**"    (X,Y : INTEGER range 0..INTEGER'LAST) return INTEGER;

      type SHORT_FLOAT is digits {implementation defined}
      type FLOAT          is digits {implementation defined}
      type LONG_FLOAT  is digits {implementation defined}
```

319

function "+" (X : FLOAT) **return** FLOAT;
function "−" (X : FLOAT) **return** FLOAT;
function abs (X : FLOAT) **return** FLOAT;

function "+" (X,Y : FLOAT) **return** FLOAT;
function "−" (X,Y : FLOAT) **return** FLOAT;
function "*" (X,Y : FLOAT) **return** FLOAT;
function "/" (X,Y : FLOAT) **return** FLOAT;
function "**" (X: : FLOAT; Y: INTEGER) **return** FLOAT;

−−Similarly for SHORT_FLOAT and LONG_FLOAT

type CHARACTER **is**
        −−The entire character set follows
        −−We will skip it here
        −−Character set goes here

package ASCII **is**
        −−All the control characters go here
        −−We will skip it here
        end ASCII;

        −−Predefined types and subtypes

subtype NATURAL **is** INTEGER **range** 1 . . INTEGER'LAST;
subtype PRIORITY **is** INTEGER **range** {implementation defined};
type STRING **is array** (NATURAL **range** <>) **of** CHARACTER;
type DURATION **is delta** {implementation defined} **range** {implementation
        defined}

−−Predefined exceptions

CONSTRAINT_ERROR : **exception**;
NUMERIC_ERROR   : **exception**;
SELECT_ERROR   : **exception**;
STORAGE_ERROR   : **exception**;
TASKING_ERROR   : **exception**;

```
package SYSTEM is   --Machine dependent
       type SYSTEM_NAME is {implementation defined enumeration type};
               NAME            : constant SYSTEM_NAME := {implementation
                                                         defined};
               STORAGE         : constant              := {implementation
                                                         defined};
               MEMORY_SIZE : constant                  := {implementation
                                                         defined};
               MIN_INT         : constant              := {implementation
                                                         defined};
               MAX_INT         : constant              := {implementation
                                                         defined};
       end SYSTEM;

       private
               for CHARACTER use   --128 ASCII character set without holes
               --We omit it here
       pragma PACK(STRING);
end STANDARD;
```

COMPARISON OF ADA AND PASCAL

Many features of Ada were derived from Pascal. In some cases minor changes in syntax have been introduced. Ada, of course, contains many powerful features for which there are no counterparts in Pascal. In this appendix we explore some of the similarities and differences between Ada and Pascal.

1. The semicolon is used in Ada as a command terminator. In Pascal the semicolon is used as a command separator.

    Pascal:
    ```
    if A < B then
            writeln('A less than B')
        else
            writeln('A is equal to or greater than B');
    ```

    Ada:
    ```
    if A < B then
            put_line("A less than B");   --Semicolon needed here
        else
            put_line("A is equal to or greater than B");
        else if;
    ```

2. Ada uses key words to terminate loops and control structures, whereas Pascal uses a compound statement nested between a "begin" and "end".

    Pascal:
    ```
    if A < B then
            begin
                    C:=D;
                    F:=H
            end;
    ```

323

```
     for I:=1 to 10 do
          begin
                 writeln('HELLO.');
                 writeln('GOODBYE.')
          end;
Ada: if A < B then
          C:=D;
          F:=H;
     end if;
     for I in 1..10 loop
          put_line("HELLO.");
          put_line("GOODBYE.");
     end loop;
```

3. In type declarations Pascal uses an equal sign, whereas Ada uses the keyword "is."

   ```
   Pascal:   type WORD = array[1..20] of CHAR;
   Ada:      type WORD is array(1..20) of CHARACTER;
   ```

   In subprogram declarations, Pascal uses the semicolon to separate the specification from the body, whereas Ada uses the word "is."

4. For array indices, Ada uses parentheses—( )—whereas Pascal uses square brackets—[ ], as illustrated above for type WORD.

5. Ada allows the logical operations "and" and "or" to be short-circuited using "and then" and "or else." In Pascal, short-circuiting is not assured. Some Pascal compilers will employ short-circuiting and some will not.

6. Pointer variables in Pascal are very similar to access variables in Ada. The syntax for Ada has been changed slightly. No pointer symbol is used in Ada.

7. Pascal has a predefined data structure called a set. The operations of union and intersection are predefined in Pascal. In Ada the data structure set is not predefined. One may be tempted to write a generic package that simulates the set structure.

8. Input and output commands differ greatly in the two languages. A TEXT_IO package will be available to support all Ada programming. The user may wish to augment this package by creating additional input/output procedures and putting them into a new input/output package. Pascal limits the user to a few predefined input/output commands such as **writeln, readln, write,** and **read.**

9. In Ada, enumeration literals may be overloaded. This is not possible in Pascal.

10. A significant difference between Ada and Pascal is that arrays with unspecified bounds may be used in Ada as subprogram parameters. In Pascal the bounds on all arrays used as subprogram parameters must be speci-

fied. This Pascal restriction limits the utility of Pascal in building scientific programming libraries.

11. The order of declarations in Ada is much less rigid than in Pascal. In Pascal, the order of declarations is label, const, type, and var. No such constraint exists in Ada.

12. Ada supports parameter matchup for subprogram calls by name as well as position. In Pascal, only calls by position are valid.

13. Pascal does not have the equivalent of Ada's binding mode ''in'' or ''out.'' Pascal's pass by reference is equivalent to Ada's binding mode ''in out.'' Ada's binding mode ''in'' differs from Pascal's ''pass by value'' inasmuch as parameters transferred using Ada's ''in'' mode act as constants in the subprogram. In Pascal's ''pass by value'' mode of transfer, the parameters are not held as constants in the Pascal subprogram.

14. The major features of Ada—namely, separate compilation, generics, packages, and tasks—have no counterpart in Pascal.

15. The overloading of operators, permitted in Ada, is not possible in Pascal.

16. Pascal does not support the use of exceptions for error handling.

17. Pascal does not support the control of floating point and fixed types that is provided by Ada.

18. Pascal does not support derived types.

ADA SYNTAX

Notation

The context-free syntax of the language is described using a simple variant of Backus-Naur Form. In particular,

(a) Lower case words, some containing embedded underscores, are used to denote syntactic categories, for example:

    adding_operator

(b) Boldface words are used to denote reserved words, for example:

    array

(c) Square brackets enclose optional items. Thus the two following rules are equivalent.

    return_statement ::=
        return [expression];
    return_statement ::=
        return; | **return** expression;

(d) Braces enclose a repeated item. The item may appear zero or more times; the repetitions occur from left to right as with an equivalent left recursive rule. Thus the two following rules are equivalent.

    term ::=
        factor {multiplying_operator factor}
    term ::=
        factor | term multiplying_operator factor

(e) A vertical bar separates alternative items, unless it occurs
     immediately after an opening brace, in which case it stands
     for itself:

```
letter_or_digit::=
    letter | digit
component_association::=
    [choice {| choice} =>] expression
```

(f) If the name of any syntactic category starts with an
     underlined part, it is equivalent to the category name
     without the underlined part. The underlined part is
     intended to convey some semantic information. For example
     type name and task name are both equivalent to name alone.

In addition, the syntax rule describing structured constructs are
presented in a form that corresponds to the recommended
paragraphing. For example, an if statement is defined as

```
if_statement ::=
    if condition then
        sequence_of_statements
    {elsif condition then
        sequence_of_statements}
    [else
        sequence_of_statements]
    end if;
```

Different lines are used for parts of a syntax rule if the
corresponding parts of the construct described by the rule are
intended to be on different lines. Indentation in the rule is a
recommendation for indentation of the corresponding part of the
construct. The preferred places for other line breaks are after
semicolons.

Syntax Summary

```
abort_statement ::=
    abort task_name {, task_name};

accept_alternative
    accept_statement [sequence_of_statements]

accept_statement ::=
    accept entry_simple_name [(expression)]
        [formal_part] [do sequence_of_statements
    end [entry_simple_name]];

access_type_definition ::=
    access subtype_indication

actual_parameter ::=
    expression | variable_name | type_mark (variable_name)

actual_parameter_part ::=
    (parameter_association {, parameter_association})
```

```
adding_operator ::=
    +  | - | &

address_clause ::=
    for simple_name use at simple_expression;

aggregate ::=
    (component_association {, component_association})

alignment_clause ::=
    at mod static simple_expression;

allocator ::=
    new subtype_indication | new qualified_expression

argument_association ::=
      [argument_identifier =>] name
    | [argument_identifier =>] expression

array_type_definition ::=
      unconstrained_array_definition
    | constrained_array_definition

assignment_statement ::=
    variable_name := expression;

attribute ::=
    prefix'attribute_designator

attribute_designator ::=
    simple_name[(universal_static_ expression)]

base ::=
    integer

based_integer ::=
    extended_digit {[underline] extended_digit}

based_literal ::=
    base # based_integer [.based_integer] # [exponent]

basic_character ::=
    basic_graphic_character | format_effector

basic_declaration ::=
      object_declaration          | number_declaration
    | type_declaration            | subtype_declaration
    | subprogram_declaration      | package_declaration
    | task_declaration            | generic_declaration
    | exception_declaration       | generic_instantiation
    | renaming_declaration        | deferred_constant_declaration

basic_declarative_item ::=
    basic_declaration | representation_clause | use_clause

basic_graphic_character ::=
      upper_case_letter | digit
    | special_character | space_character

basic_loop ::=
    loop
       sequence_of_statements
    end loop
```

```
block_statement ::=
    [block_simple_name:]
        [declare
            declarative_part]
        begin
            sequence_of_statements
        [exception
            exception_handler
           {exception_handler}]
        end [block_simple_name];

body ::=
    proper_body | body_stub

body_stub ::=
        subprogram_specification is separate;
    | package body package_simple_name is separate;
    | task body task_simple_name is separate;

case_statement ::=
    case expression is
        case_statement_alternative
       { case_statement_alternative}
    end case;

case_statement_alternative ::=
    when choice {| choice } =>
        sequence_of_statements

character_literal ::=
    'graphic_character'

choice ::=
        simple_expression | discrete_range | others
    | component_simple_name

code_statement ::=
    type_mark'record_aggregate;

compilation ::=
    {compilation_unit}

compilation_unit ::=
    context_clause library_unit | context_clause secondary_unit

component_association ::=
    [choice {| choice} =>] expression

component_clause ::=
    component_name at static_simple_expression
    range static_range;

component_declaration ::=
    identifier_list:component_subtype_definition [:= expression];

component_list ::=
        component_declaration {component_declaration}
    | {component_declaration} variant_part
    | null;

component_subtype_definition ::=
    subtype_indication
```

```
compound_statement ::=
      if_statement                | case_statement
    | loop_statement              | block_statement
    | accept_statement            | select_statement

condition ::=
    boolean_expression

conditional_entry_call ::=
    select
        entry_call_statement
      [sequence_of_statements]
    else
        sequence_of_statements
    end select;

constrained_array_definition ::=
    array index_constraint of component_subtype_indication

constraint ::=
        range_constraint        | floating_point_constraint
      | fixed_point_constraint | index_constraint
      | discriminant_constraint

context_clause ::=
    {with_clause {use_clause}}

decimal_literal ::=
    integer [.integer] [exponent]

declarative_part ::=
    {basic_declartive_item}  {later_declarative_item}

deferred_constant_declaration ::=
    identifier_list : constant type_mark;

delay_alternative ::=
    delay_statement  [sequence_of_statements]

delay_statement ::=
    delay simple_expression;

derived_type_definition ::=
    new subtype_indication

designator ::=
    identifier | operator_symbol

discrete_range ::=
    discrete_subtype_indication | range

discriminant_association ::=
    [discriminant_simple_name {| discriminant_simple_name} =>]
    expression

discriminant_constraint ::=
    (discriminant_association {, discriminant_association})

discriminant_part ::=
    (discriminant_specification {; discriminant_specification})

discriminant_specifiction ::=
    identifier_list  :  type_mark [:= expression]
```

```
entry_call_statement ::=
    entry_name [actual_parameter_part];

entry_declaration ::=
    entry identifier [(discrete_range)] [formal_part];

enumeration_literal ::=
    identifier | character_literal

enumeration_literal_specification ::=
    enumeration_literal

enumeration_representation_clause ::=
    for type_simple_name use aggregate;

enumeration_type_definition ::=
    (enumeration_literal_specification
        {, enumeration_literal_specification})

exception_choice ::=
    exception_name | others

exception_declaration ::=
    identifier_list : exception;

exception_handler ::=
    when exception_choice {| exception_choice} =>
        sequence_of_statements

exit_statement ::=
    exit [loop_name]  [when condition];

exponent ::=
    E [+] integer | E - integer

exponentiating_operator ::=
    **

expression ::=
      relation {and relation} | relation {or relation}
    | relation {xor relation} | relation {and then relation}
    | relation {or else relation}

extended_digit ::=
    digit | letter

factor ::=
    primary [exponentiating_operator primary]

fixed_accuracy_definition ::=
    delta static_simple_expression

fixed_point_constraint ::=
    fixed_accuracy_definition [range_constraint]

floating_accuracy_definition ::=
    digits static_simple_expression

floating_point_constraint ::=
    floating_accuracy_definition [range_constraint]

formal_parameter ::=
    parameter_simple_name
```

```
formal_part ::=
    (parameter_specification {; parameter_specification})

full_type_declaration ::=
    type identifier [discriminant_part] is type_definition;

function_call ::=
    function_name [actual_parameter_part]

generic_actual_parameter ::=
        expression        | variable_name
    | subprogram_name  | entry_name        | type_mark

generic_actual_part ::=
    (generic_association {, generic_association})

generic_association ::=
    [generic_formal_parameter =>] generic_actual_parameter

generic_declaration ::=
    generic_specification;

generic_formal_parameter ::=
    parameter_simple_name | operator_symbol

generic_formal_part ::=
    generic {generic_parameter_declaration}

generic_instantiation ::=
        package identifier is
            new generic_package_name [generic_actual_part];
    | procedure identifier is
            new generic_procedure_name [generic_actual_part];
    | function designator is
            new generic_function_name [generic_actual_part];

generic_parameter_declaration ::=
        identifier_list : [in [out]] type_mark [:= expression];
    | type identifier   is generic_type_definition;
    | private_type_declaration
    | with subprogram_specification [is name];
    | with subprogram_specification [is <>];

generic_specification ::=
        generic_formal_part subprogram_specification
    | generic_formal_part package_specification

generic_type_definition ::=
        (<>) | range <> | digits <> | delta <>
    | array_type_definition | access_type_definition

goto_statement ::=
    goto label_name;

graphic_character ::=
        basic_graphic_character
    | lower_case_letter | other_special_character

identifier ::=
    letter {[underline] letter_or_digit}

identifier_list ::=
    identifier {, identifier}
```

```
if_statement ::=
    if condition then
        sequence_of_statements
    {elsif condition then
        sequence_of_statements}
    [else
        sequence_of_statements]
     end if;

incomplete_type_declaration ::=
    type identifier [discriminant_part];

index_constraint ::=
    (discrete_range {, discrete_range})

index_subtype_definition ::=
    type_mark range <>

indexed_component ::=
    prefix(expression {, expression})

integer ::=
    digit {[underline] digit}

integer_type_definition ::=
    range_constraint

iteration_rule ::=
      while condition
    | for loop_parameter_specification

label ::=
    <<label_simple_name>>

later_declarative_item ::=
      body | subprogram_declaration    | package_declaration
    | task_declaration                 | generic_declaration
    | use_clause                       | generic_instantiation

length_clause ::=
    for attribute use simple_expression;

letter ::=
    upper_case_letter | lower_case_letter

letter_or_digit ::=
    letter | digit

library_unit ::=
      subprogram_declaration        | package_declaration
    | generic_declaration           | generic_instantiation
    | subprogram_body

logical_operator ::=
    and | or | xor

loop_parameter_specification ::=
    identifier in [reverse] discrete_range

loop_statement ::=
    [loop_simple_name:]
        [iteration_rule]
        basic_loop [loop_simple_name];
```

```
mode ::=
    [in] | in out | out

multiplying_operator ::=
    *  | /  | mod | rem

name ::=
      simple_name | character_literal   | operator_symbol
    | indexed_component                 | slice
    | selected_component                | attribute

null_statement ::=
    null;

number_declaration ::=
    identifier_list : constant := universal_static_expression;

numeric_literal ::=
    decimal_literal | based_literal

object_declaration ::=
      identifier_list : [constant] subtype_indication
                        [:= expression];
    | identifier_list : [constant] constrained_array_definition
                        [:= expression];

operator_symbol ::=
    string_literal

package_body ::=
    package body package_simple_name is
        [declarative_part]
      [begin
         sequence_of_statements
      [exception
         exception_handler
        {exception_handler}]]
      end [package_simple_name];

package_declaration ::=
    package_specification;

package_specification ::=
    package identifier is
       {basic_declarative_item}
    [private
       {basic_declarative_item}
    end [package_simple_name]

parameter_association ::=
    [formal_parameter =>] actual_parameter

parameter_specification ::=
    identifier_list : mode type_mark [:= expression]

pragma ::=
    pragma identifier [(argument_association
                           {, argument_association})]

prefix ::=
    name | function_call
```

```
primary ::=
      numeric_literal        | null            | aggregate
    | string_literal         | name            | allocator
    | function_call          | type_conversion
    | qualified_expression   | (expression)

private_type_declaration ::=
    type identifier [discriminant_part] is [limited] private;

procedure_call_statement ::=
    procedure_name [actual_parameter_part];

proper_body ::=
    subprogram_body | package_body | task_body

qualified_expression ::=
    type_mark'(expression) | type_mark'aggregate

raise_statement ::=
    raise [exception_name];

range ::=
      range_attribute
    | simple_expression .. simple_expression

range_constraint ::=
    range range

real_type_definition ::=
    floating_point_constraint | fixed_point_constraint

record_representation_clause ::=
    for type_simple_name use
        record [alignmnt_clause]
           {component_clause}
        end record;

record_type_definition ::=
    record
        component_list
    end record

relation ::=
      simple_expression [relational_operator simple_expression]
    | simple_expression [not] in range
    | simple_expression [not] in type_mark

relational_operator ::=
    = | /= | < | <= | > | >=

renaming_declaration ::=
      identifier : type_mark        renames object_name;
    | identifier : exception        renames exception_name;
    | package identifier            renames package_name;
    | subprogram_specification renames subprogram_or_entry_name;

representation_clause ::=
      length_clause          | enumeration_representation_clause
    | address_clause         | record_representation_clause
```

```
return_statement ::=
    return [expression];

secondary_unit ::=
    subprogram_body | package_body | subunit

select_alternative ::=
    [when condition =>]
        selective_wait_alternative

select_statement ::=
        selective_wait
    | conditional_entry_call | timed_entry_call

selected_component ::=
    prefix.selector

selective_wait ::=
    select
        select_alternative
    {or
        select_alternative}
    [else
        sequence_of_statements]
    end select;

selective_wait_alternative ::=
        accept_alternative | delay_alternative
    | terminate_alternative

selector ::=
        simple_name       | character_literal
    | operator_symbol | all

sequence_of_statements ::=
    statement {statement}

simple_expression ::=
    [unary_operator] term {adding_operator term}

simple_name ::=
    identifier

simple_statement ::=
        null_statement
    | assignment_statement          | procedure_call_statement
    | exit_statement                | return_statement
    | goto_statement                | entry_call_statement
    | delay_statement               | abort_statement
    | raise_statement               | code_statement

slice ::=
    prefix(discrete_range)

statement ::=
    {label} simple_statement | {label} compound_statement

string_literal ::=
    "{graphic_character}"
```

```
subprogram_body ::=
    subprogram_specification is
        [declarative_part]
    begin
        sequence_of_statements
    [exception
        exception_handler
        {exception_handler}]
    end [designator];

subprogram_declaration ::=
    subprogram_specification;

subprogram_specification ::=
        procedure identifier [formal_part]
    | function designator  [formal_part] return type_mark

subtype_declaration ::=
    subtype identifier is subtype_indication;

subtype_indication ::=
    type_mark [constraint]

subunit ::=
    separate (parent_unit_name) proper_body

task_body ::=
    task body task_simple_name is
        [declarative_part]
    begin
        sequence_of_statements
    [exception
        exception_handler
        {exception_handler}]
    end [task_simple_name];

task_declaration ::=
    task_specification;

task_specification ::=
    task [type] identifier [is
        {entry_declaration}
        {representation_clause}
    end [task_simple_name]]

term ::=
    factor {multiplying_operator factor}

terminate_alternative ::=
    terminate;

timed_entry_call ::=
    select
        entry_call_statement
        [sequence_of_statements]
    or
        delay_alternative
     end select;

type_conversion ::=
    type_mark(expression)
```

```
type_declaration ::=
      full_type_declaration
    | incomplete_type_declaration  | private_type_declaration

type_definition ::=
      enumeration_type_definition   | integer_type_definition
    | real_type_definition          | array_type_definition
    | record_type_definition        | access_type_definition
    | derived_type_definition

type_mark ::=
    type_name | subtype_name

unary_operator ::=
    + | - | abs | not

unconstrained_array_definition ::=
    array (index_subtype_definition {, index_subtype_definition})
       of component_subtype_indication

use_clause ::=
    use package_name {, package_name};

variant ::=
    when choice {| choice} =>
       component_list

variant_part ::=
    case discriminant_simple_name is
        variant
        {variant}
    end case;

with_clause ::=
    with unit_simple_name {, unit_simple_name};
```

REFERENCES

1. Barnes, J. G. P. *Programming in Ada*. Addison-Wesley, 1982.
2. Military Standard, MIL-STD-1815, Ada Programming Language (Language Reference Manual). December 1980. Draft Revised. July 1982.
3. Pyle, I. C. *The Ada Programming Language*. Prentice-Hall, 1981.
4. Tenenbaum, A. M., and M. J. Augenstein. *Data Structures Using Pascal*. Prentice-Hall, 1981.
5. Vandergraft, James W. *Introduction to Numerical Computations*, Academic Press, 1978.
6. Wegner, Peter. *Programming with Ada—An Introduction by Means of Graduated Example*. Prentice-Hall, 1980.

INDEX

\

WIENER
PROGRAMMING IN ADA

AMA 13/17   2HR   MOHLT